DISCIPLES

FANTAGRAPHICS BOOKS PRESENTS

A TRADITIONAL COMICS AND
NEOTEXT BOOKS PRODUCTION

WRITTEN BY

DAVID BIRKE & NICHOLAS MCCARTHY

ILLUSTRATED BY

BENJAMIN MARRA

TRADITIONAL COMICS

FANTAGRAPHICS

NEOTEXT

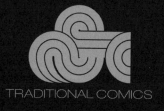

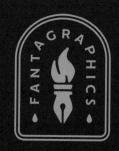

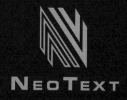

MARIN COUNTY
CALIFORNIA
DECEMBER 1978

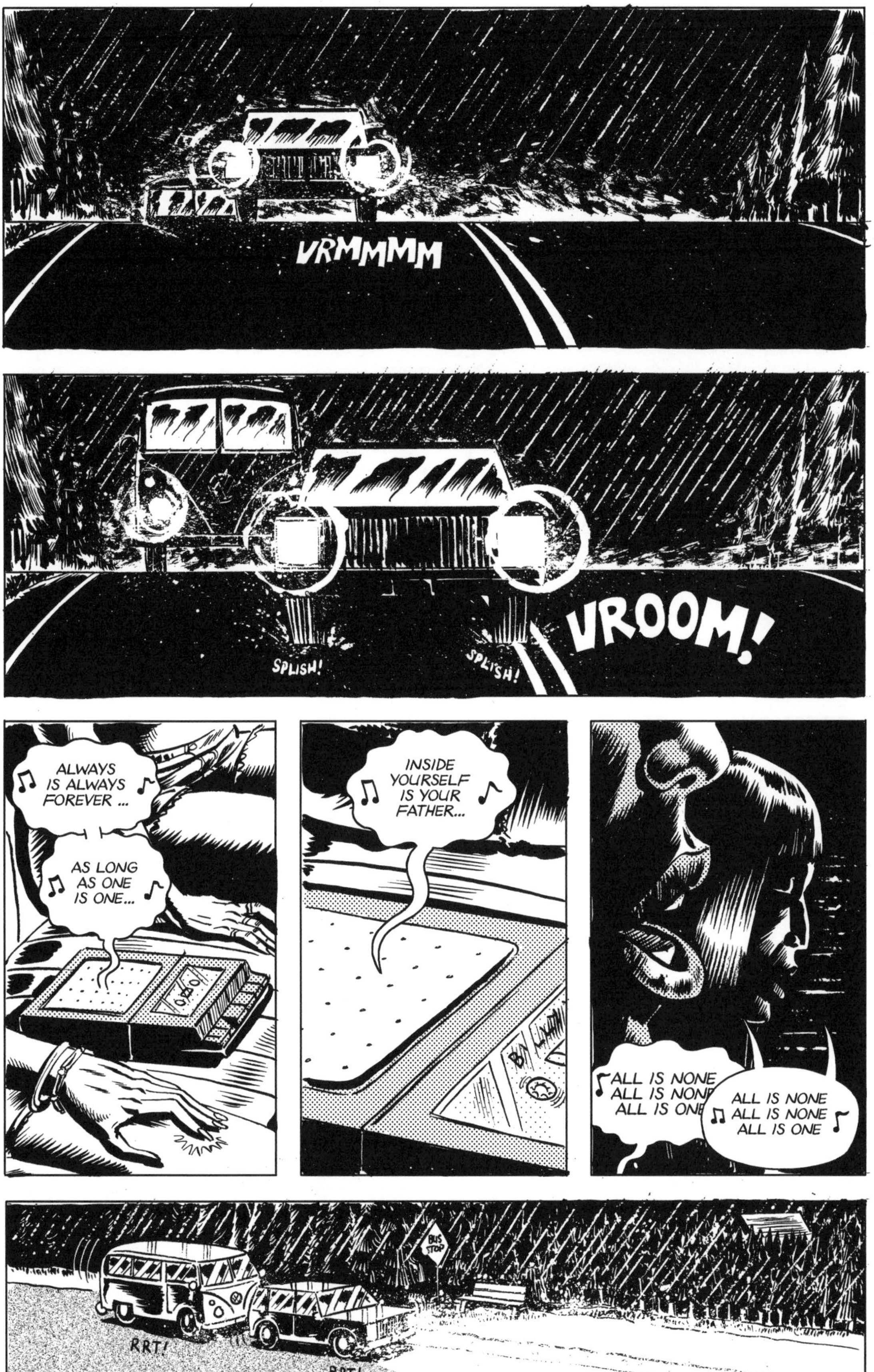
VRMMMM
SPLISH!
SPLISH!
VROOM!
ALWAYS IS ALWAYS FOREVER ...
AS LONG AS ONE IS ONE...
INSIDE YOURSELF IS YOUR FATHER...
ALL IS NONE ALL IS NONE ALL IS ONE
ALL IS NONE ALL IS NONE ALL IS ONE
BUS STOP
RRT!
RRT!

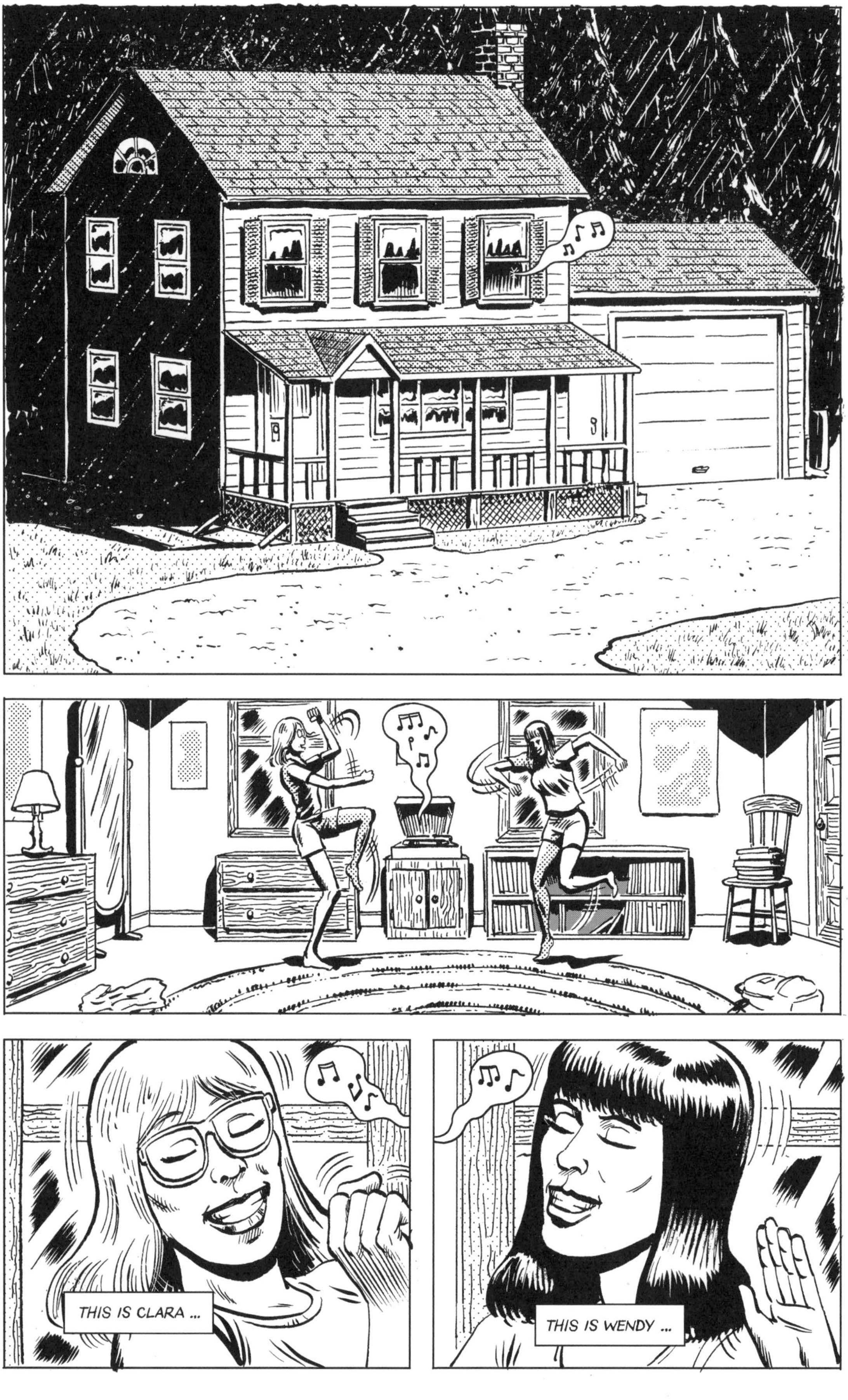
THIS IS CLARA ...
THIS IS WENDY ...

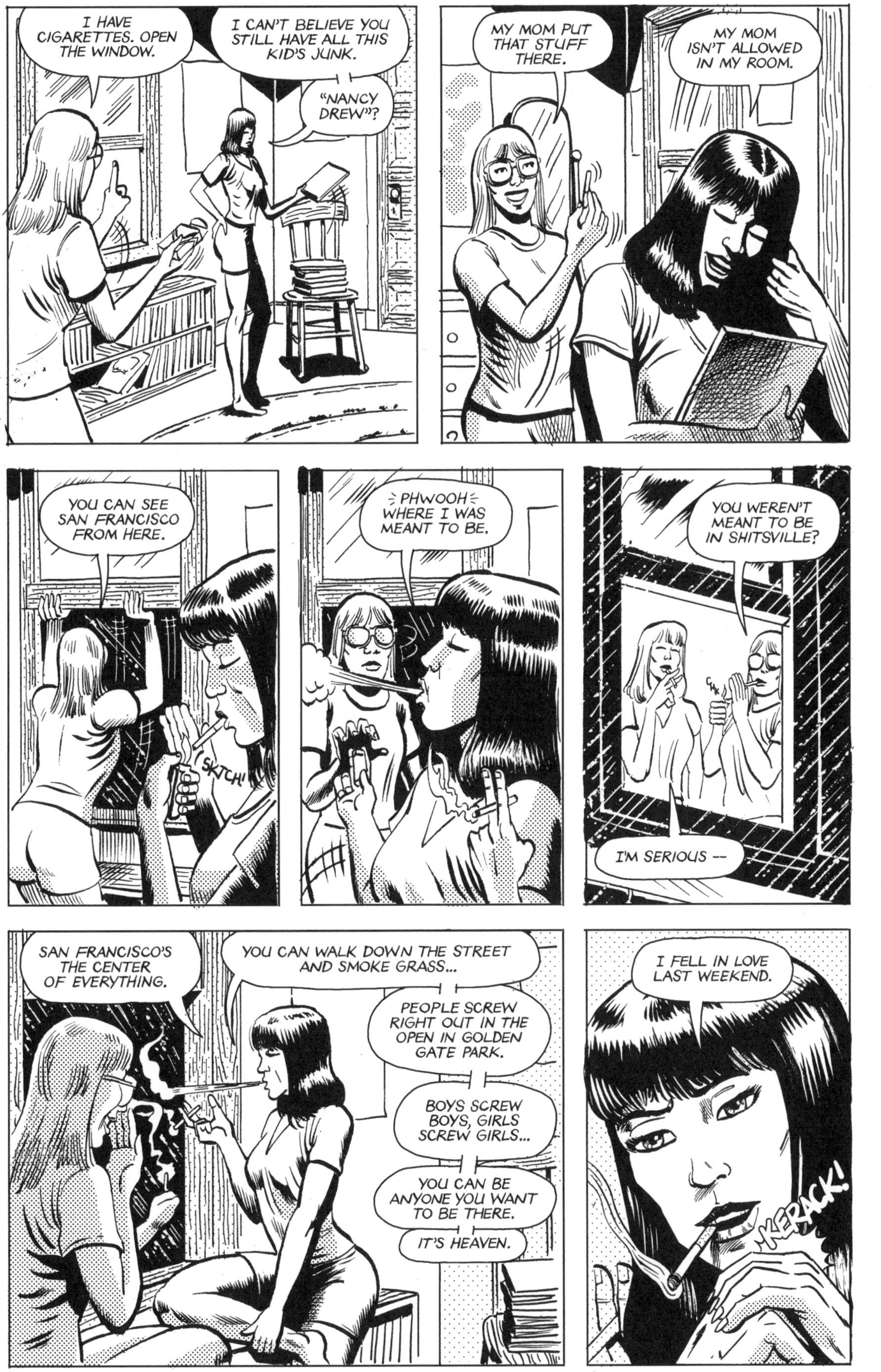
I HAVE CIGARETTES. OPEN THE WINDOW.
I CAN'T BELIEVE YOU STILL HAVE ALL THIS KID'S JUNK.
"NANCY DREW"?
MY MOM PUT THAT STUFF THERE.
MY MOM ISN'T ALLOWED IN MY ROOM.
YOU CAN SEE SAN FRANCISCO FROM HERE.
SKTCH!
PHWOOH
WHERE I WAS MEANT TO BE.
YOU WEREN'T MEANT TO BE IN SHITSVILLE?
I'M SERIOUS --
SAN FRANCISCO'S THE CENTER OF EVERYTHING.
YOU CAN WALK DOWN THE STREET AND SMOKE GRASS...
PEOPLE SCREW RIGHT OUT IN THE OPEN IN GOLDEN GATE PARK.
BOYS SCREW BOYS, GIRLS SCREW GIRLS...
YOU CAN BE ANYONE YOU WANT TO BE THERE.
IT'S HEAVEN.
I FELL IN LOVE LAST WEEKEND.
KKERACK!

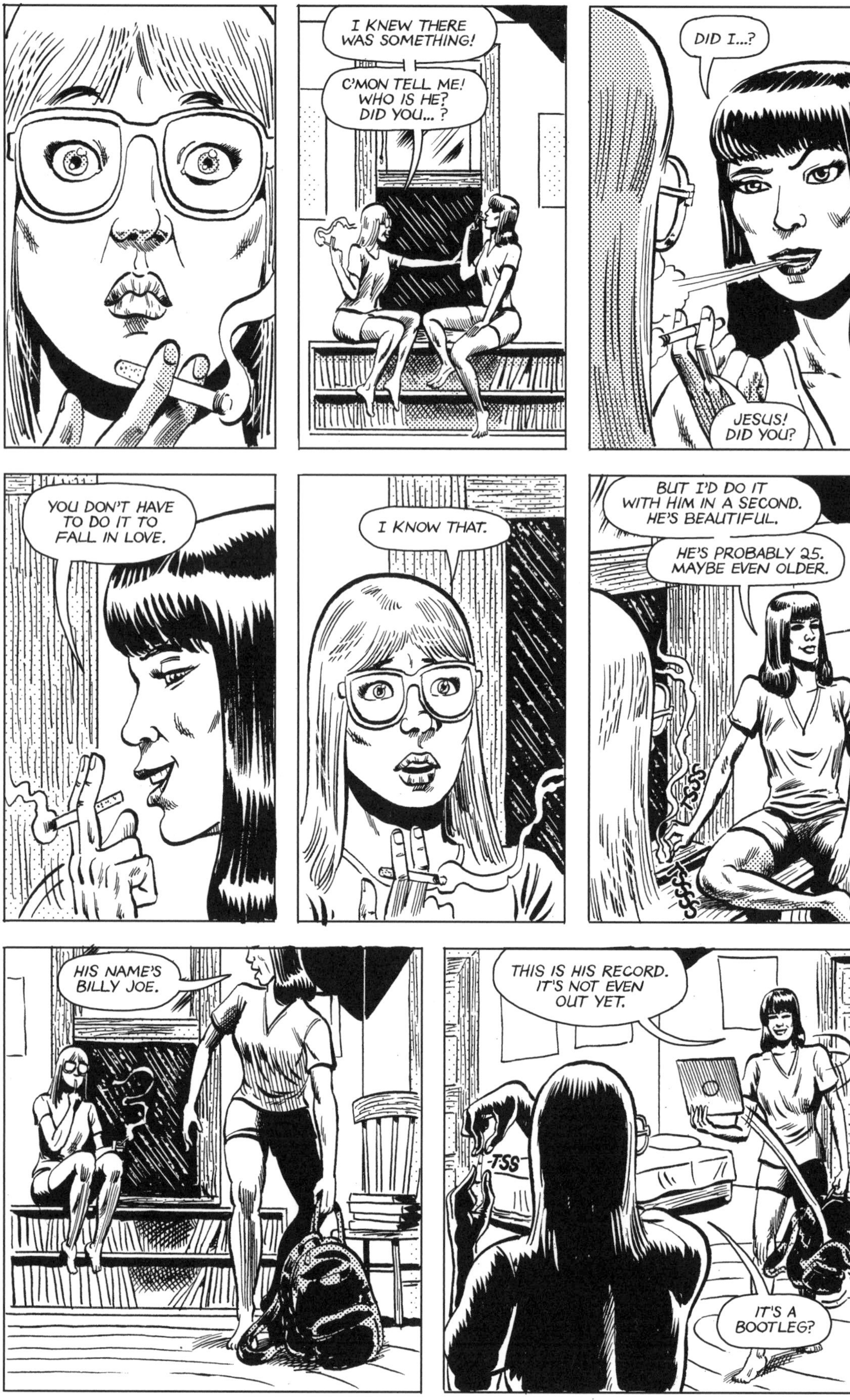
I KNEW THERE WAS SOMETHING!
C'MON TELL ME! WHO IS HE? DID YOU... ?
DID I...?
JESUS! DID YOU?
YOU DON'T HAVE TO DO IT TO FALL IN LOVE.
I KNOW THAT.
BUT I'D DO IT WITH HIM IN A SECOND. HE'S BEAUTIFUL.
HE'S PROBABLY 25. MAYBE EVEN OLDER.
TSSS
TSSSSS
HIS NAME'S BILLY JOE.
THIS IS HIS RECORD. IT'S NOT EVEN OUT YET.
TSS
IT'S A BOOTLEG?

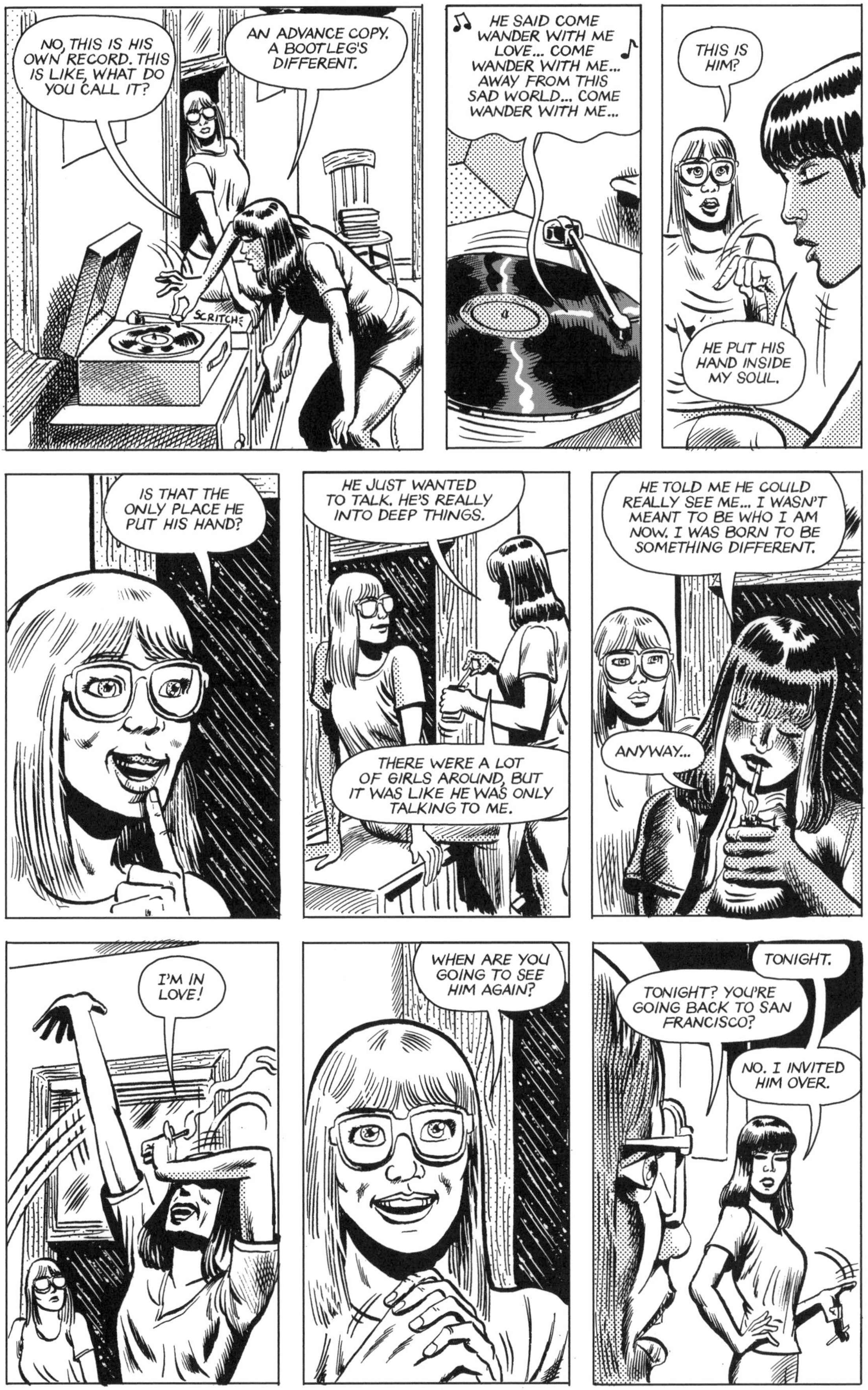
NO, THIS IS HIS OWN RECORD. THIS IS LIKE, WHAT DO YOU CALL IT?
AN ADVANCE COPY. A BOOTLEG'S DIFFERENT.
SCRITCH
HE SAID COME WANDER WITH ME LOVE... COME WANDER WITH ME... AWAY FROM THIS SAD WORLD... COME WANDER WITH ME...
THIS IS HIM?
HE PUT HIS HAND INSIDE MY SOUL.
IS THAT THE ONLY PLACE HE PUT HIS HAND?
HE JUST WANTED TO TALK. HE'S REALLY INTO DEEP THINGS.
THERE WERE A LOT OF GIRLS AROUND, BUT IT WAS LIKE HE WAS ONLY TALKING TO ME.
HE TOLD ME HE COULD REALLY SEE ME... I WASN'T MEANT TO BE WHO I AM NOW. I WAS BORN TO BE SOMETHING DIFFERENT.
ANYWAY...
I'M IN LOVE!
WHEN ARE YOU GOING TO SEE HIM AGAIN?
TONIGHT.
TONIGHT? YOU'RE GOING BACK TO SAN FRANCISCO?
NO. I INVITED HIM OVER.

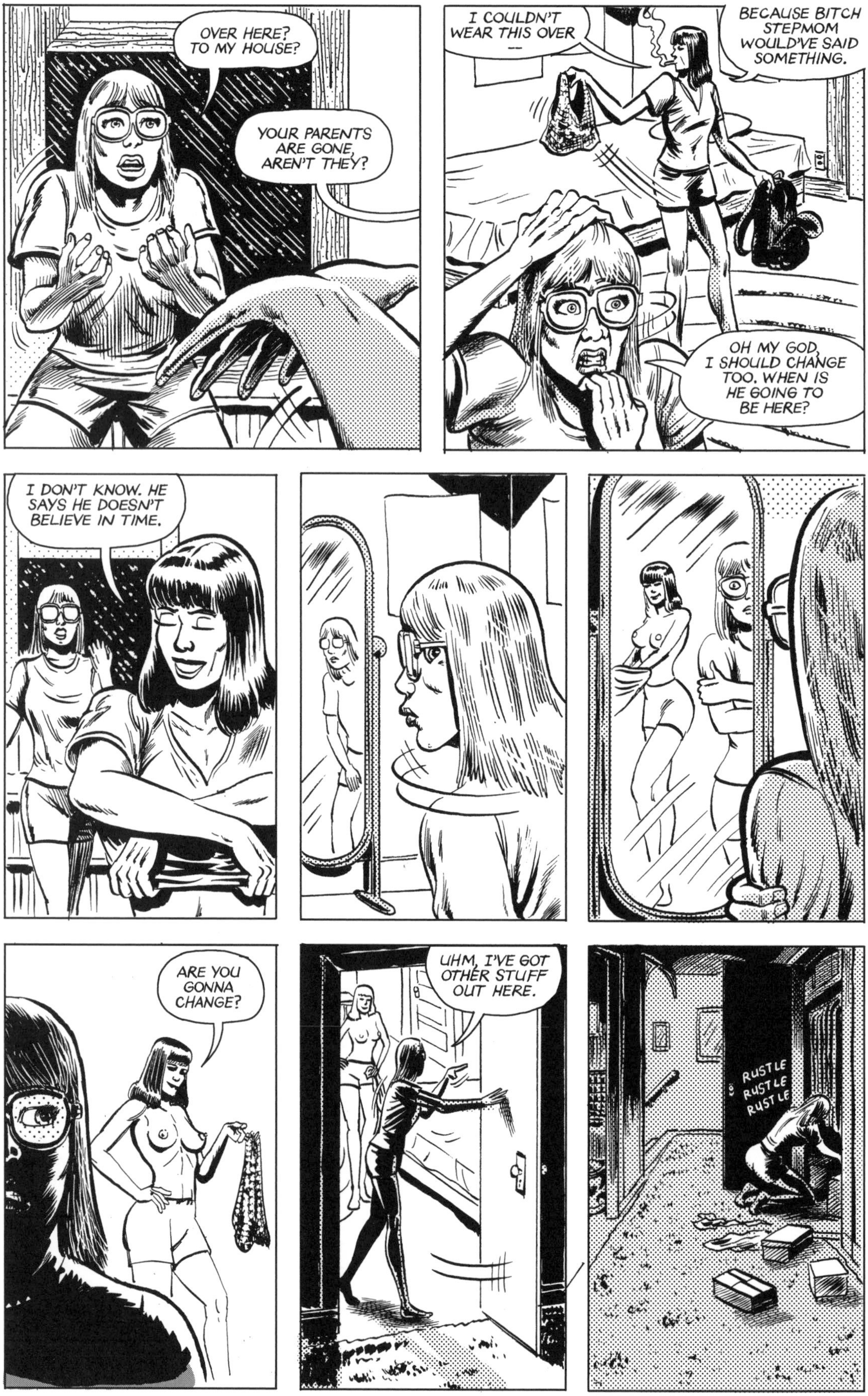
OVER HERE? TO MY HOUSE?
YOUR PARENTS ARE GONE, AREN'T THEY?
I COULDN'T WEAR THIS OVER --
BECAUSE BITCH STEPMOM WOULD'VE SAID SOMETHING.
OH MY GOD, I SHOULD CHANGE TOO. WHEN IS HE GOING TO BE HERE?
I DON'T KNOW. HE SAYS HE DOESN'T BELIEVE IN TIME.
ARE YOU GONNA CHANGE?
UHM, I'VE GOT OTHER STUFF OUT HERE.
RUSTLE RUSTLE RUSTLE

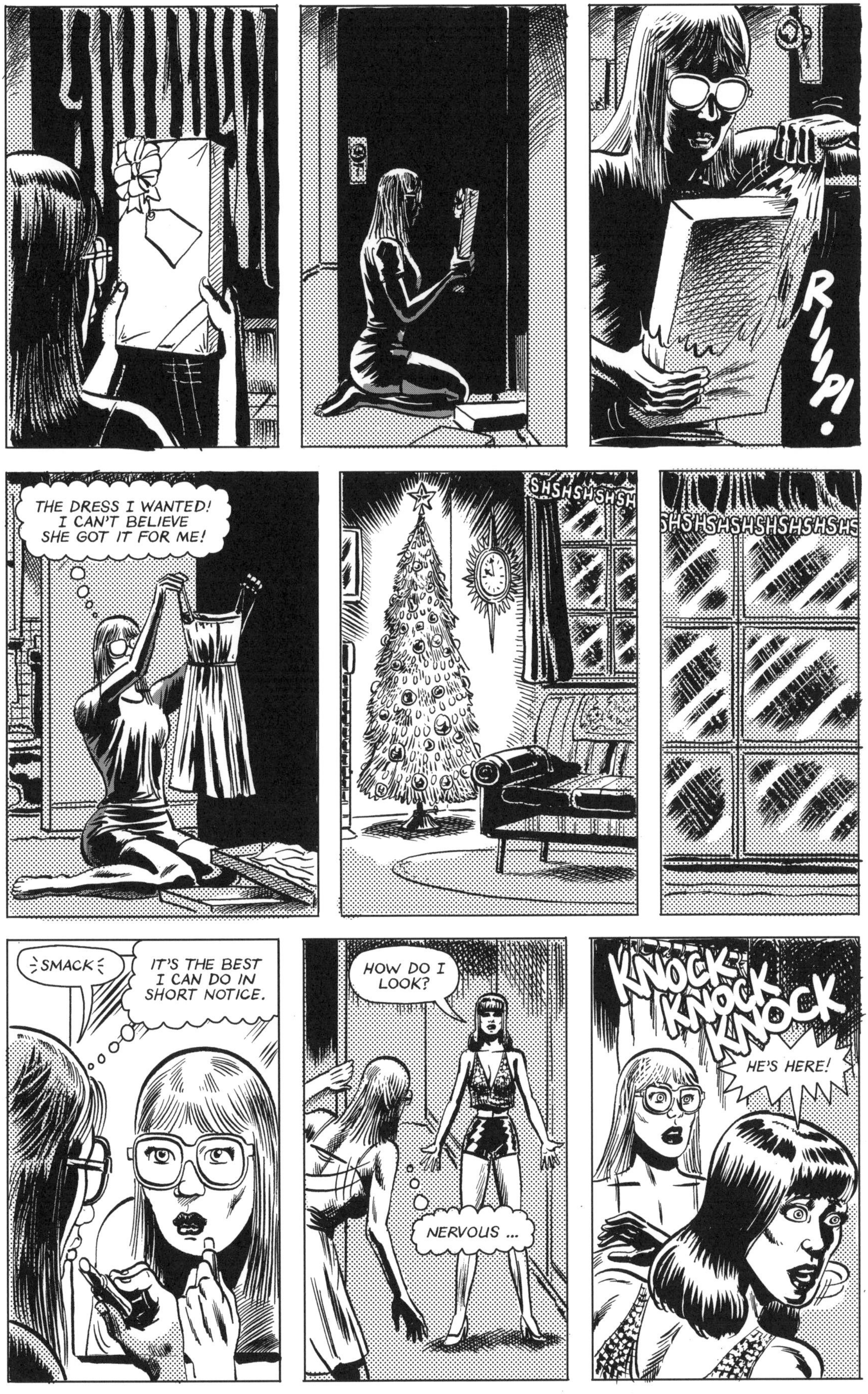
RIIIP!
THE DRESS I WANTED! I CAN'T BELIEVE SHE GOT IT FOR ME!
SHSHSHSHSH
SHSHSHSHSHSHSHSHS
SMACK
IT'S THE BEST I CAN DO IN SHORT NOTICE.
HOW DO I LOOK?
NERVOUS ...
KNOCK KNOCK KNOCK
HE'S HERE!

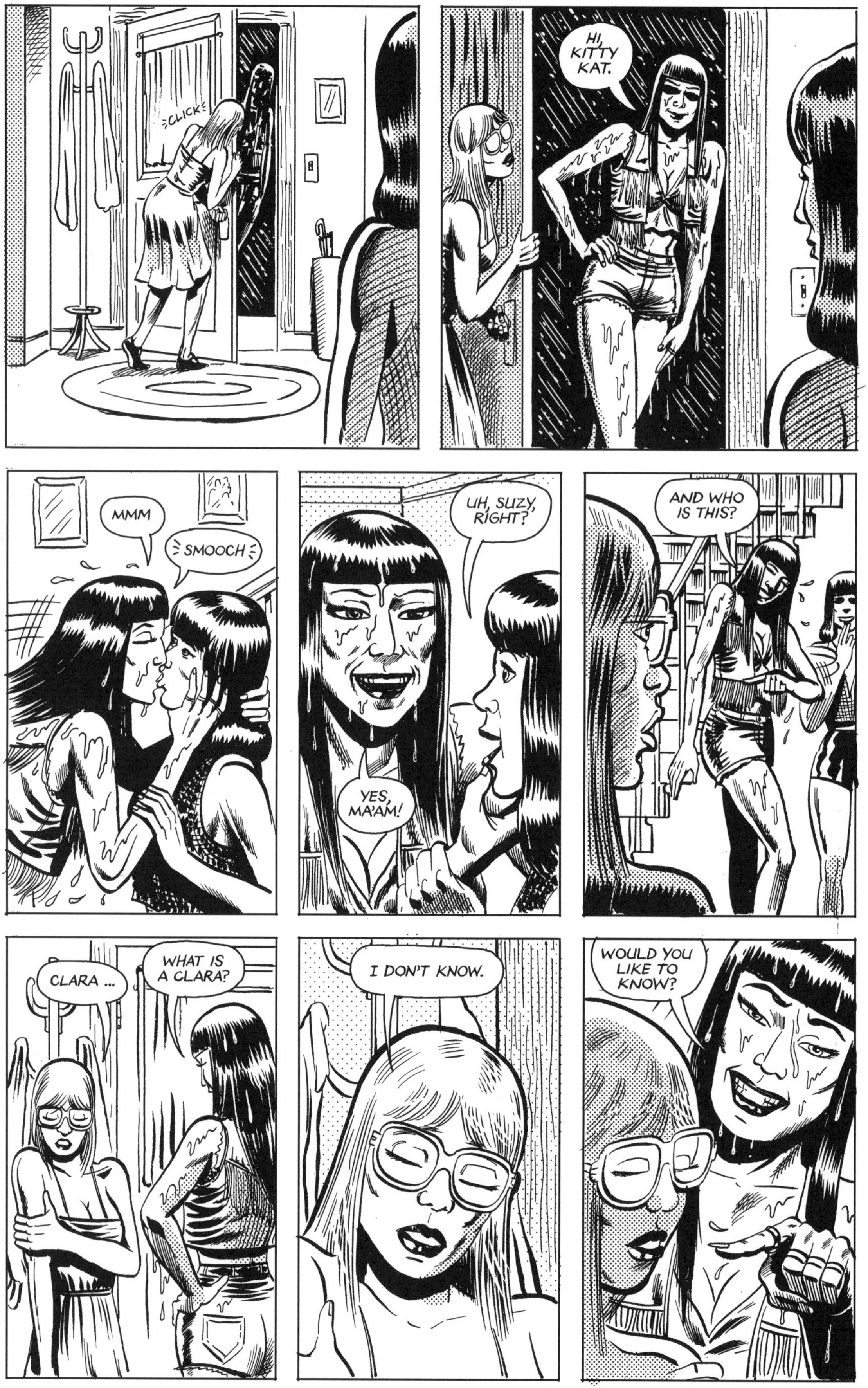
CLICK
HI, KITTY KAT.
MMM
SMOOCH
UH, SUZY, RIGHT?
YES, MA'AM!
AND WHO IS THIS?
CLARA ...
WHAT IS A CLARA?
I DON'T KNOW.
WOULD YOU LIKE TO KNOW?

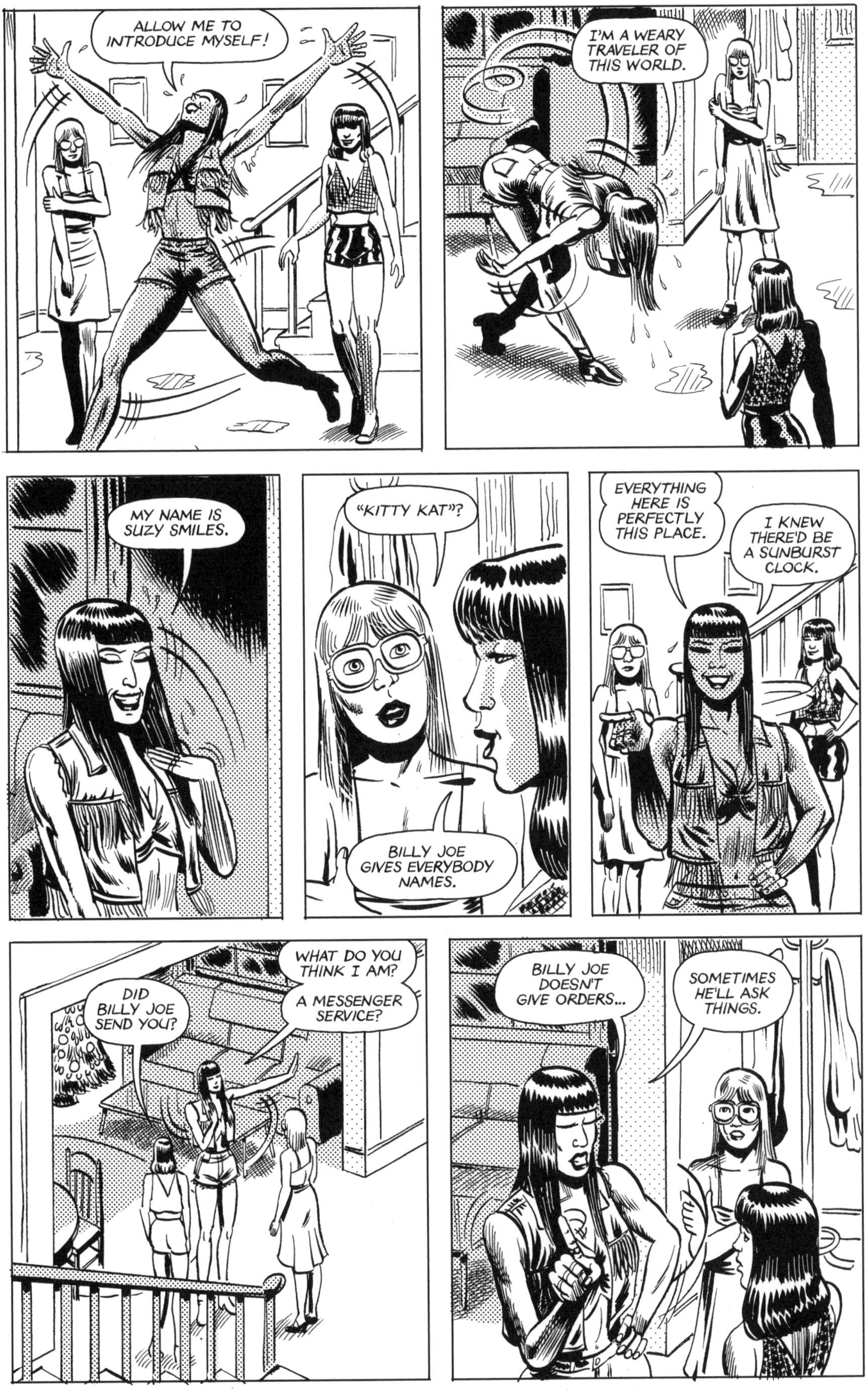
ALLOW ME TO INTRODUCE MYSELF!
I'M A WEARY TRAVELER OF THIS WORLD.
MY NAME IS SUZY SMILES.
"KITTY KAT"?
BILLY JOE GIVES EVERYBODY NAMES.
EVERYTHING HERE IS PERFECTLY THIS PLACE.
I KNEW THERE'D BE A SUNBURST CLOCK.
DID BILLY JOE SEND YOU?
WHAT DO YOU THINK I AM?
A MESSENGER SERVICE?
BILLY JOE DOESN'T GIVE ORDERS...
SOMETIMES HE'LL ASK THINGS.

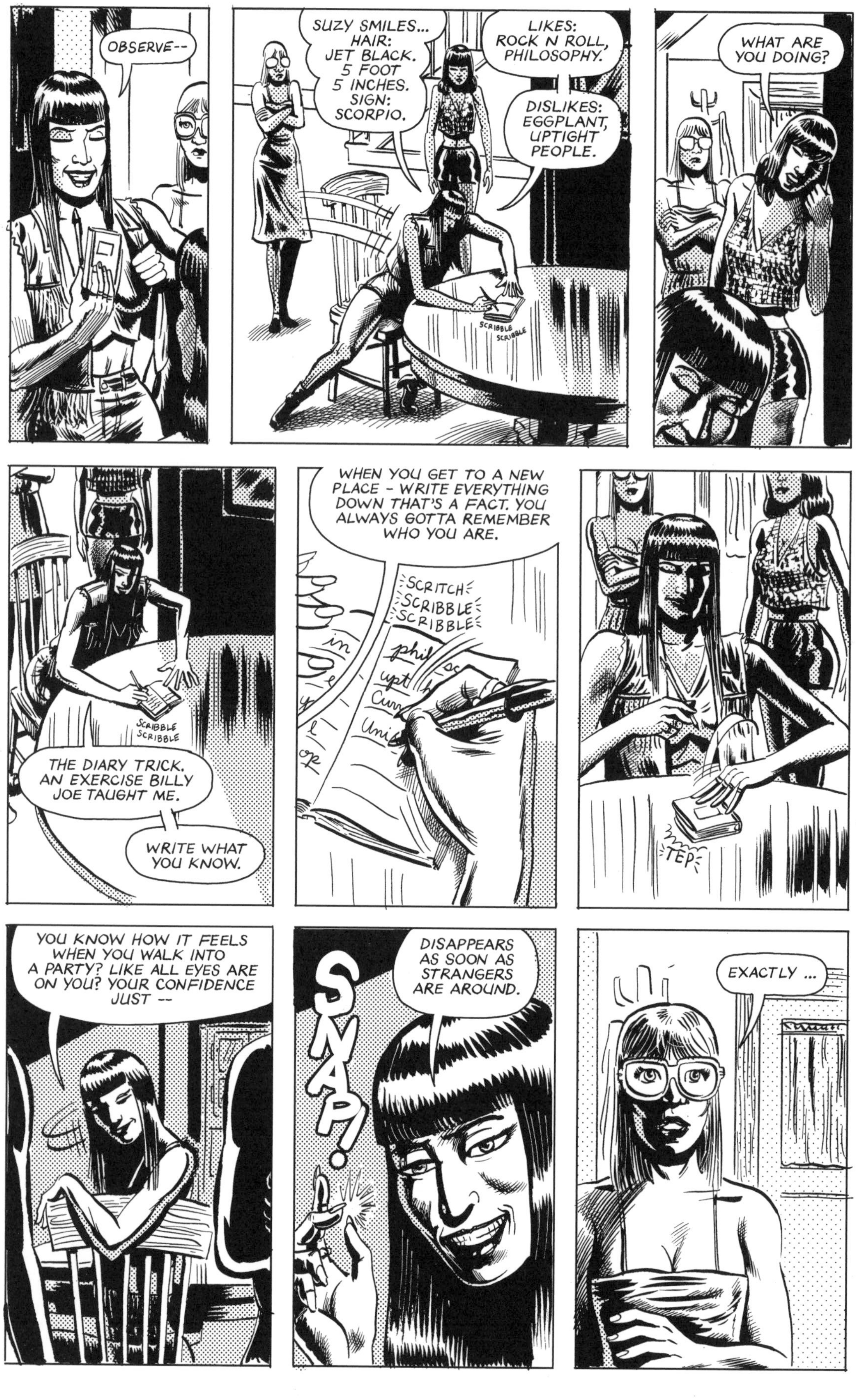
OBSERVE--
SUZY SMILES... HAIR: JET BLACK. 5 FOOT 5 INCHES. SIGN: SCORPIO.
LIKES: ROCK N ROLL, PHILOSOPHY.
DISLIKES: EGGPLANT, UPTIGHT PEOPLE.
SCRIBBLE SCRIBBLE
WHAT ARE YOU DOING?
SCRIBBLE SCRIBBLE
THE DIARY TRICK. AN EXERCISE BILLY JOE TAUGHT ME.
WRITE WHAT YOU KNOW.
WHEN YOU GET TO A NEW PLACE - WRITE EVERYTHING DOWN THAT'S A FACT. YOU ALWAYS GOTTA REMEMBER WHO YOU ARE.
SCRITCH SCRIBBLE SCRIBBLE
TEP
YOU KNOW HOW IT FEELS WHEN YOU WALK INTO A PARTY? LIKE ALL EYES ARE ON YOU? YOUR CONFIDENCE JUST --
SNAP!
DISAPPEARS AS SOON AS STRANGERS ARE AROUND.
EXACTLY ...

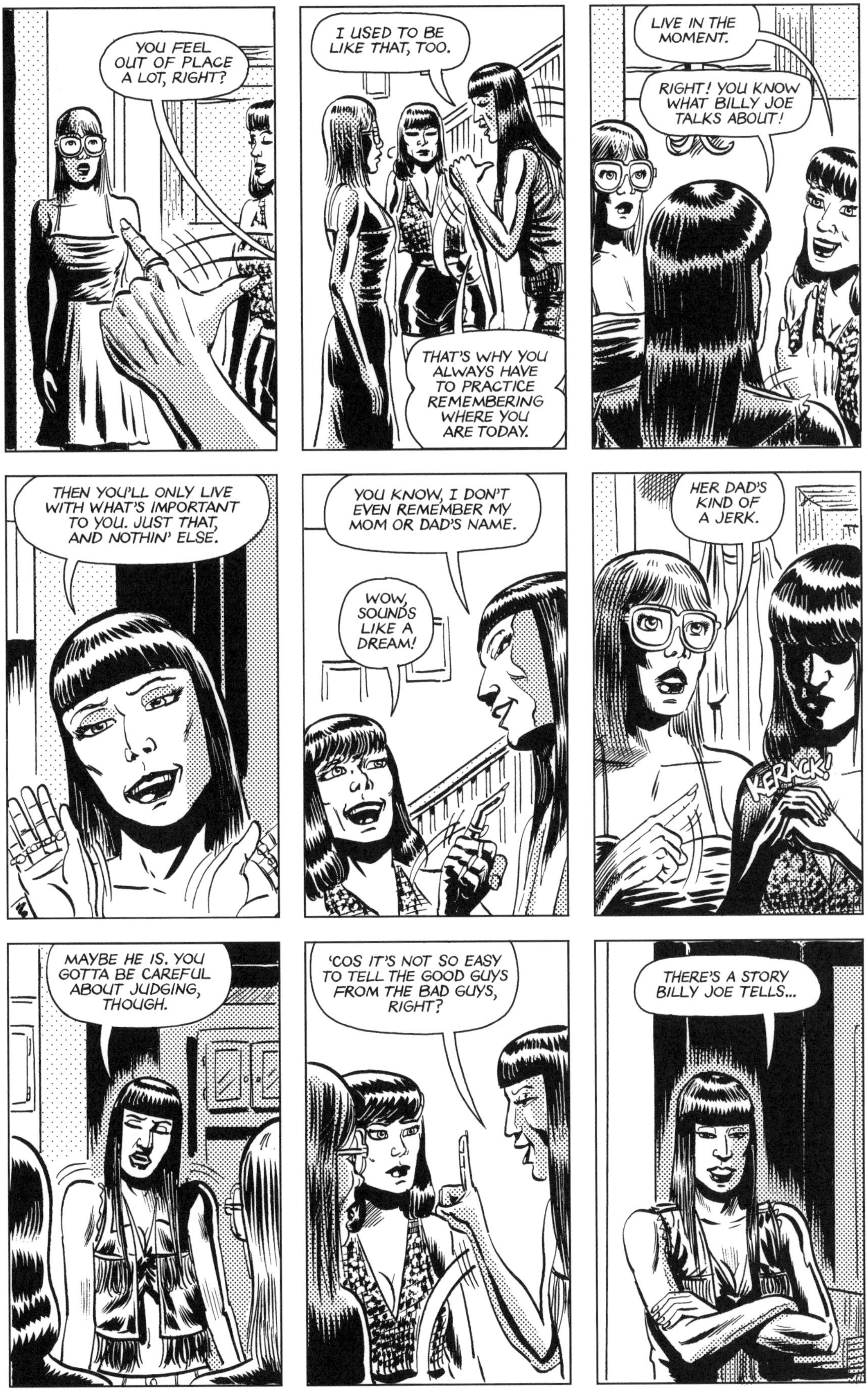
YOU FEEL OUT OF PLACE A LOT, RIGHT?
I USED TO BE LIKE THAT, TOO.
THAT'S WHY YOU ALWAYS HAVE TO PRACTICE REMEMBERING WHERE YOU ARE TODAY.
LIVE IN THE MOMENT.
RIGHT! YOU KNOW WHAT BILLY JOE TALKS ABOUT!
THEN YOU'LL ONLY LIVE WITH WHAT'S IMPORTANT TO YOU. JUST THAT, AND NOTHIN' ELSE.
YOU KNOW, I DON'T EVEN REMEMBER MY MOM OR DAD'S NAME.
WOW, SOUNDS LIKE A DREAM!
HER DAD'S KIND OF A JERK.
KERACK!
MAYBE HE IS. YOU GOTTA BE CAREFUL ABOUT JUDGING, THOUGH.
'COS IT'S NOT SO EASY TO TELL THE GOOD GUYS FROM THE BAD GUYS, RIGHT?
THERE'S A STORY BILLY JOE TELLS...

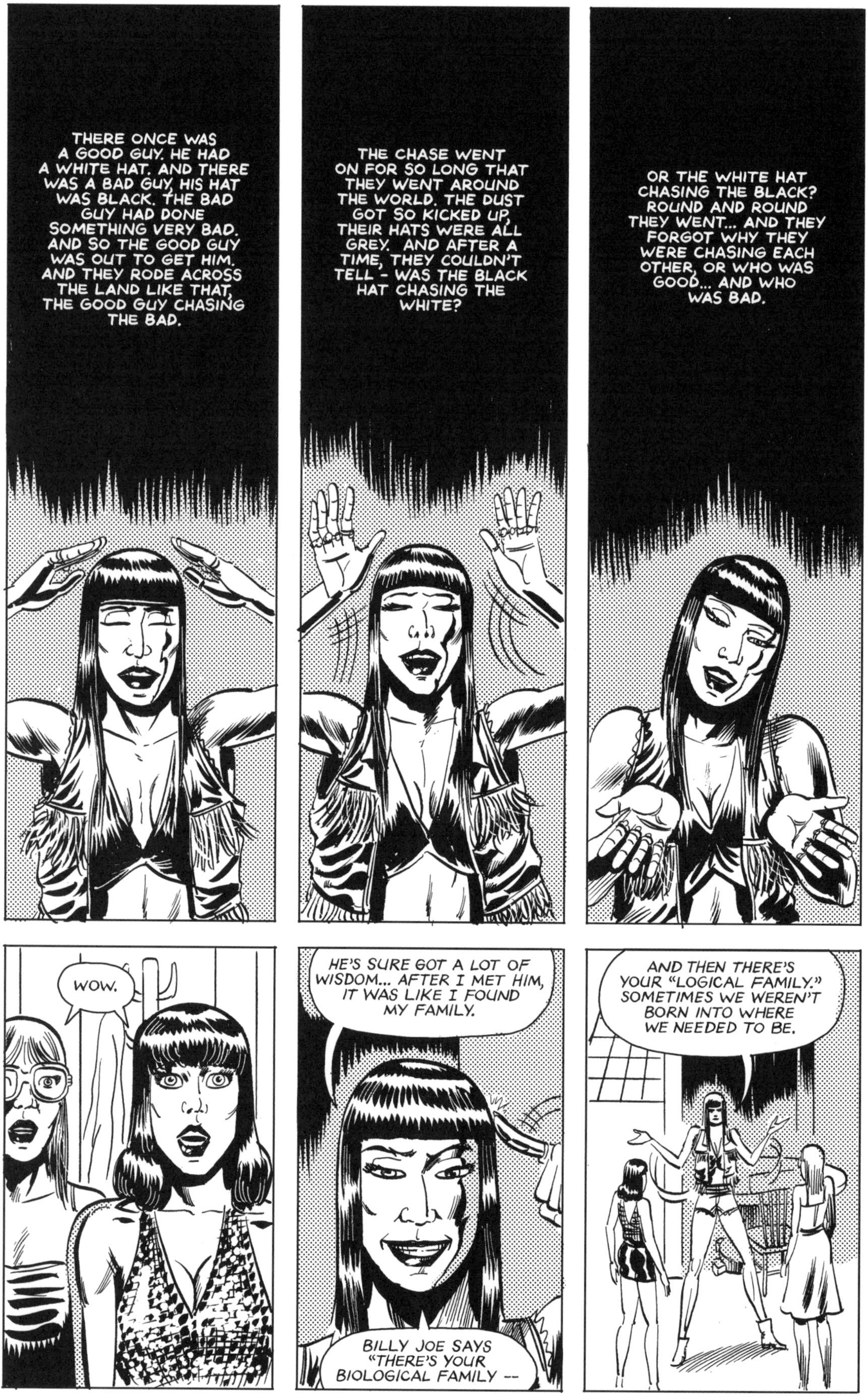
THERE ONCE WAS A GOOD GUY. HE HAD A WHITE HAT. AND THERE WAS A BAD GUY, HIS HAT WAS BLACK. THE BAD GUY HAD DONE SOMETHING VERY BAD. AND SO THE GOOD GUY WAS OUT TO GET HIM. AND THEY RODE ACROSS THE LAND LIKE THAT, THE GOOD GUY CHASING THE BAD.
THE CHASE WENT ON FOR SO LONG THAT THEY WENT AROUND THE WORLD. THE DUST GOT SO KICKED UP, THEIR HATS WERE ALL GREY. AND AFTER A TIME, THEY COULDN'T TELL - WAS THE BLACK HAT CHASING THE WHITE?
OR THE WHITE HAT CHASING THE BLACK? ROUND AND ROUND THEY WENT... AND THEY FORGOT WHY THEY WERE CHASING EACH OTHER, OR WHO WAS GOOD... AND WHO WAS BAD.
WOW.
HE'S SURE GOT A LOT OF WISDOM... AFTER I MET HIM, IT WAS LIKE I FOUND MY FAMILY.
BILLY JOE SAYS "THERE'S YOUR BIOLOGICAL FAMILY --
AND THEN THERE'S YOUR "LOGICAL FAMILY." SOMETIMES WE WEREN'T BORN INTO WHERE WE NEEDED TO BE.

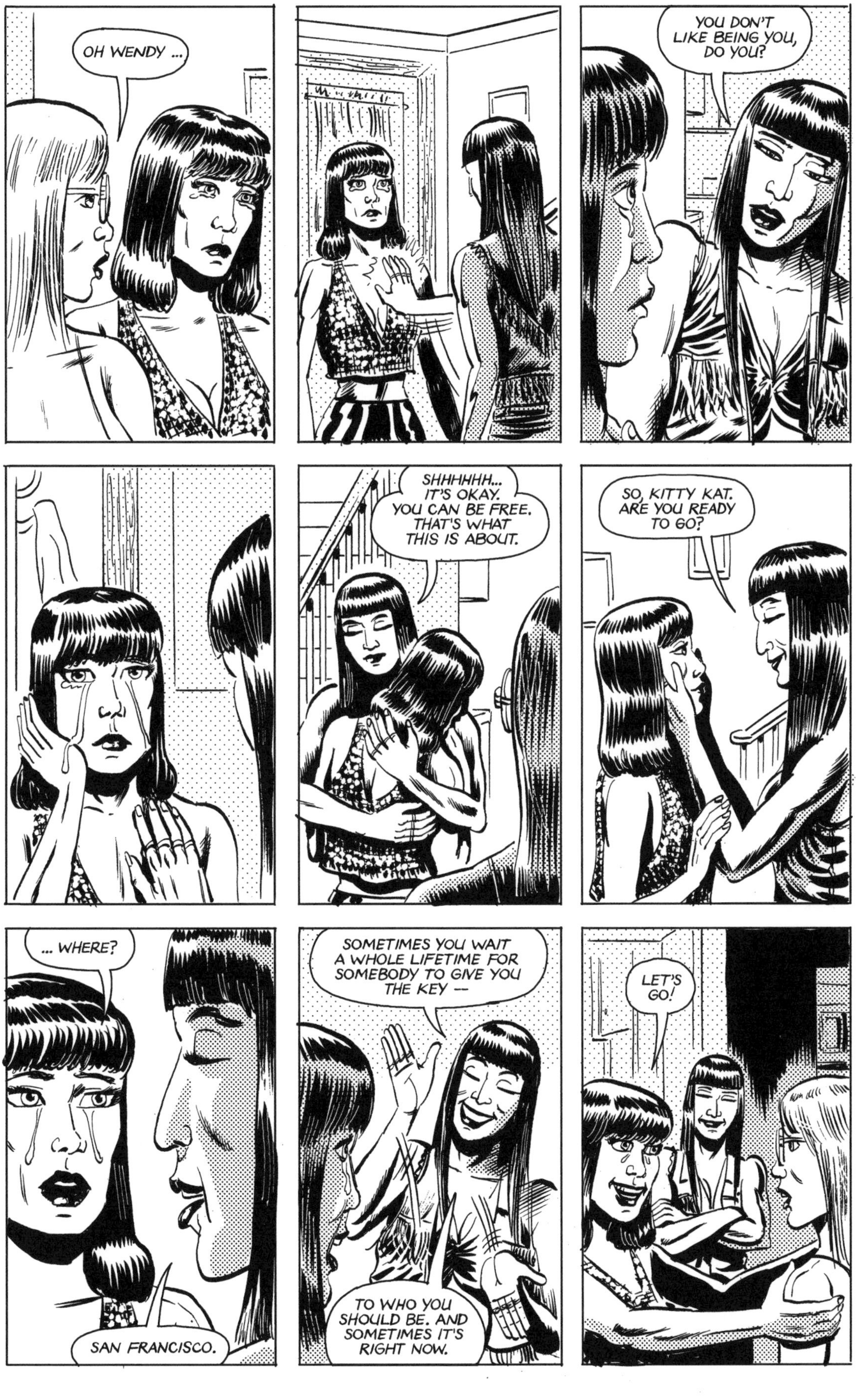
OH WENDY ...
YOU DON'T LIKE BEING YOU, DO YOU?
SHHHHHH... IT'S OKAY. YOU CAN BE FREE. THAT'S WHAT THIS IS ABOUT.
SO, KITTY KAT. ARE YOU READY TO GO?
... WHERE?
SAN FRANCISCO.
SOMETIMES YOU WAIT A WHOLE LIFETIME FOR SOMEBODY TO GIVE YOU THE KEY --
TO WHO YOU SHOULD BE. AND SOMETIMES IT'S RIGHT NOW.
LET'S GO!

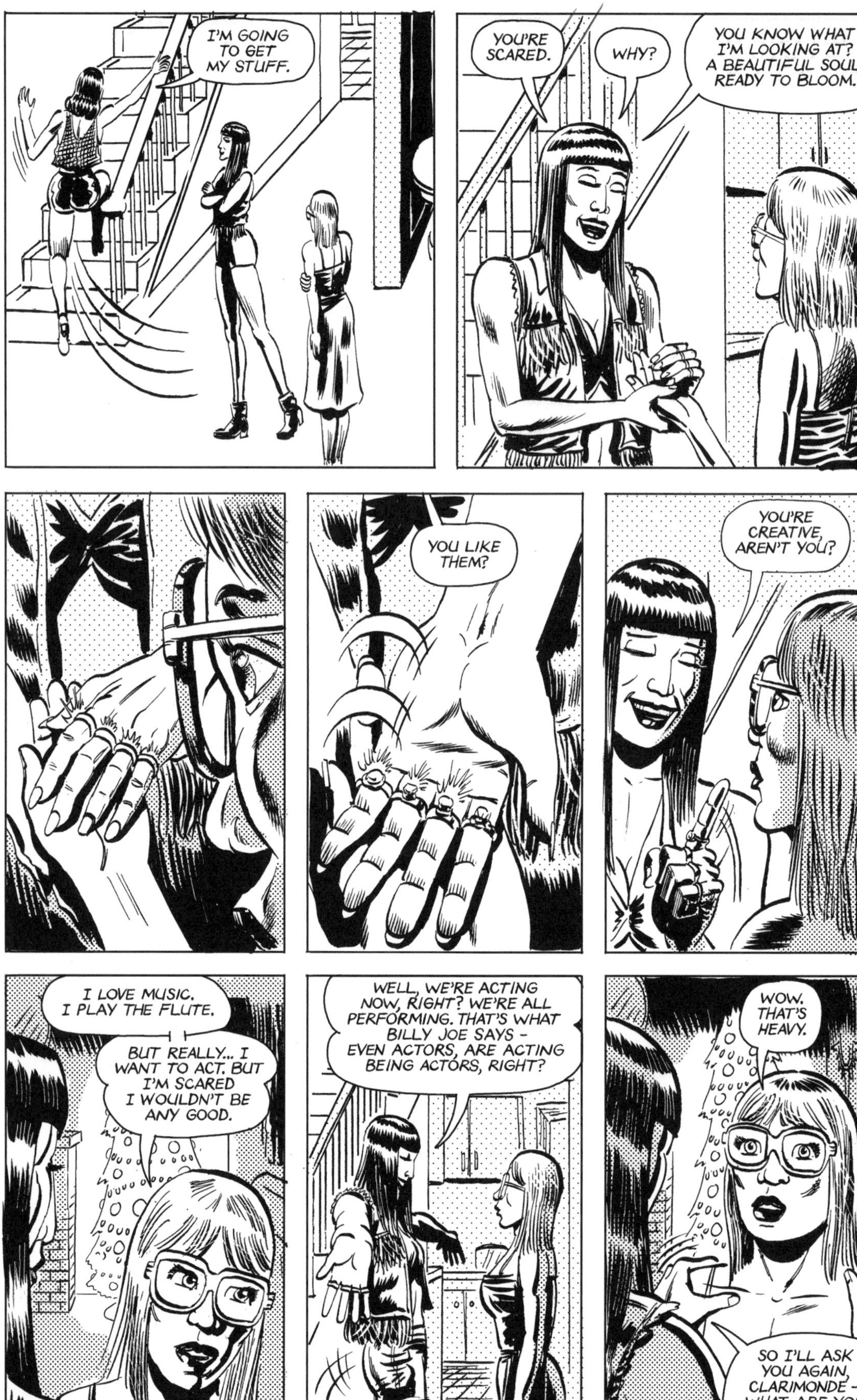
I'M GOING TO GET MY STUFF.
YOU'RE SCARED.
WHY?
YOU KNOW WHAT I'M LOOKING AT? A BEAUTIFUL SOUL, READY TO BLOOM.
YOU LIKE THEM?
YOU'RE CREATIVE, AREN'T YOU?
I LOVE MUSIC. I PLAY THE FLUTE.
BUT REALLY... I WANT TO ACT. BUT I'M SCARED I WOULDN'T BE ANY GOOD.
WELL, WE'RE ACTING NOW, RIGHT? WE'RE ALL PERFORMING. THAT'S WHAT BILLY JOE SAYS - EVEN ACTORS, ARE ACTING BEING ACTORS, RIGHT?
WOW. THAT'S HEAVY.
SO I'LL ASK YOU AGAIN, CLARIMONDE - WHAT ARE YOU AFRAID OF?

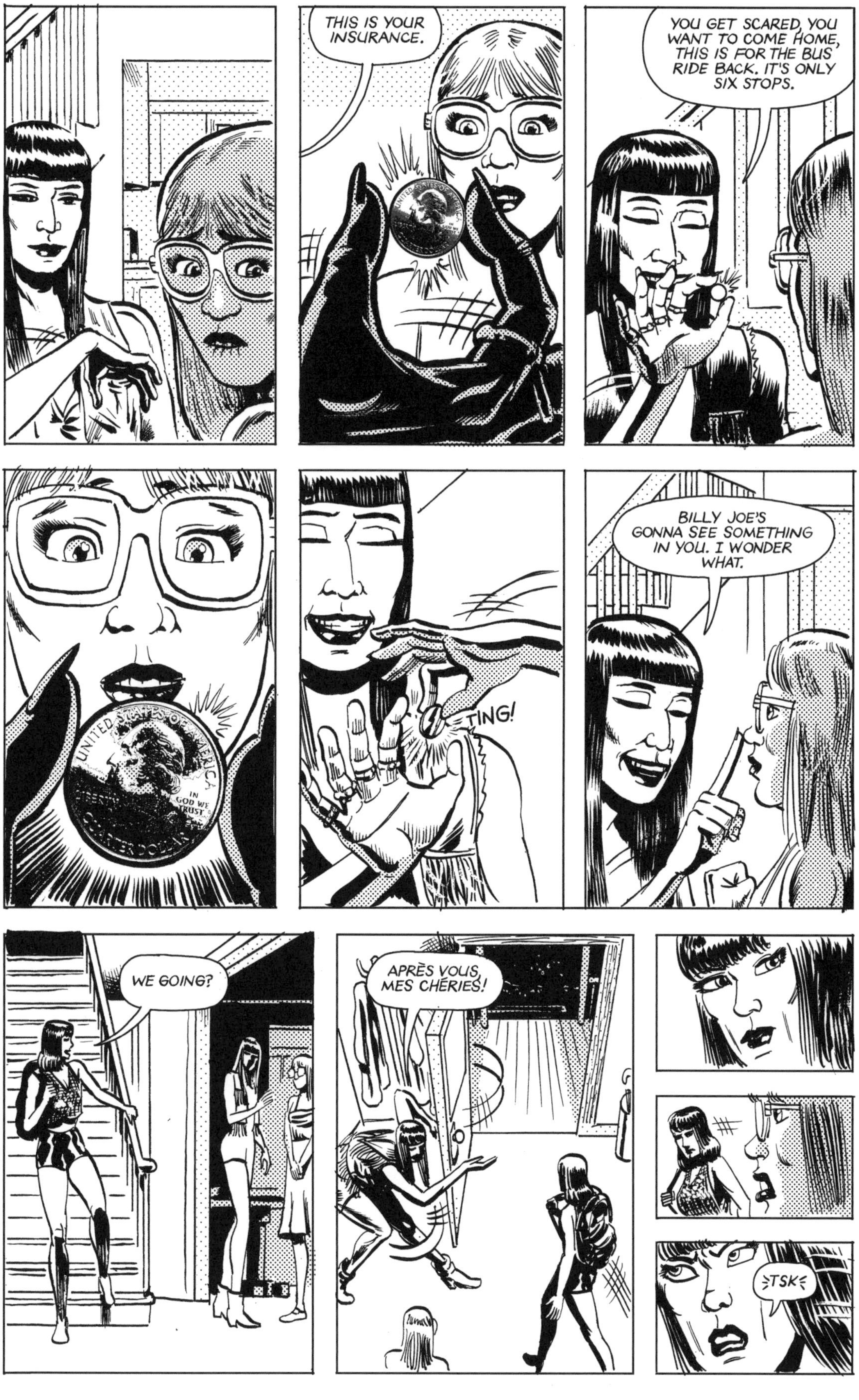
THIS IS YOUR INSURANCE.
YOU GET SCARED, YOU WANT TO COME HOME, THIS IS FOR THE BUS RIDE BACK. IT'S ONLY SIX STOPS.
UNITED STATES OF AMERICA
LIBERTY
IN GOD WE TRUST
QUARTER DOLLAR
TING!
BILLY JOE'S GONNA SEE SOMETHING IN YOU. I WONDER WHAT.
WE GOING?
APRÈS VOUS, MES CHÉRIES!
TSK

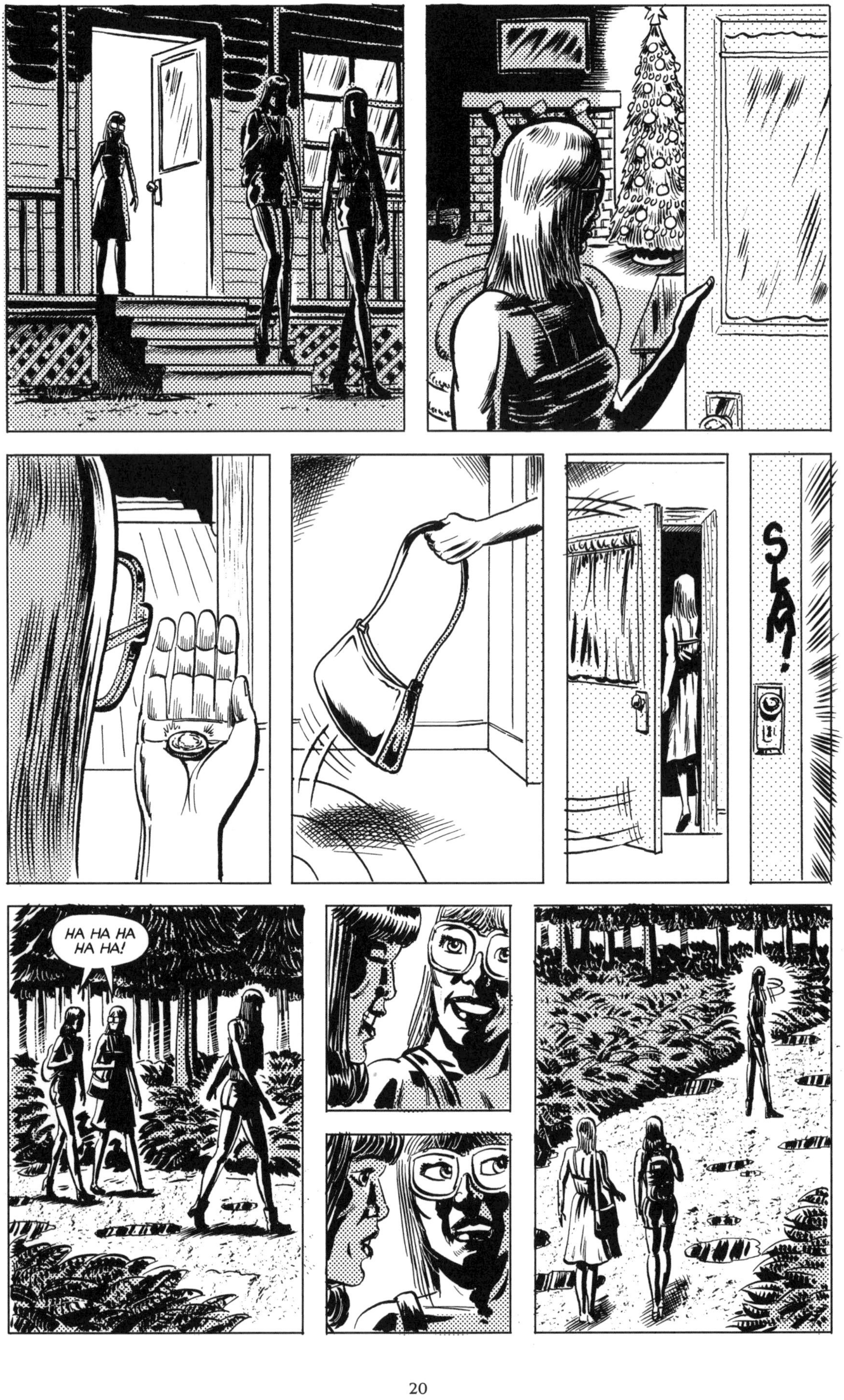
SLAM!
HA HA HA HA HA!

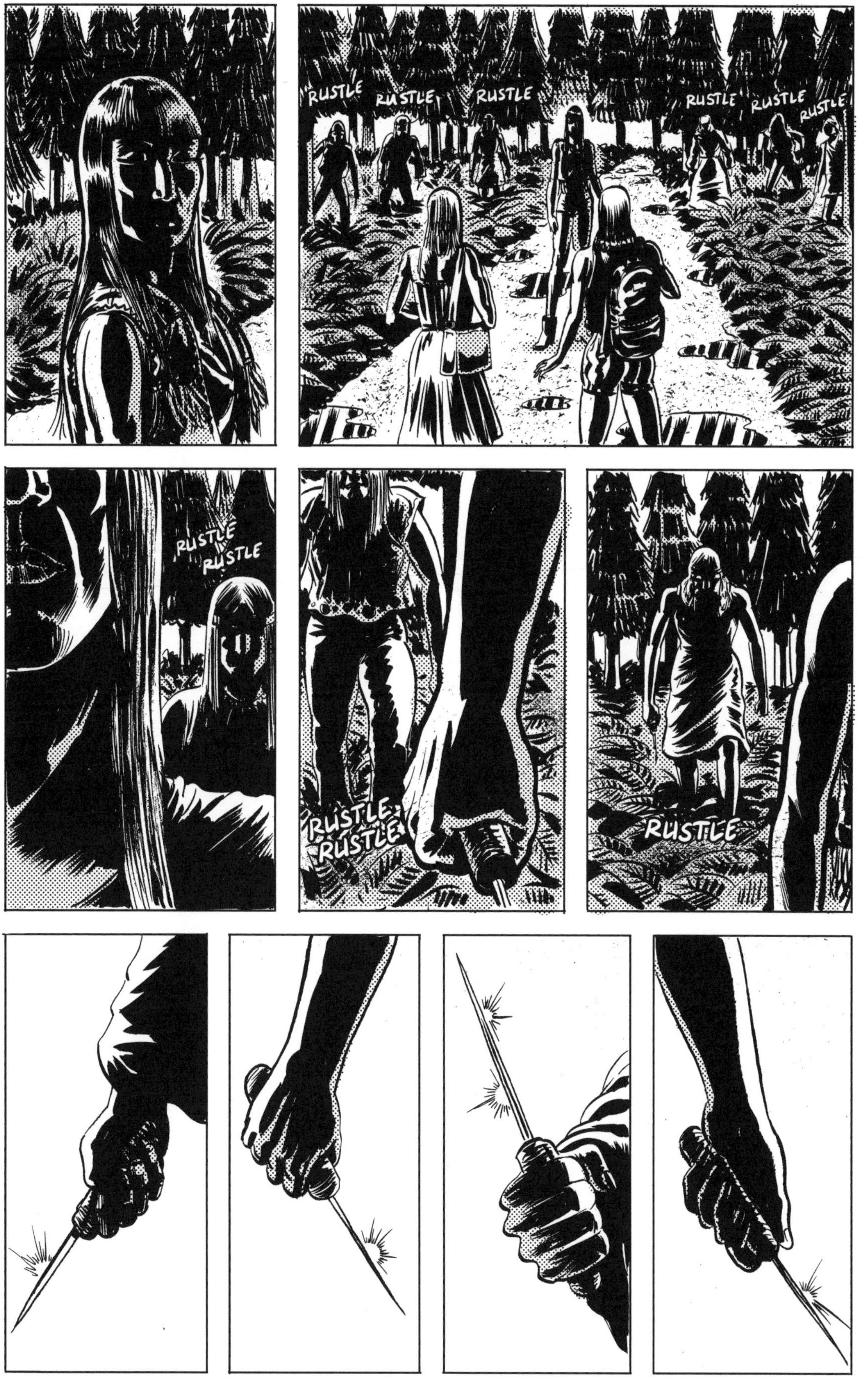
RUSTLE
RUSTLE
RUSTLE
RUSTLE
RUSTLE
RUSTLE
RUSTLE
RUSTLE
RUSTLE
RUSTLE
RUSTLE

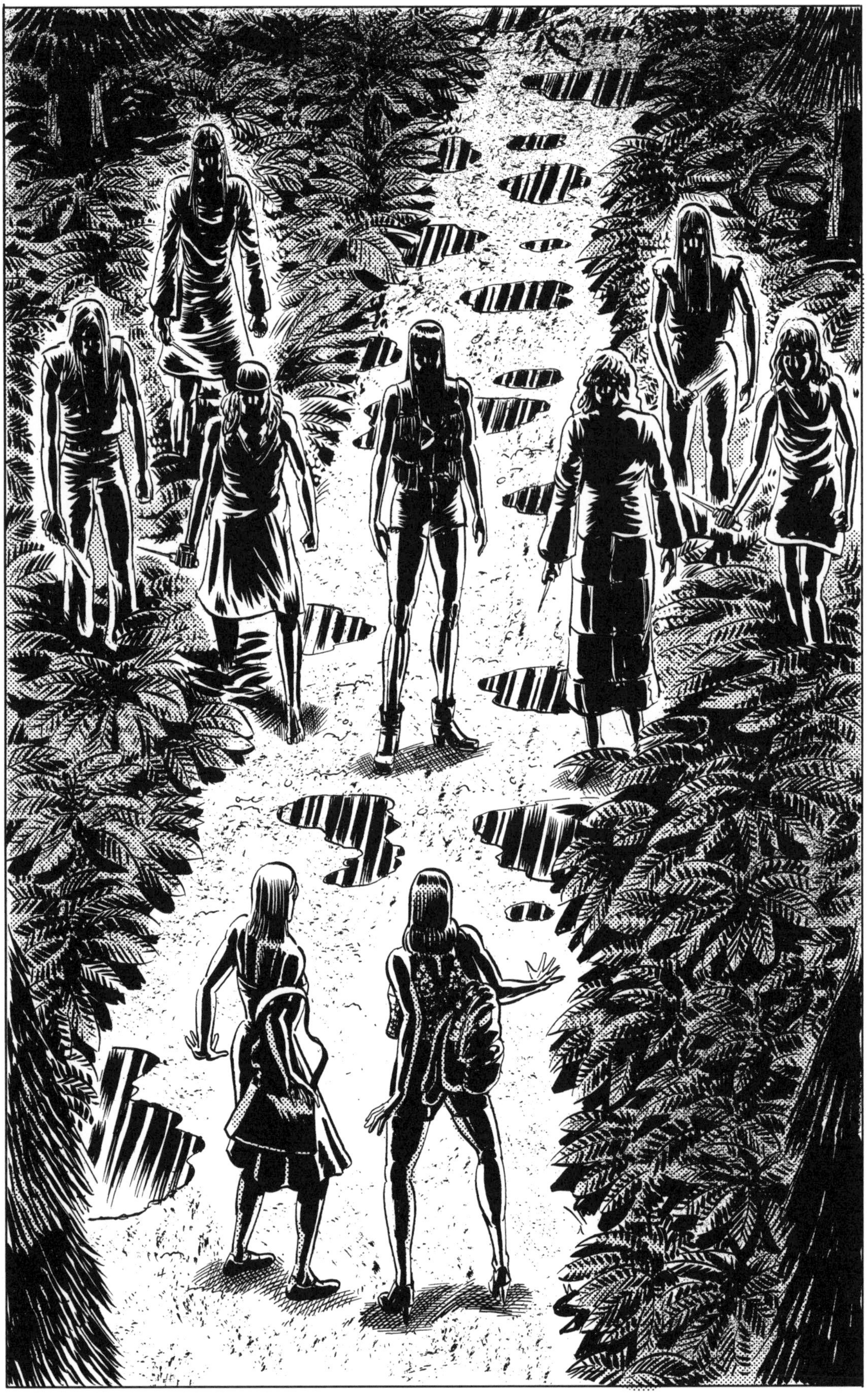

FIVE MONTHS LATER

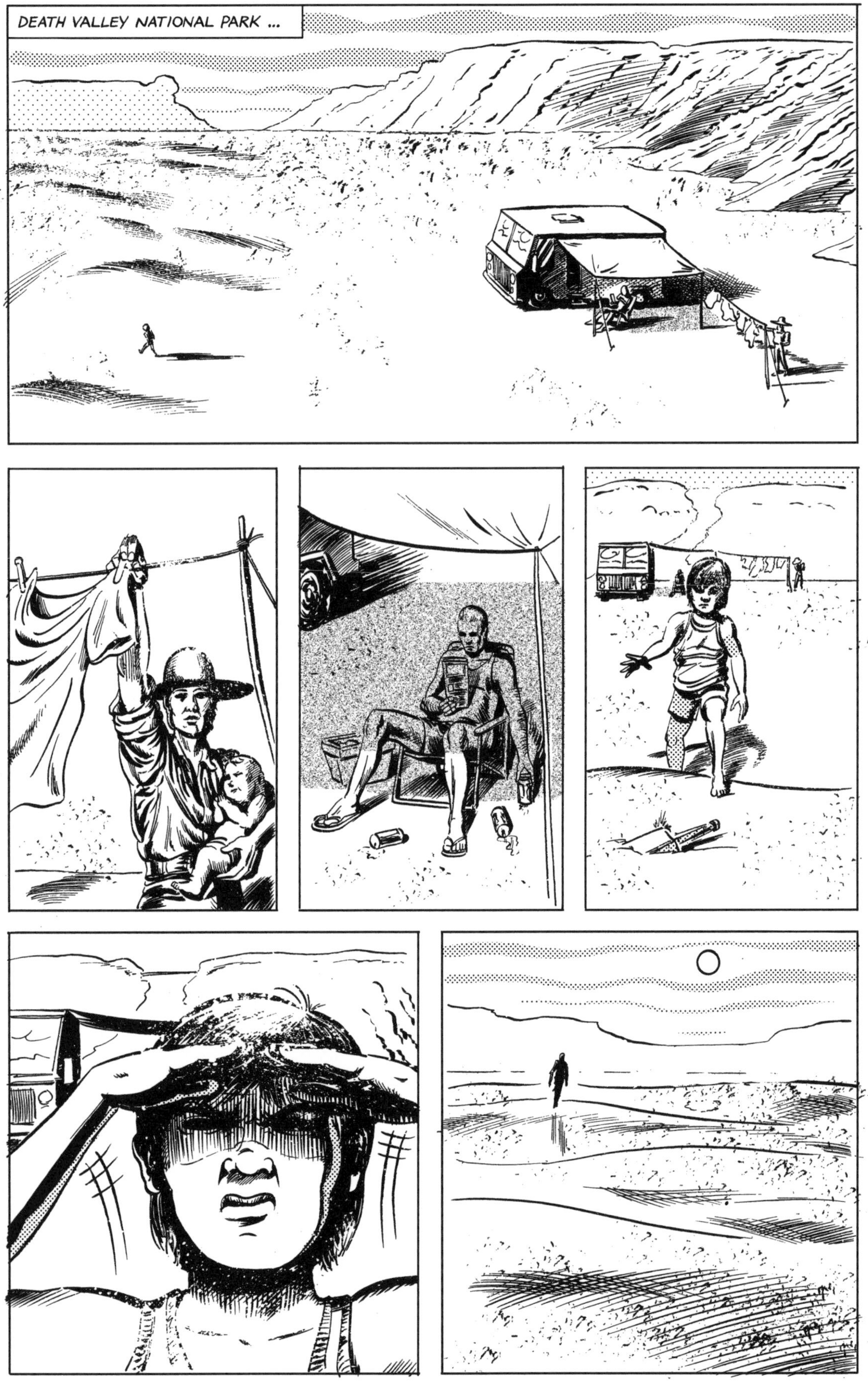
DEATH VALLEY NATIONAL PARK ...

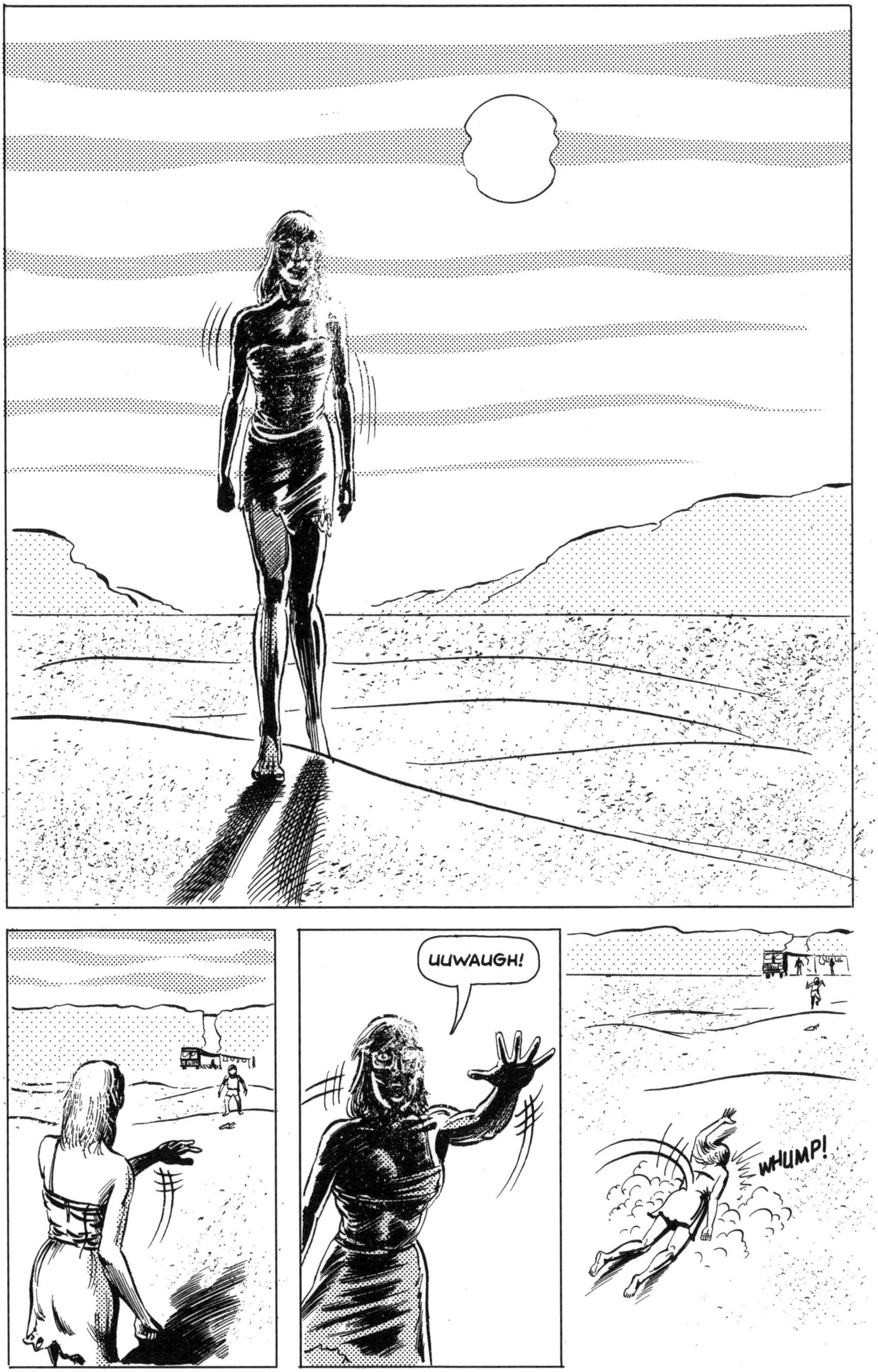
UUWAUGH!
WHUMP!

PRESENT DAY

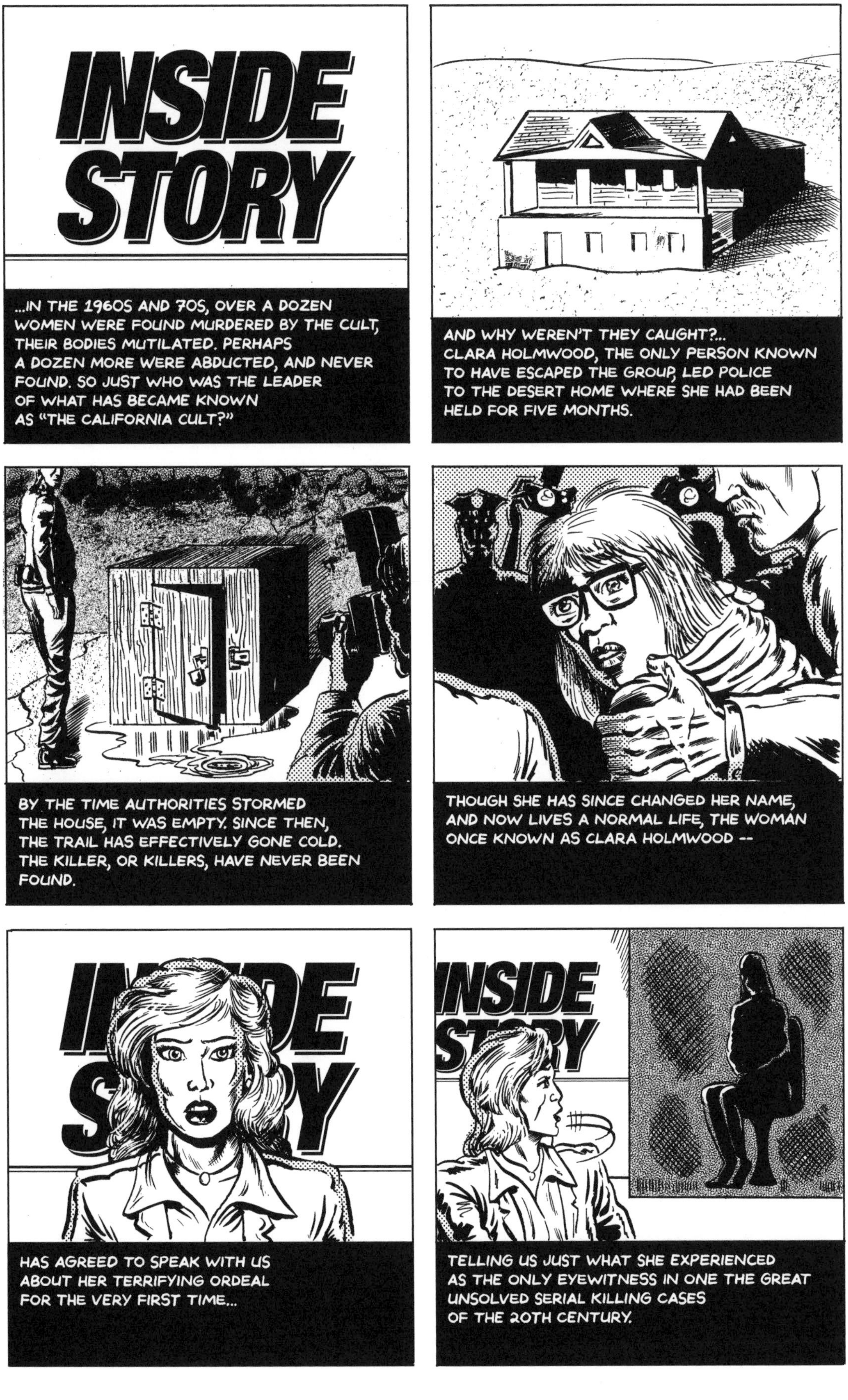
INSIDE STORY
...IN THE 1960S AND 70S, OVER A DOZEN WOMEN WERE FOUND MURDERED BY THE CULT, THEIR BODIES MUTILATED. PERHAPS A DOZEN MORE WERE ABDUCTED, AND NEVER FOUND. SO JUST WHO WAS THE LEADER OF WHAT HAS BECAME KNOWN AS "THE CALIFORNIA CULT?"
AND WHY WEREN'T THEY CAUGHT?... CLARA HOLMWOOD, THE ONLY PERSON KNOWN TO HAVE ESCAPED THE GROUP, LED POLICE TO THE DESERT HOME WHERE SHE HAD BEEN HELD FOR FIVE MONTHS.
BY THE TIME AUTHORITIES STORMED THE HOUSE, IT WAS EMPTY. SINCE THEN, THE TRAIL HAS EFFECTIVELY GONE COLD. THE KILLER, OR KILLERS, HAVE NEVER BEEN FOUND.
THOUGH SHE HAS SINCE CHANGED HER NAME, AND NOW LIVES A NORMAL LIFE, THE WOMAN ONCE KNOWN AS CLARA HOLMWOOD --
HAS AGREED TO SPEAK WITH US ABOUT HER TERRIFYING ORDEAL FOR THE VERY FIRST TIME...
INSIDE STORY
TELLING US JUST WHAT SHE EXPERIENCED AS THE ONLY EYEWITNESS IN ONE THE GREAT UNSOLVED SERIAL KILLING CASES OF THE 20TH CENTURY.

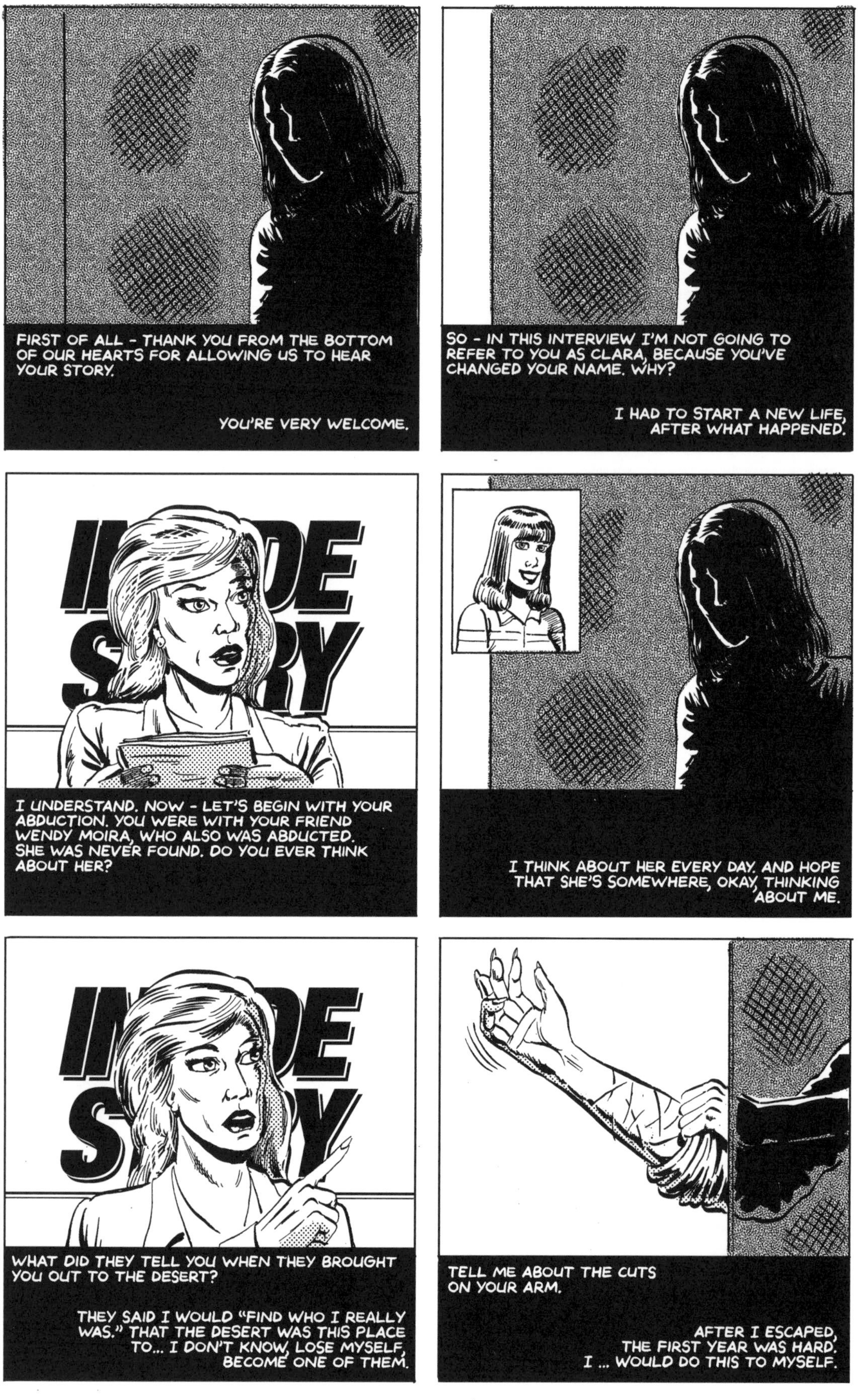
FIRST OF ALL - THANK YOU FROM THE BOTTOM OF OUR HEARTS FOR ALLOWING US TO HEAR YOUR STORY.
YOU'RE VERY WELCOME.
SO - IN THIS INTERVIEW I'M NOT GOING TO REFER TO YOU AS CLARA, BECAUSE YOU'VE CHANGED YOUR NAME. WHY?
I HAD TO START A NEW LIFE, AFTER WHAT HAPPENED.
I UNDERSTAND. NOW - LET'S BEGIN WITH YOUR ABDUCTION. YOU WERE WITH YOUR FRIEND WENDY MOIRA, WHO ALSO WAS ABDUCTED. SHE WAS NEVER FOUND. DO YOU EVER THINK ABOUT HER?
I THINK ABOUT HER EVERY DAY. AND HOPE THAT SHE'S SOMEWHERE, OKAY, THINKING ABOUT ME.
WHAT DID THEY TELL YOU WHEN THEY BROUGHT YOU OUT TO THE DESERT?
THEY SAID I WOULD "FIND WHO I REALLY WAS." THAT THE DESERT WAS THIS PLACE TO... I DON'T KNOW, LOSE MYSELF, BECOME ONE OF THEM.
TELL ME ABOUT THE CUTS ON YOUR ARM.
AFTER I ESCAPED, THE FIRST YEAR WAS HARD. I ... WOULD DO THIS TO MYSELF.

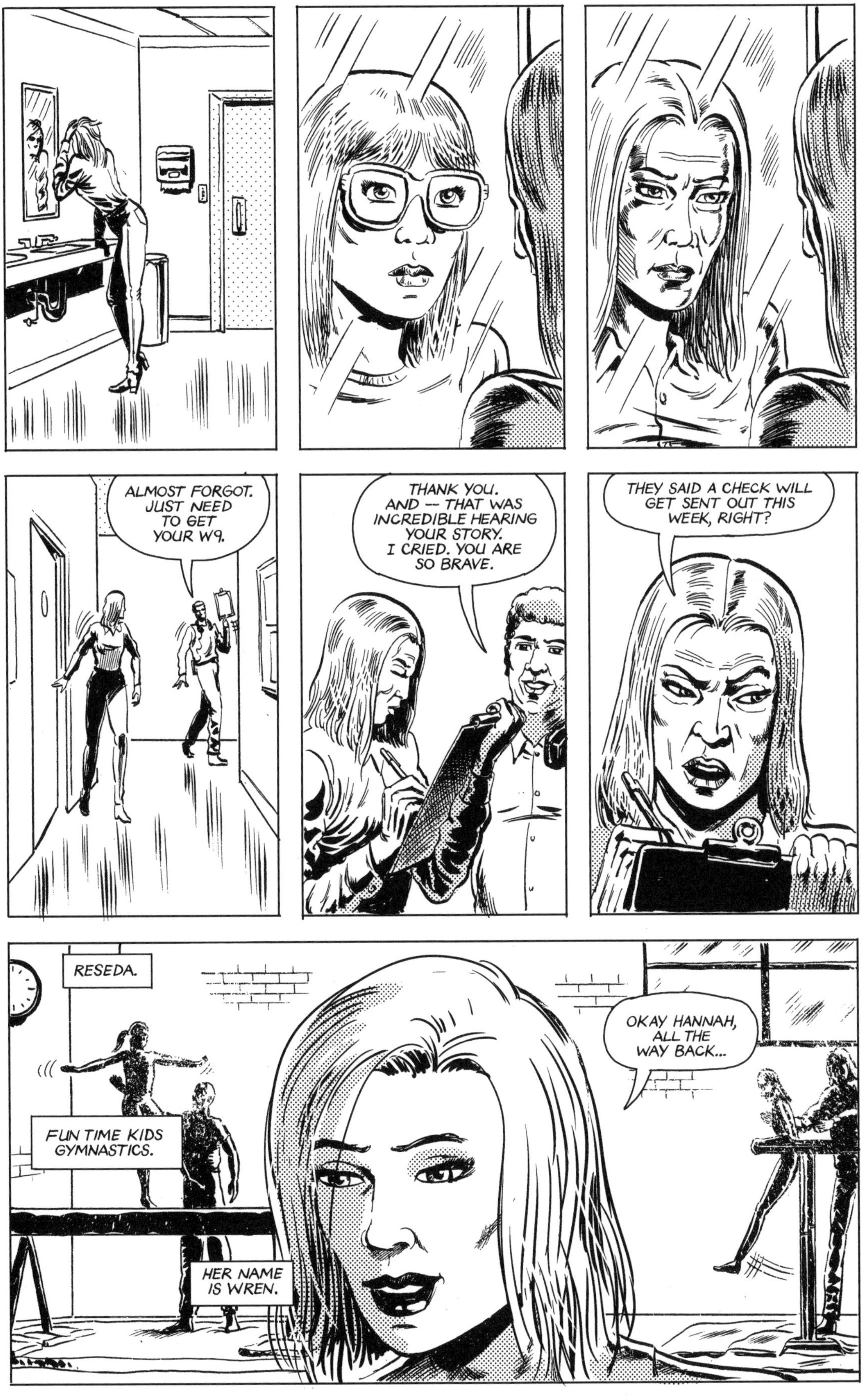
ALMOST FORGOT. JUST NEED TO GET YOUR W9.
THANK YOU. AND -- THAT WAS INCREDIBLE HEARING YOUR STORY. I CRIED. YOU ARE SO BRAVE.
THEY SAID A CHECK WILL GET SENT OUT THIS WEEK, RIGHT?
RESEDA.
FUN TIME KIDS GYMNASTICS.
OKAY HANNAH, ALL THE WAY BACK...
HER NAME IS WREN.

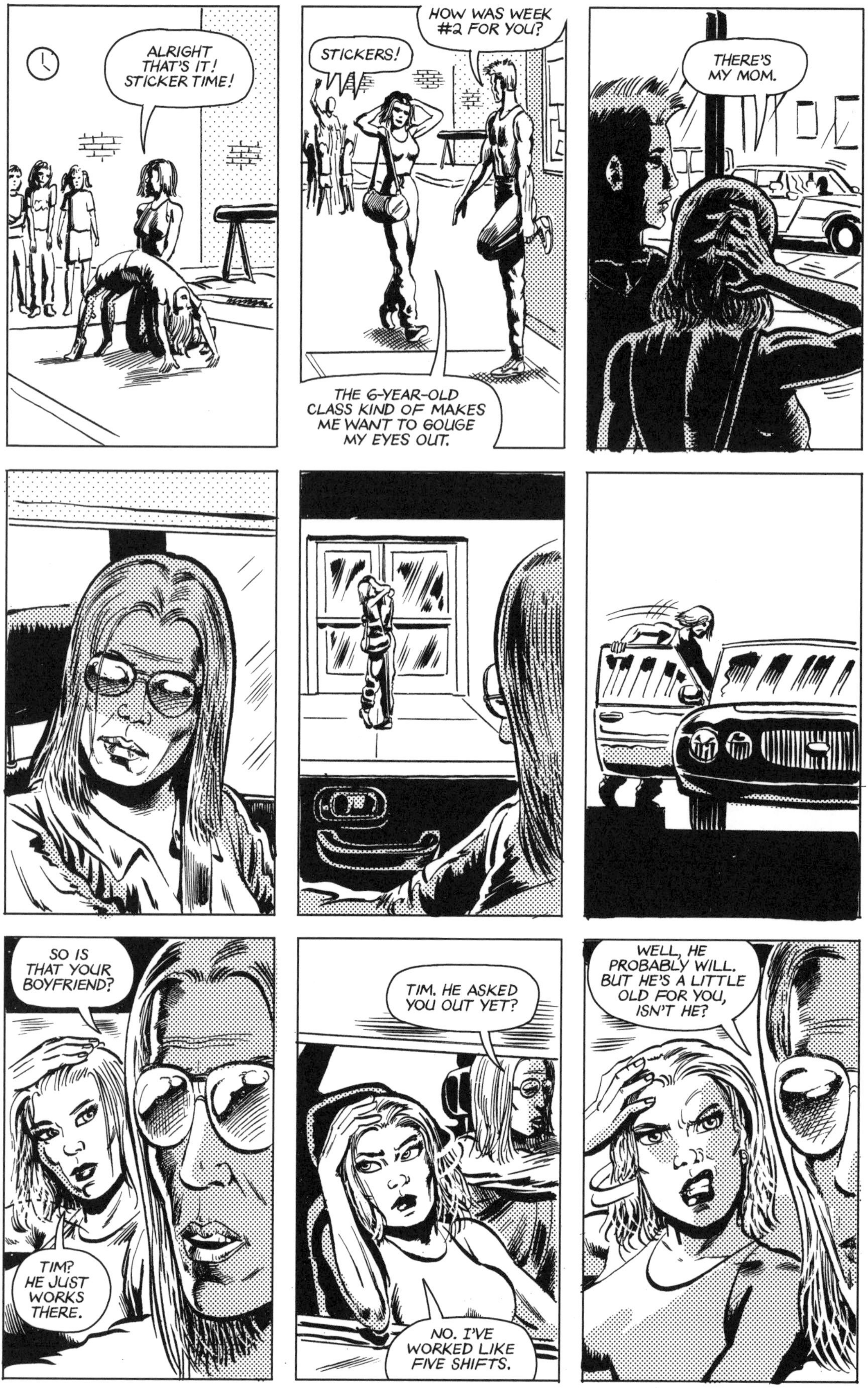
ALRIGHT THAT'S IT! STICKER TIME!
HOW WAS WEEK #2 FOR YOU?
STICKERS!
THE 6-YEAR-OLD CLASS KIND OF MAKES ME WANT TO GOUGE MY EYES OUT.
THERE'S MY MOM.
SO IS THAT YOUR BOYFRIEND?
TIM? HE JUST WORKS THERE.
TIM. HE ASKED YOU OUT YET?
NO. I'VE WORKED LIKE FIVE SHIFTS.
WELL, HE PROBABLY WILL. BUT HE'S A LITTLE OLD FOR YOU, ISN'T HE?

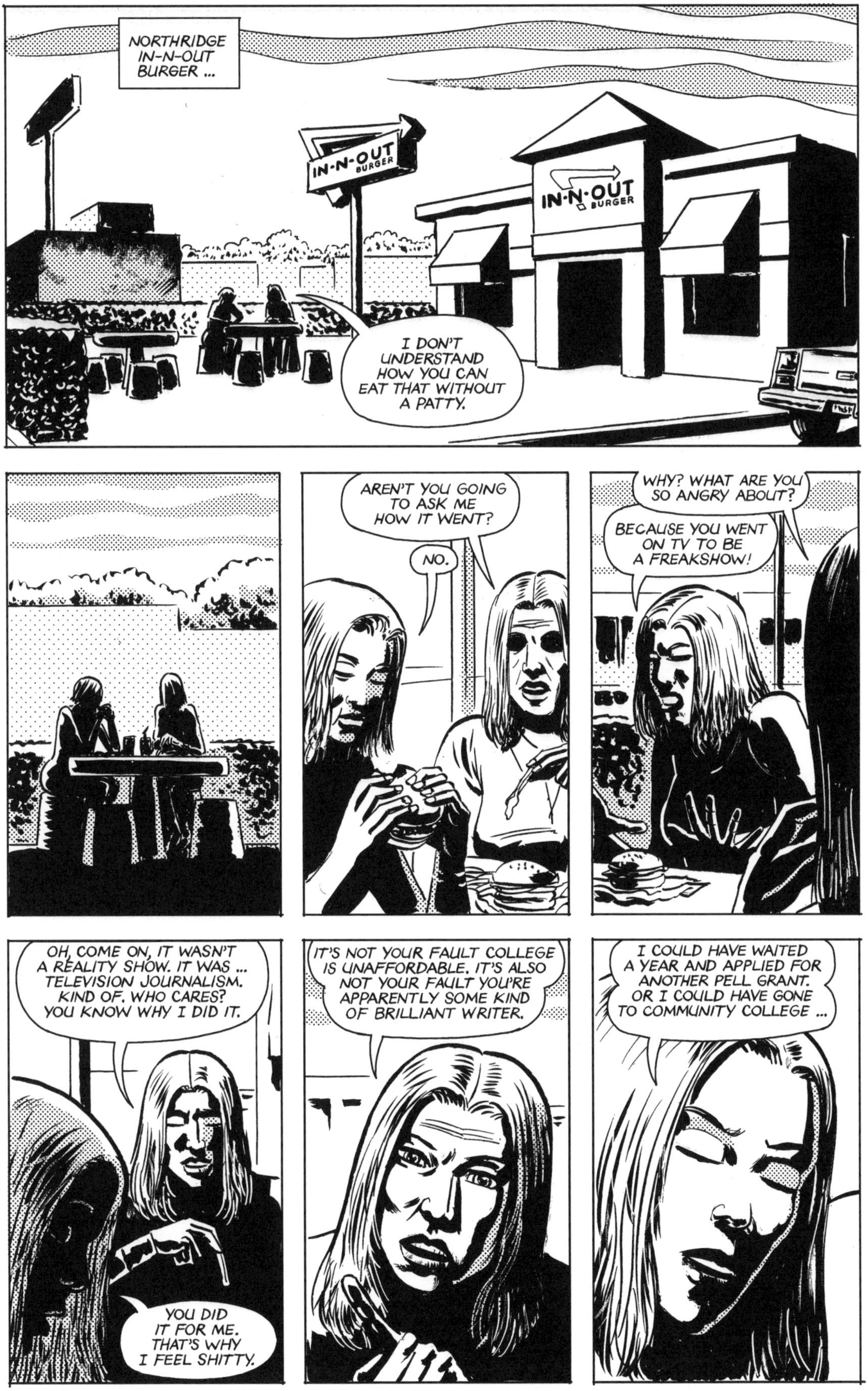
NORTHRIDGE IN-N-OUT BURGER ...
IN-N-OUT BURGER
IN-N-OUT BURGER
I DON'T UNDERSTAND HOW YOU CAN EAT THAT WITHOUT A PATTY.
AREN'T YOU GOING TO ASK ME HOW IT WENT?
NO.
WHY? WHAT ARE YOU SO ANGRY ABOUT?
BECAUSE YOU WENT ON TV TO BE A FREAKSHOW!
OH, COME ON, IT WASN'T A REALITY SHOW. IT WAS ... TELEVISION JOURNALISM. KIND OF. WHO CARES? YOU KNOW WHY I DID IT.
YOU DID IT FOR ME. THAT'S WHY I FEEL SHITTY.
IT'S NOT YOUR FAULT COLLEGE IS UNAFFORDABLE. IT'S ALSO NOT YOUR FAULT YOU'RE APPARENTLY SOME KIND OF BRILLIANT WRITER.
I COULD HAVE WAITED A YEAR AND APPLIED FOR ANOTHER PELL GRANT. OR I COULD HAVE GONE TO COMMUNITY COLLEGE ...

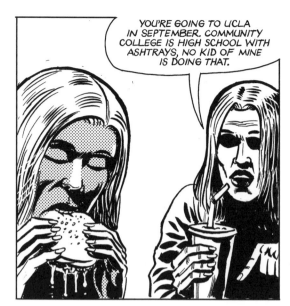

YOU'RE GOING TO UCLA IN SEPTEMBER. COMMUNITY COLLEGE IS HIGH SCHOOL WITH ASHTRAYS, NO KID OF MINE IS DOING THAT.

THAT IS AN EXTREMELY DATED REFERENCE.

MUNCH MUNCH

SLURP!

I'M AN EXTREMELY DATED REFERENCE.

YOU STILL LIKE THAT BRACELET?

MUNCH MUNCH

YEAH, YEAH, I DO. I THINK IT'S COOL.

CHATSWORTH.

DEEP IN THE SAN FERNANDO VALLEY.

ROWS OF 1970S BUILDS LINE THE ROADS.

INCLUDING LUCY'S HOUSE.

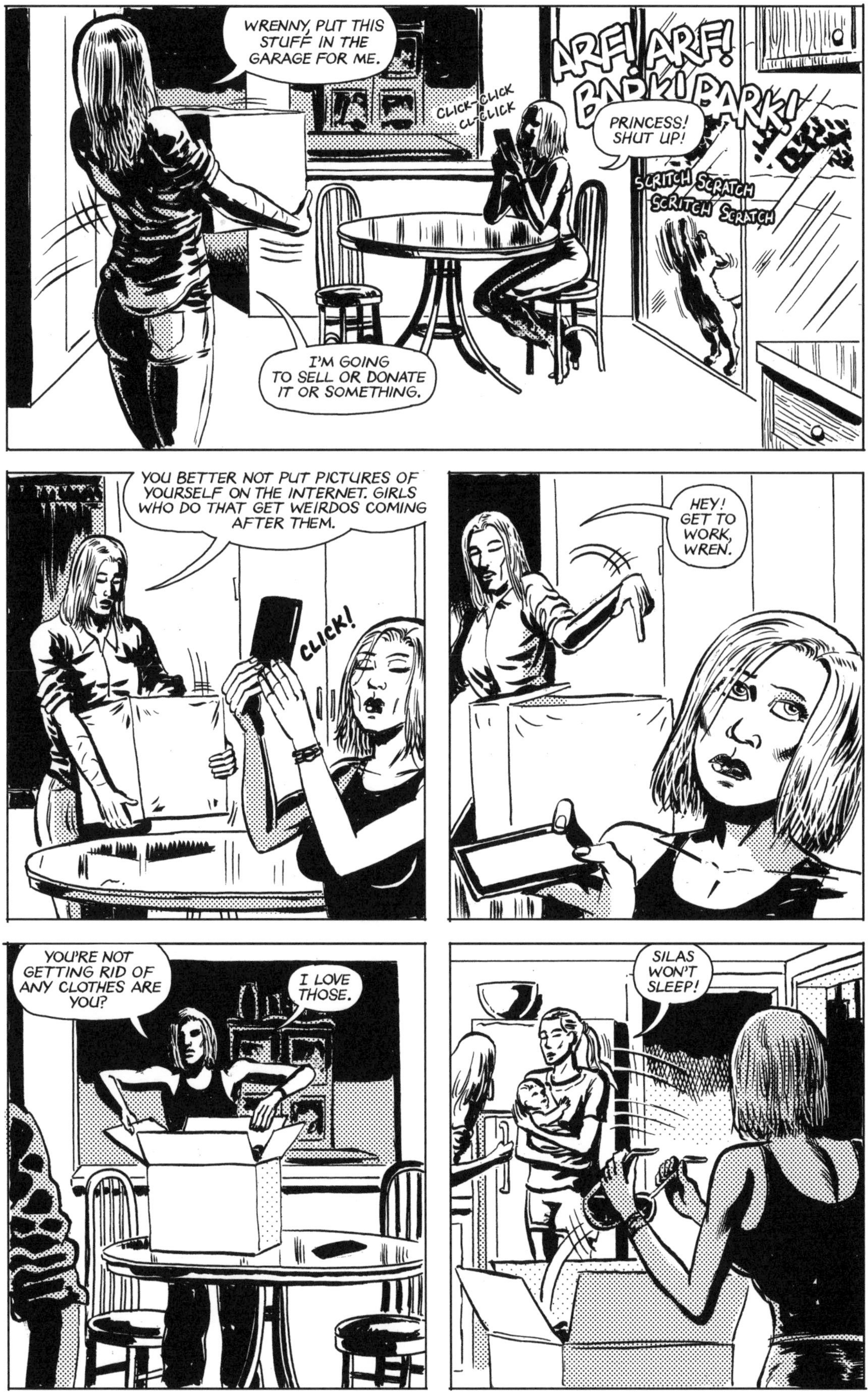
WRENNY, PUT THIS STUFF IN THE GARAGE FOR ME.
CLICK-CLICK CL-CLICK
ARF! ARF! BARK! BARK!
PRINCESS! SHUT UP!
SCRITCH SCRATCH SCRITCH SCRATCH
I'M GOING TO SELL OR DONATE IT OR SOMETHING.
YOU BETTER NOT PUT PICTURES OF YOURSELF ON THE INTERNET. GIRLS WHO DO THAT GET WEIRDOS COMING AFTER THEM.
CLICK!
HEY! GET TO WORK, WREN.
YOU'RE NOT GETTING RID OF ANY CLOTHES ARE YOU?
I LOVE THOSE.
SILAS WON'T SLEEP!

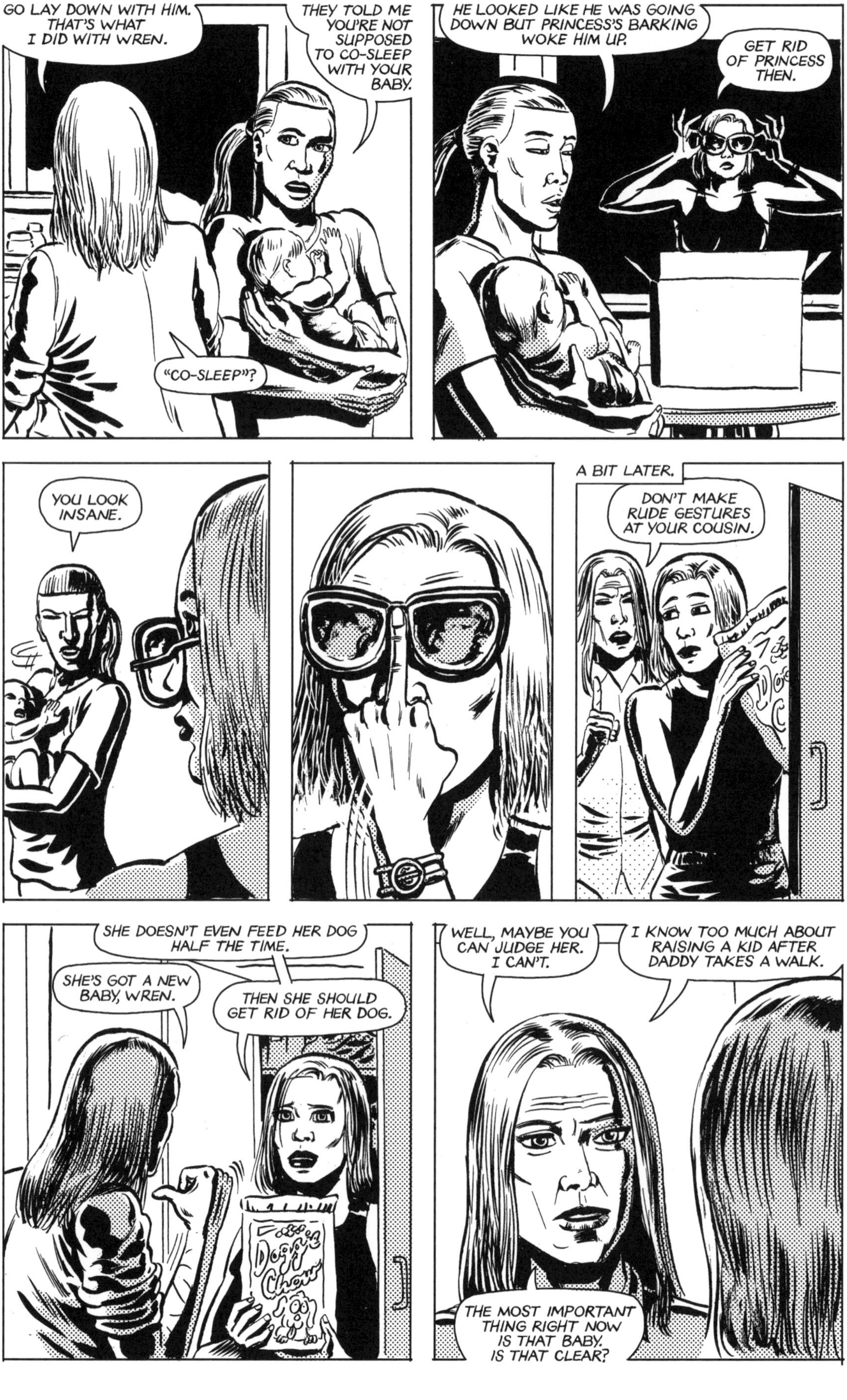
GO LAY DOWN WITH HIM. THAT'S WHAT I DID WITH WREN.
THEY TOLD ME YOU'RE NOT SUPPOSED TO CO-SLEEP WITH YOUR BABY.
"CO-SLEEP"?
HE LOOKED LIKE HE WAS GOING DOWN BUT PRINCESS'S BARKING WOKE HIM UP.
GET RID OF PRINCESS THEN.
YOU LOOK INSANE.
A BIT LATER.
DON'T MAKE RUDE GESTURES AT YOUR COUSIN.
SHE DOESN'T EVEN FEED HER DOG HALF THE TIME.
SHE'S GOT A NEW BABY, WREN.
THEN SHE SHOULD GET RID OF HER DOG.
WELL, MAYBE YOU CAN JUDGE HER. I CAN'T.
I KNOW TOO MUCH ABOUT RAISING A KID AFTER DADDY TAKES A WALK.
THE MOST IMPORTANT THING RIGHT NOW IS THAT BABY. IS THAT CLEAR?

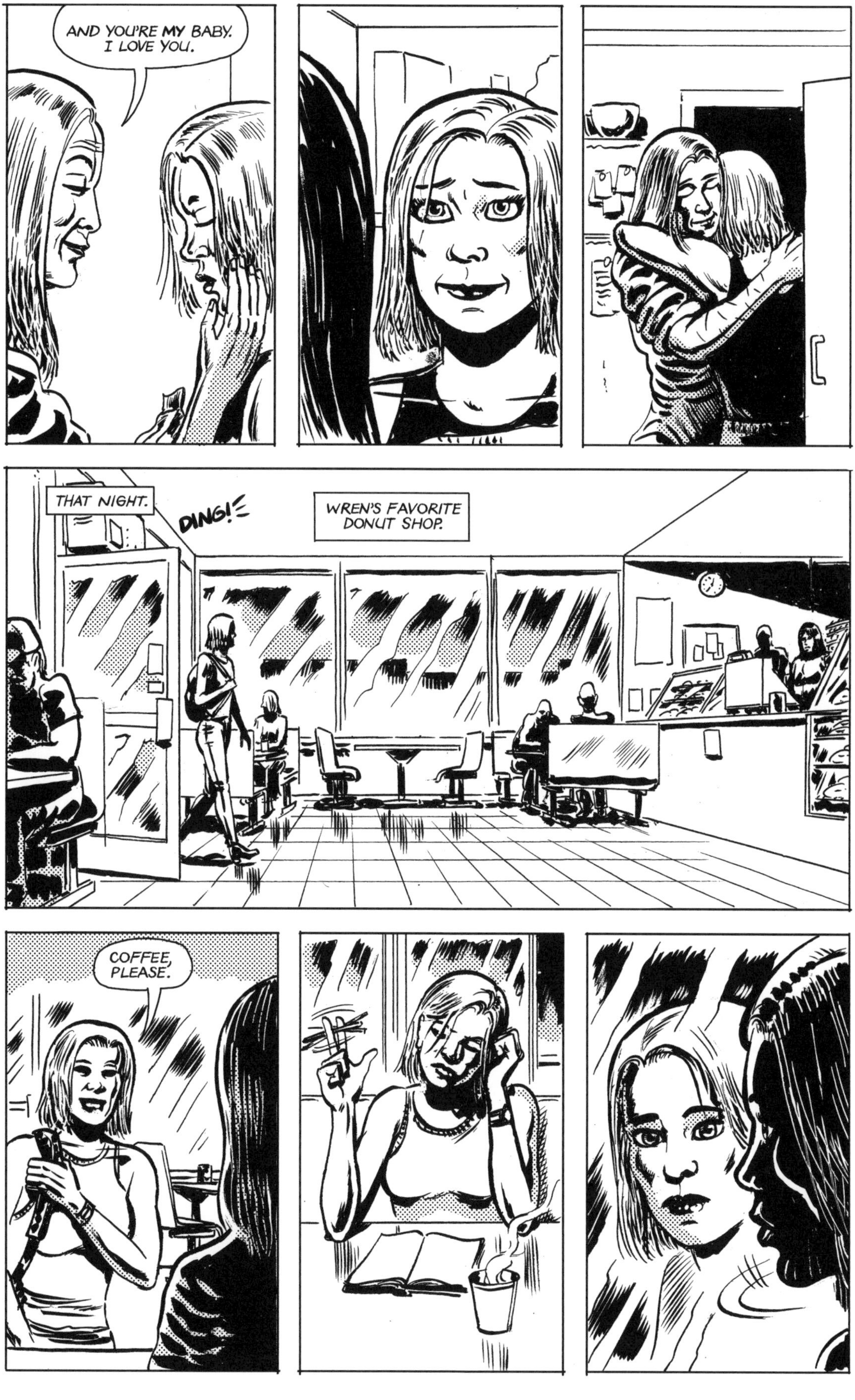
AND YOU'RE MY BABY. I LOVE YOU.
THAT NIGHT.
DING!
WREN'S FAVORITE DONUT SHOP.
COFFEE, PLEASE.

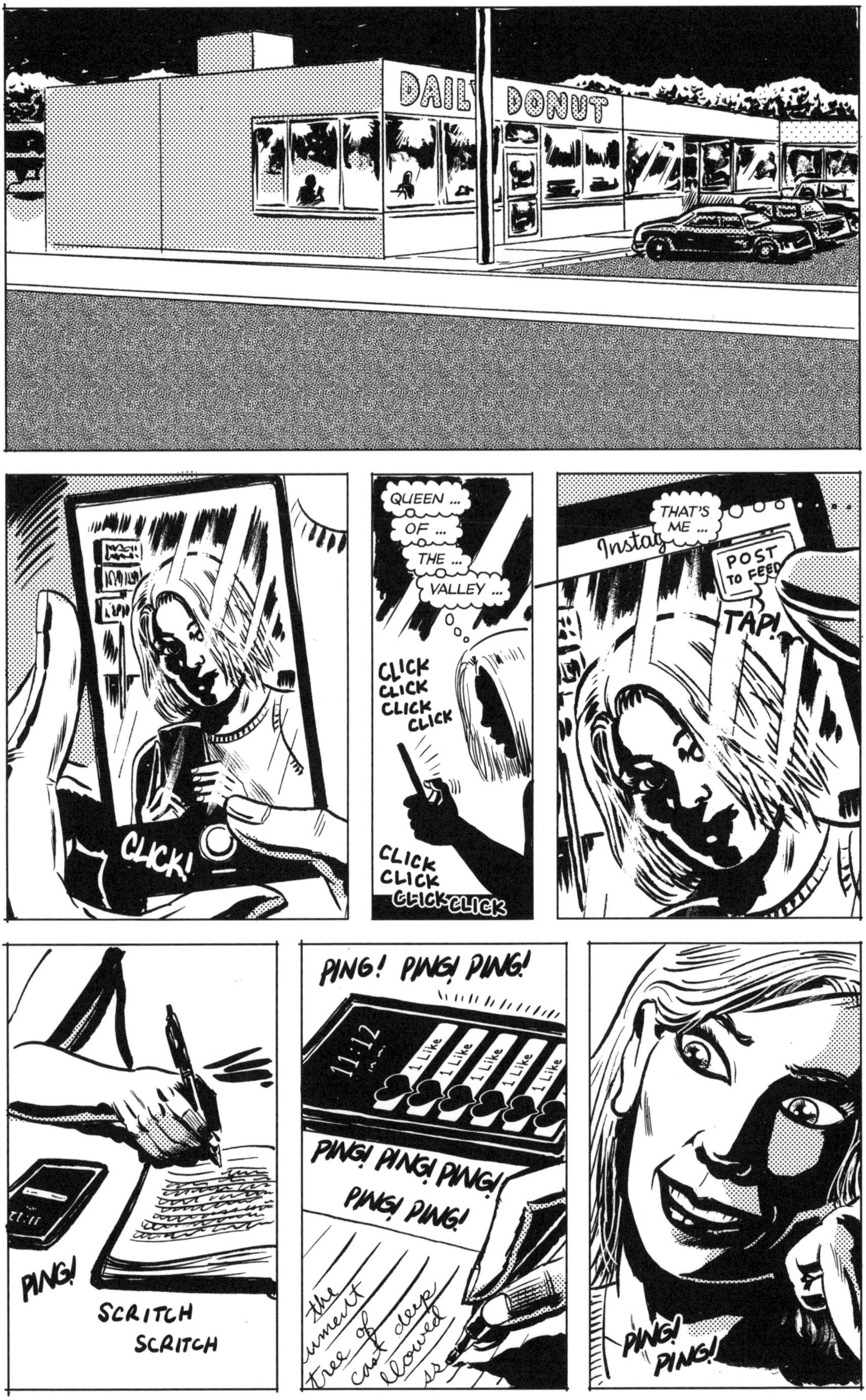
DAILY DONUT
CLICK!
QUEEN ...
OF ...
THE ...
VALLEY ...
CLICK CLICK CLICK CLICK
CLICK CLICK CLICK CLICK
THAT'S ME ...
Instag
POST TO FEED
TAP!
PING!
SCRITCH SCRITCH
PING! PING! PING!
11:12
1 Like
1 Like
1 Like
1 Like
1 Like
PING! PING! PING!
PING! PING!
PING! PING!

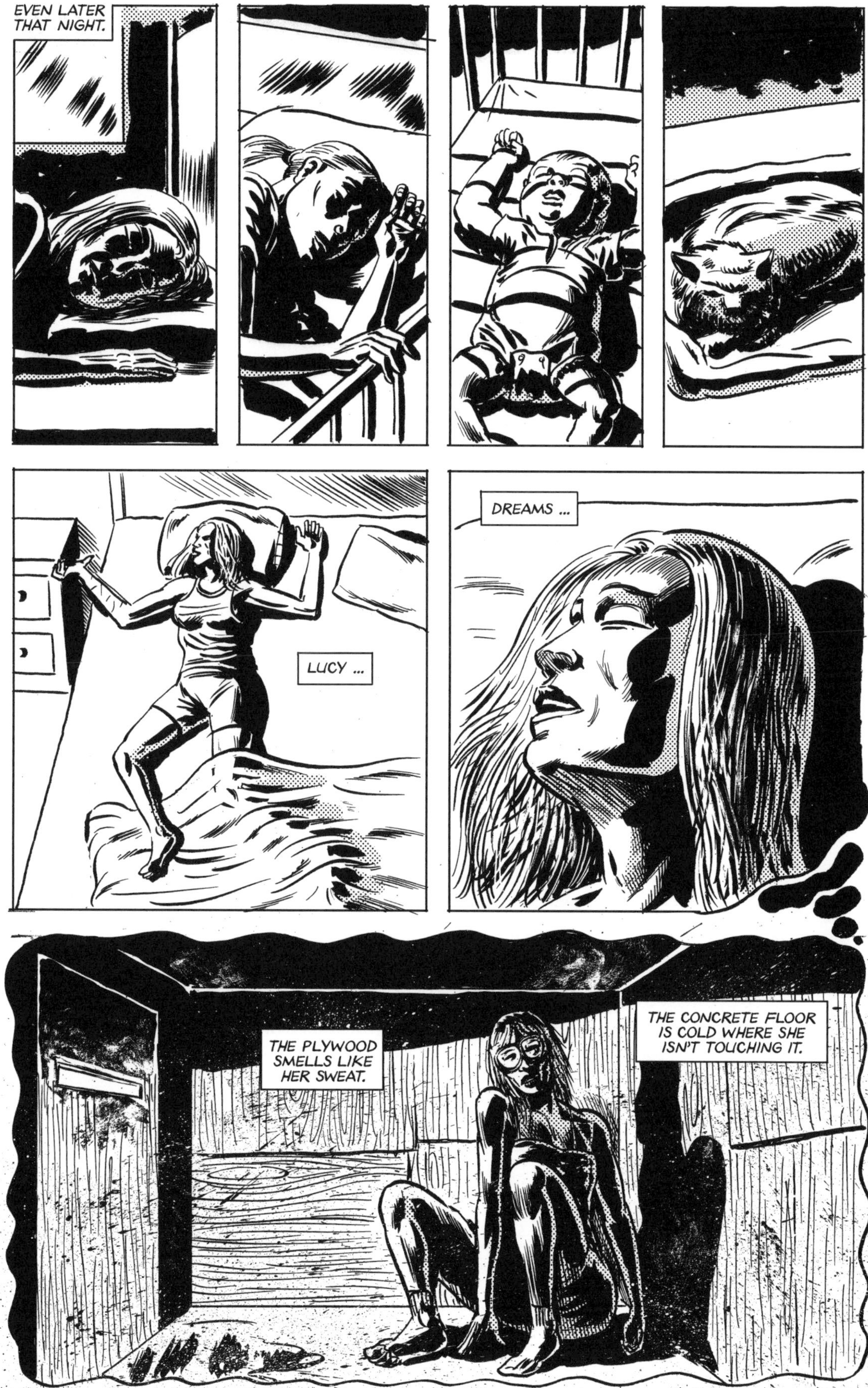
EVEN LATER THAT NIGHT.
LUCY ...
DREAMS ...
THE PLYWOOD SMELLS LIKE HER SWEAT.
THE CONCRETE FLOOR IS COLD WHERE SHE ISN'T TOUCHING IT.

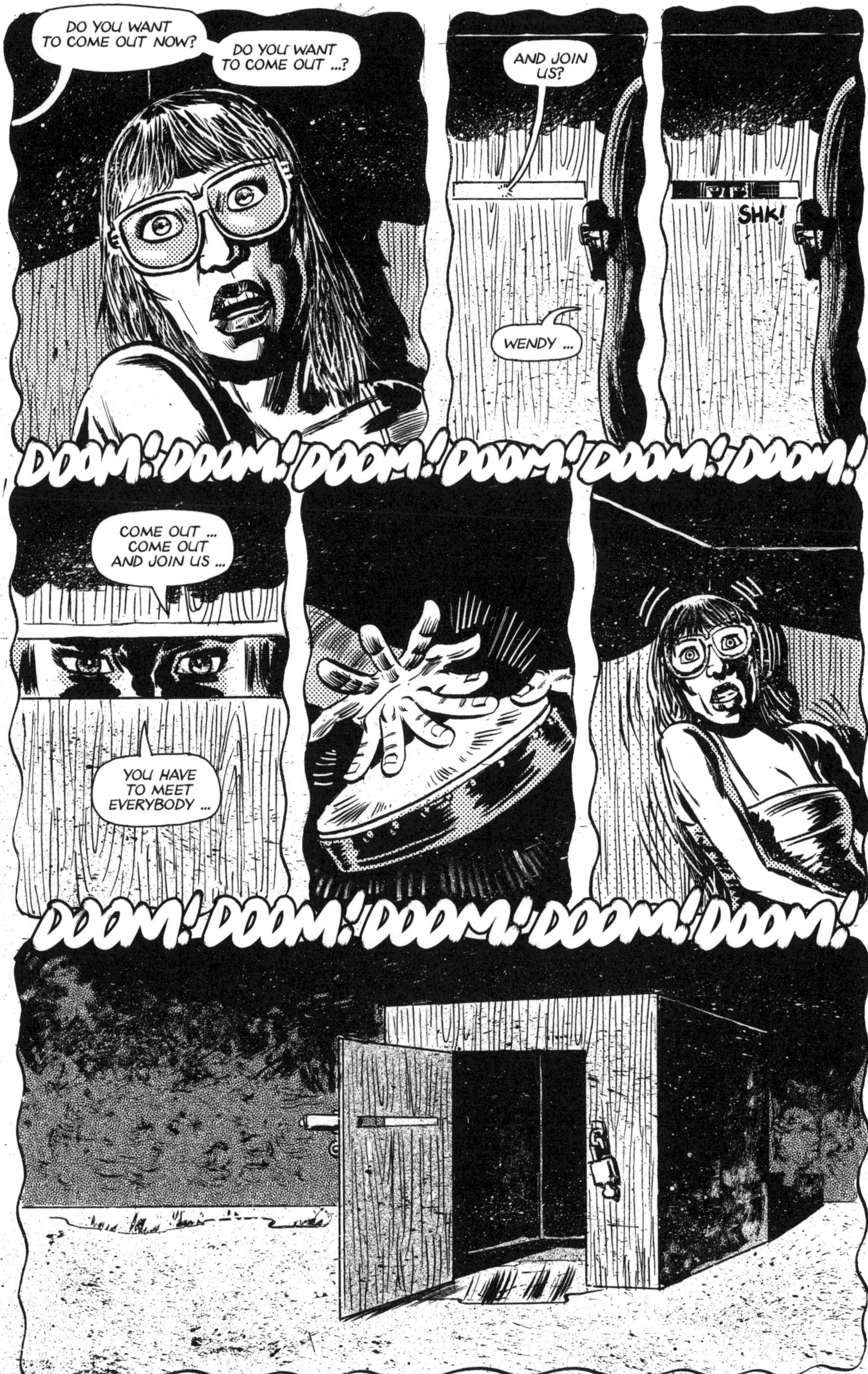
DO YOU WANT TO COME OUT NOW?
DO YOU WANT TO COME OUT ...?
AND JOIN US?
WENDY ...
SHK!
DOOM! DOOM! DOOM! DOOM! DOOM! DOOM!
COME OUT ... COME OUT AND JOIN US ...
YOU HAVE TO MEET EVERYBODY ...
DOOM! DOOM! DOOM! DOOM! DOOM!

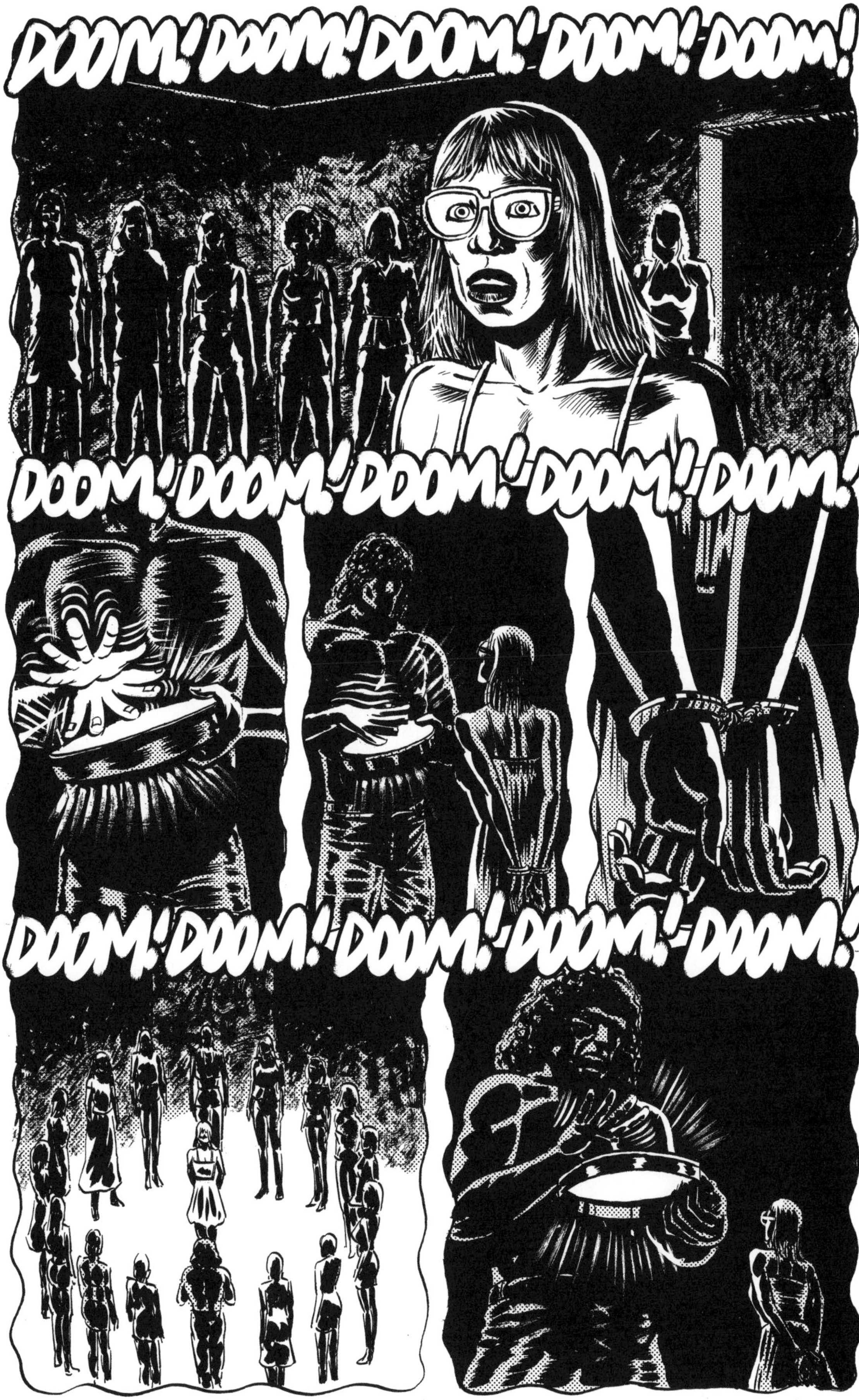
DOOM! DOOM! DOOM! DOOM! DOOM!
DOOM! DOOM! DOOM! DOOM! DOOM!
DOOM! DOOM! DOOM! DOOM! DOOM!

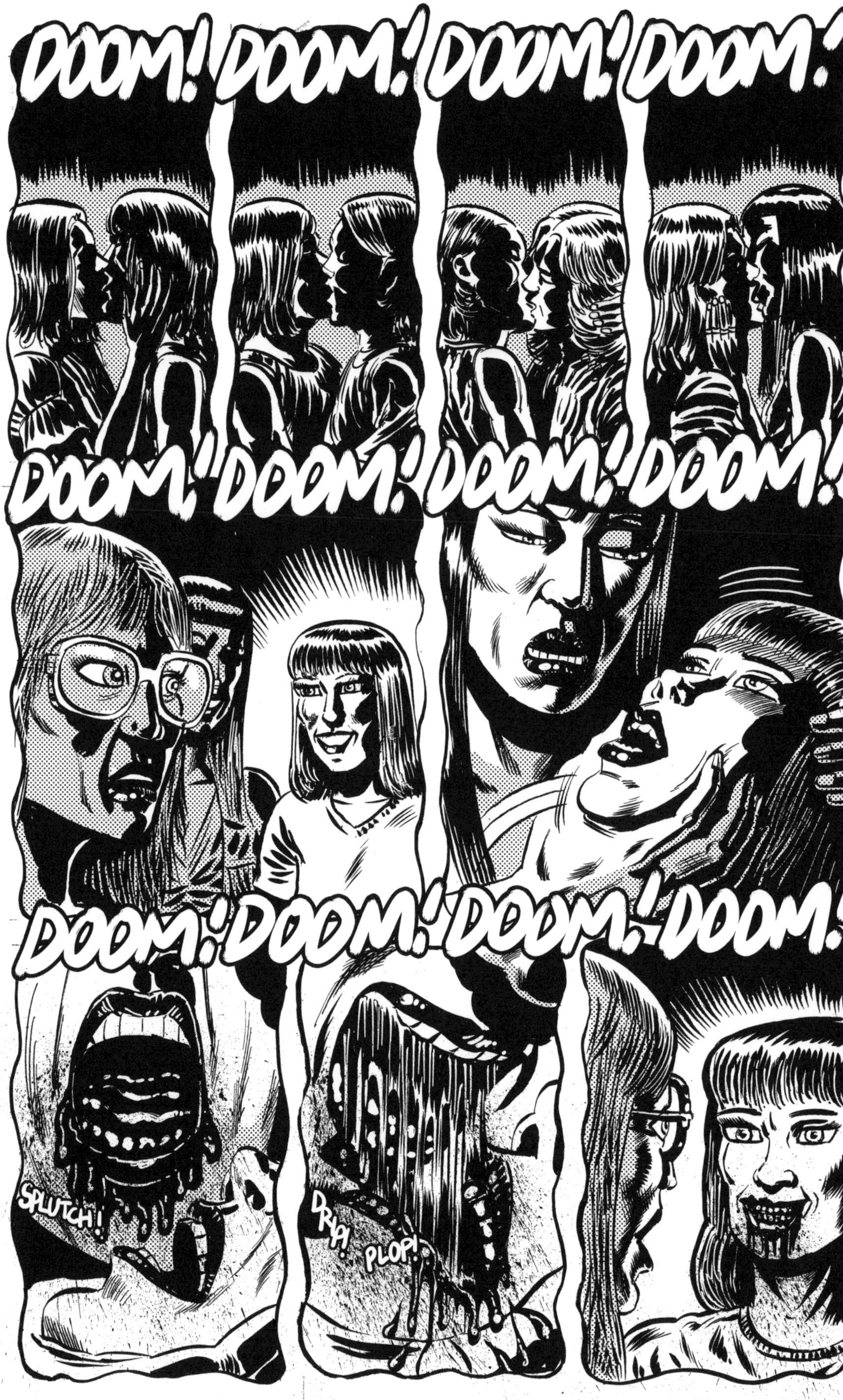
DOOM! DOOM! DOOM! DOOM!
DOOM! DOOM! DOOM! DOOM!
DOOM! DOOM! DOOM! DOOM!
SPLUTCH!
DRIP! PLOP!

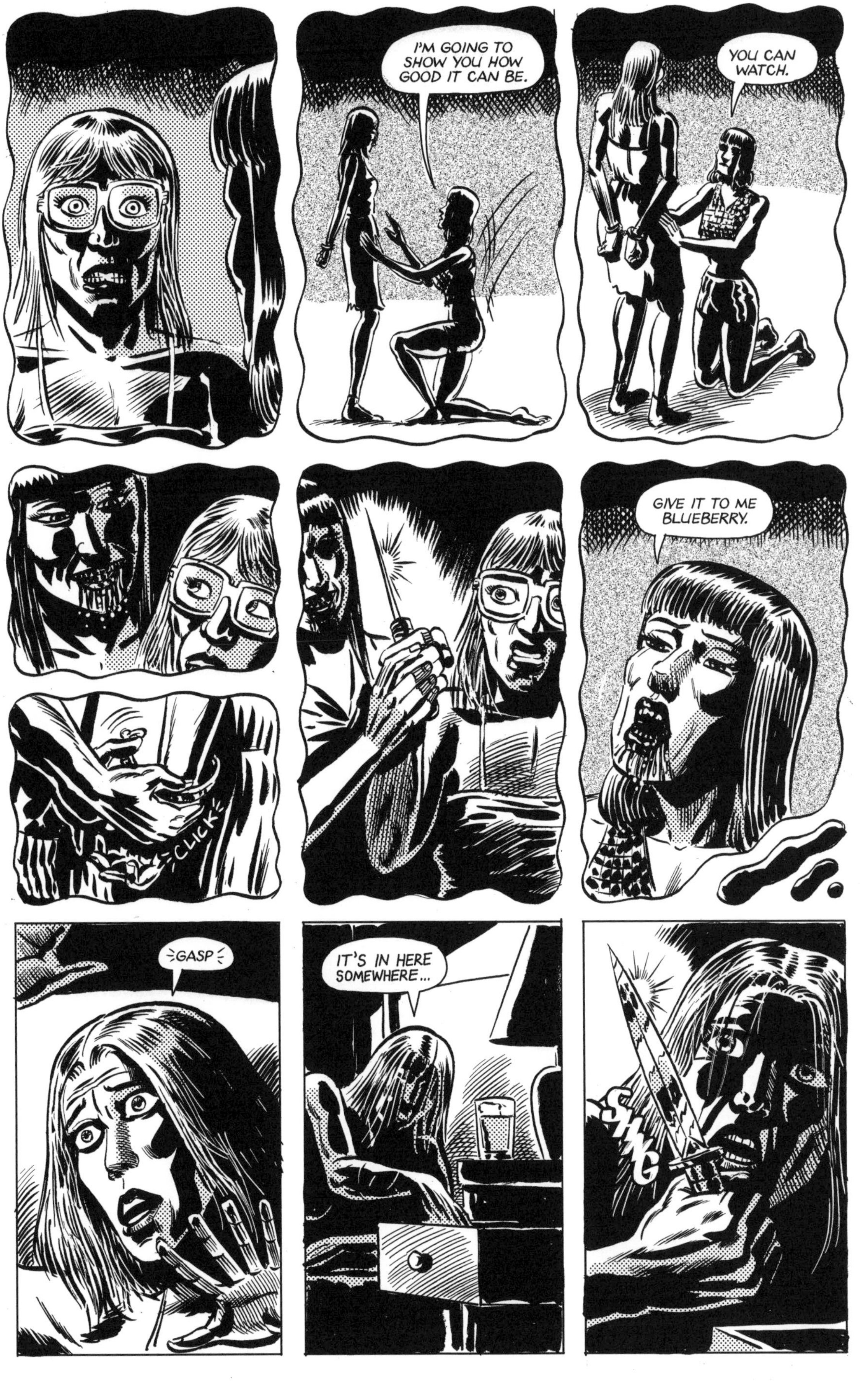
I'M GOING TO SHOW YOU HOW GOOD IT CAN BE.
YOU CAN WATCH.
CLICK
GIVE IT TO ME BLUEBERRY.
GASP
IT'S IN HERE SOMEWHERE...
SHG

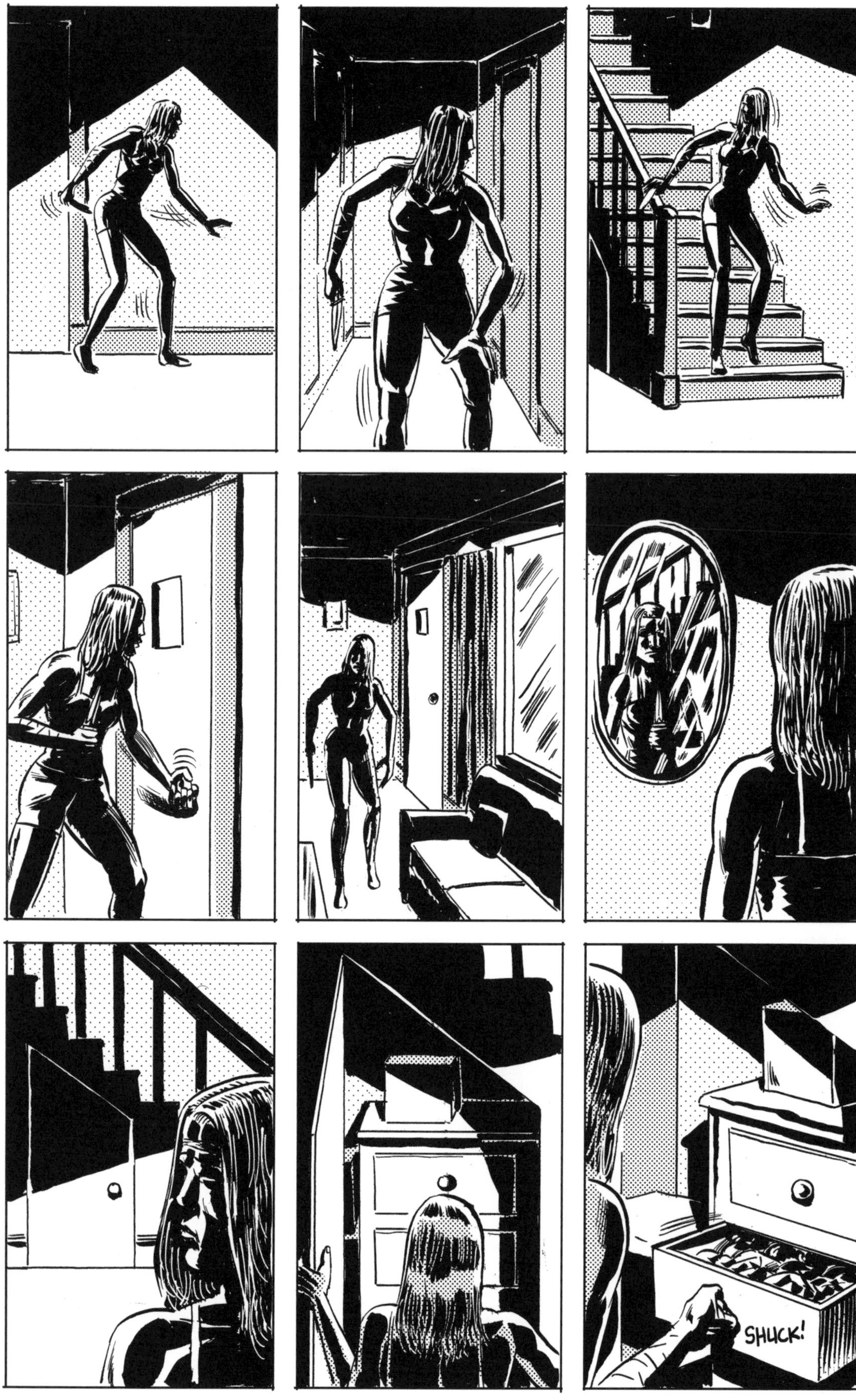
SHUCK!

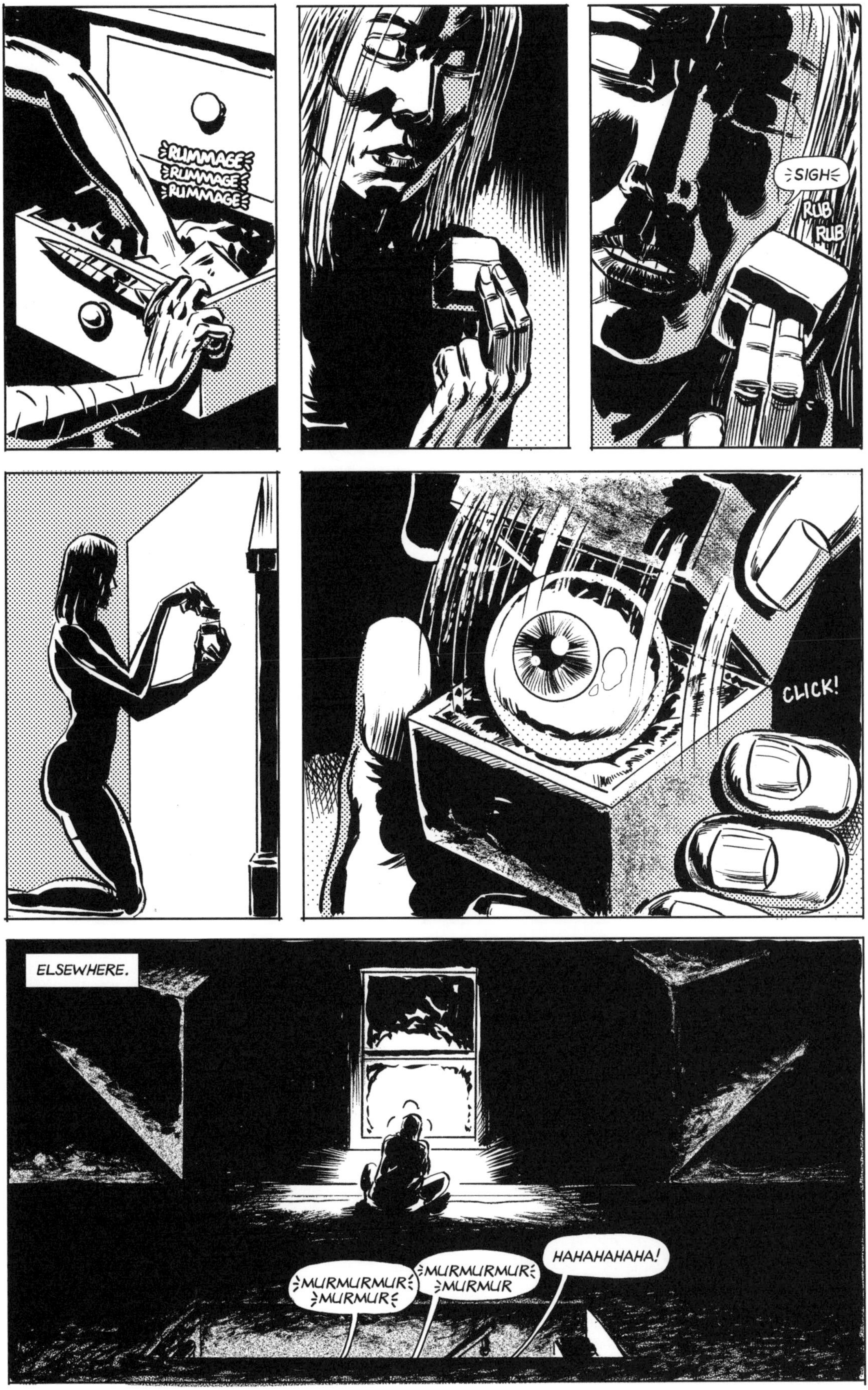
RUMMAGE
RUMMAGE
RUMMAGE
SIGH
RUB
RUB
CLICK!
ELSEWHERE.
MURMURMUR MURMUR
MURMURMUR MURMUR
HAHAHAHAHA!

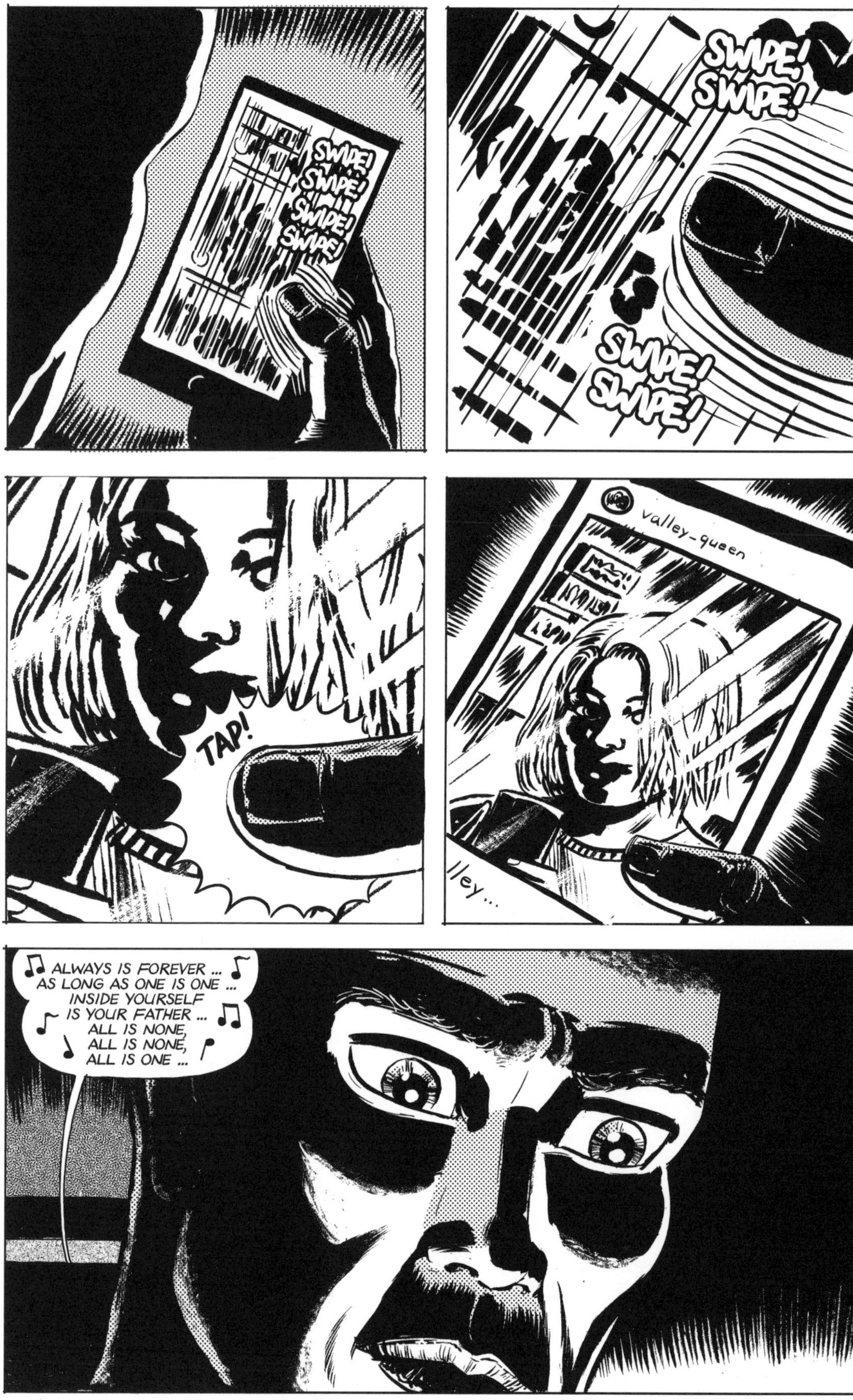
SWIPE!
SWIPE!
SWIPE!
SWIPE!
SWIPE!
SWIPE!
SWIPE!
SWIPE!
TAP!
valley_queen
lley...
ALWAYS IS FOREVER ... AS LONG AS ONE IS ONE ... INSIDE YOURSELF IS YOUR FATHER ... ALL IS NONE, ALL IS NONE, ALL IS ONE ...

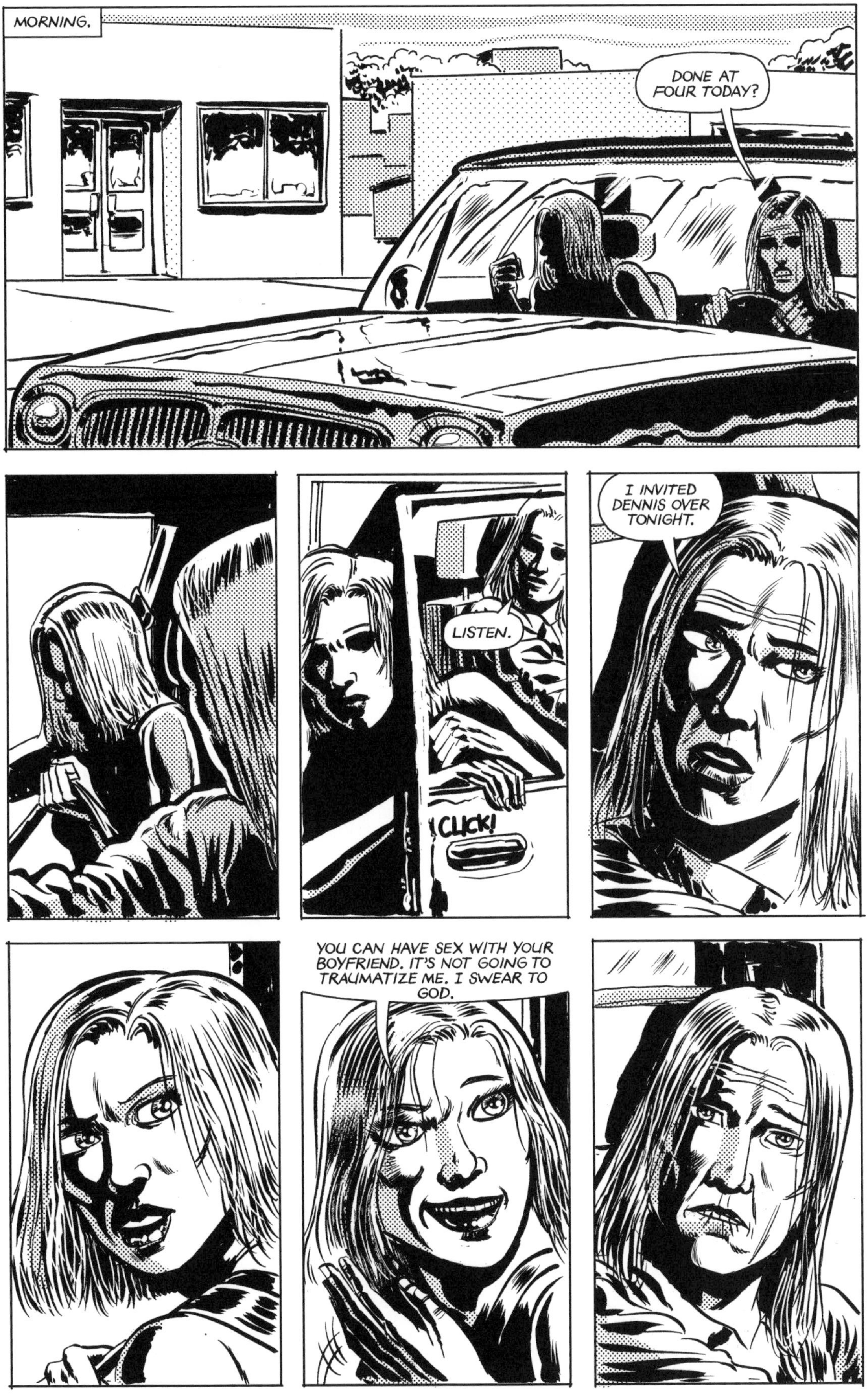
MORNING.
DONE AT FOUR TODAY?
LISTEN.
CLICK!
I INVITED DENNIS OVER TONIGHT.
YOU CAN HAVE SEX WITH YOUR BOYFRIEND. IT'S NOT GOING TO TRAUMATIZE ME. I SWEAR TO GOD.

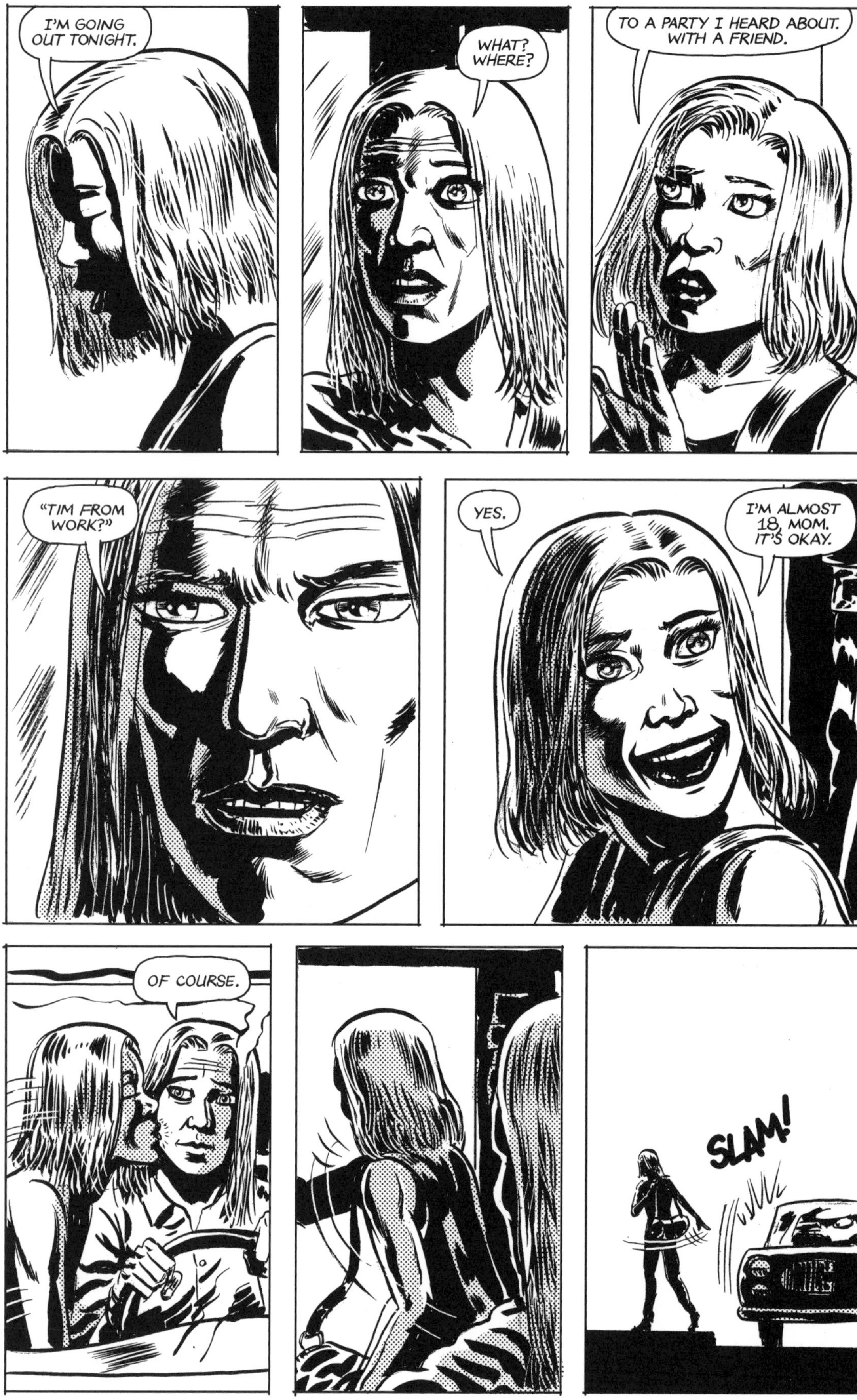
I'M GOING OUT TONIGHT.
WHAT? WHERE?
TO A PARTY I HEARD ABOUT. WITH A FRIEND.
"TIM FROM WORK?"
YES.
I'M ALMOST 18, MOM. IT'S OKAY.
OF COURSE.
SLAM!

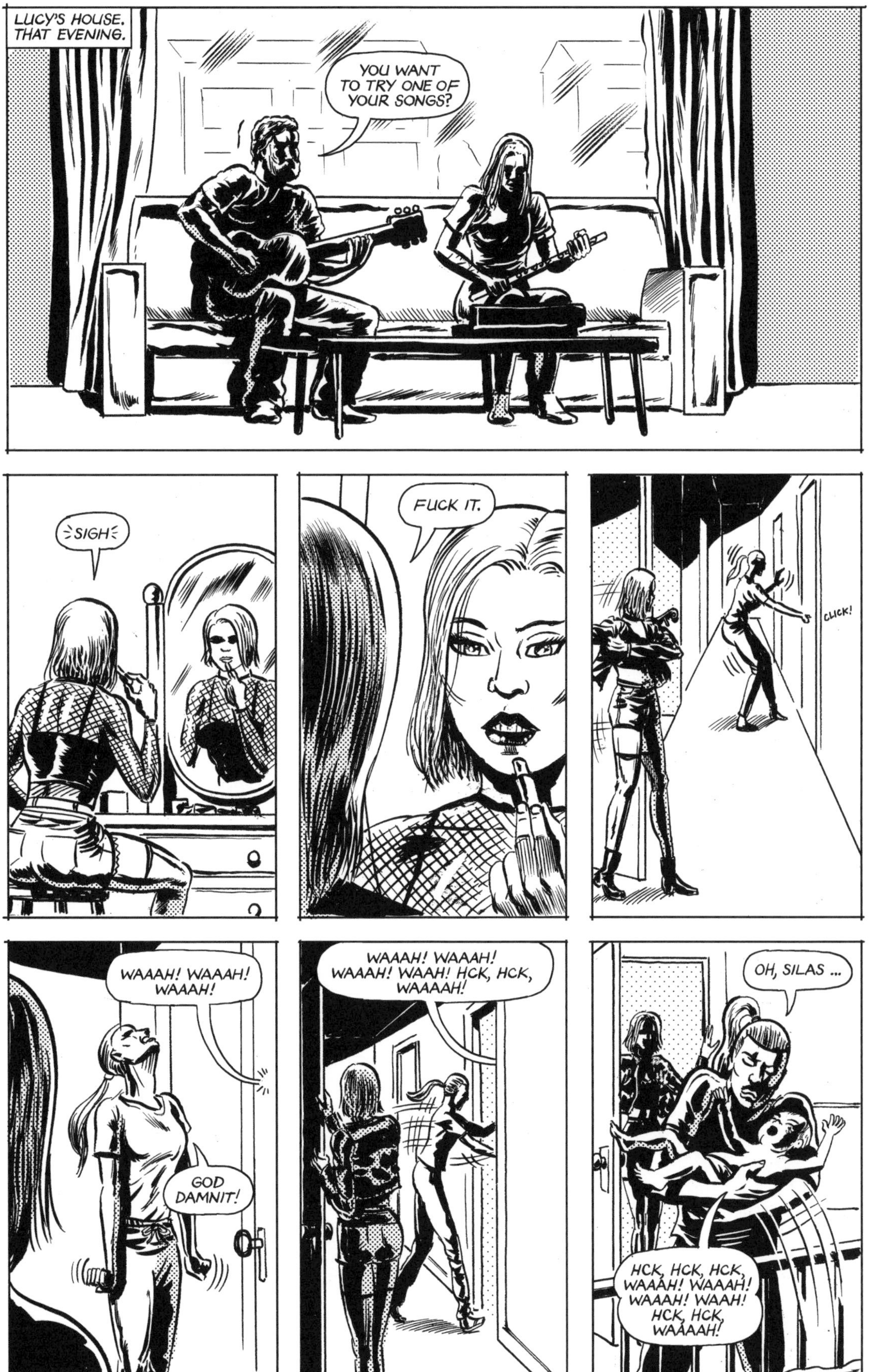
LUCY'S HOUSE. THAT EVENING.
YOU WANT TO TRY ONE OF YOUR SONGS?
SIGH
FUCK IT.
CLICK!
WAAAH! WAAAH! WAAAH!
GOD DAMNIT!
WAAAH! WAAAH! WAAAH! WAAH! HCK, HCK, WAAAAH!
OH, SILAS ...
HCK, HCK, HCK, WAAAH! WAAAH! WAAAH! WAAH! HCK, HCK, WAAAAH!

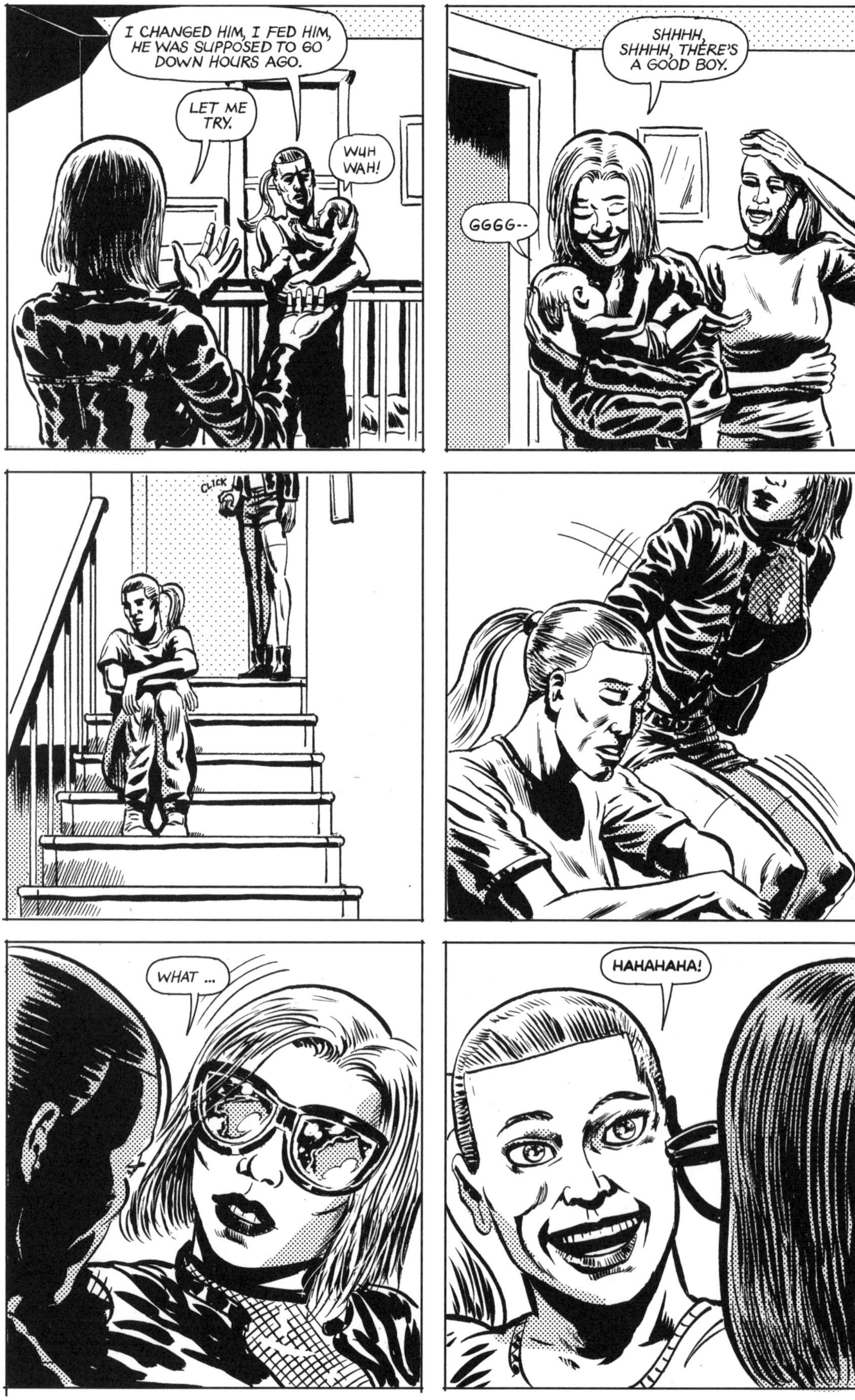
I CHANGED HIM, I FED HIM, HE WAS SUPPOSED TO GO DOWN HOURS AGO.
LET ME TRY.
WUH WAH!
SHHHH, SHHHH, THERE'S A GOOD BOY.
GGGG--
CLICK
WHAT ...
HAHAHAHA!

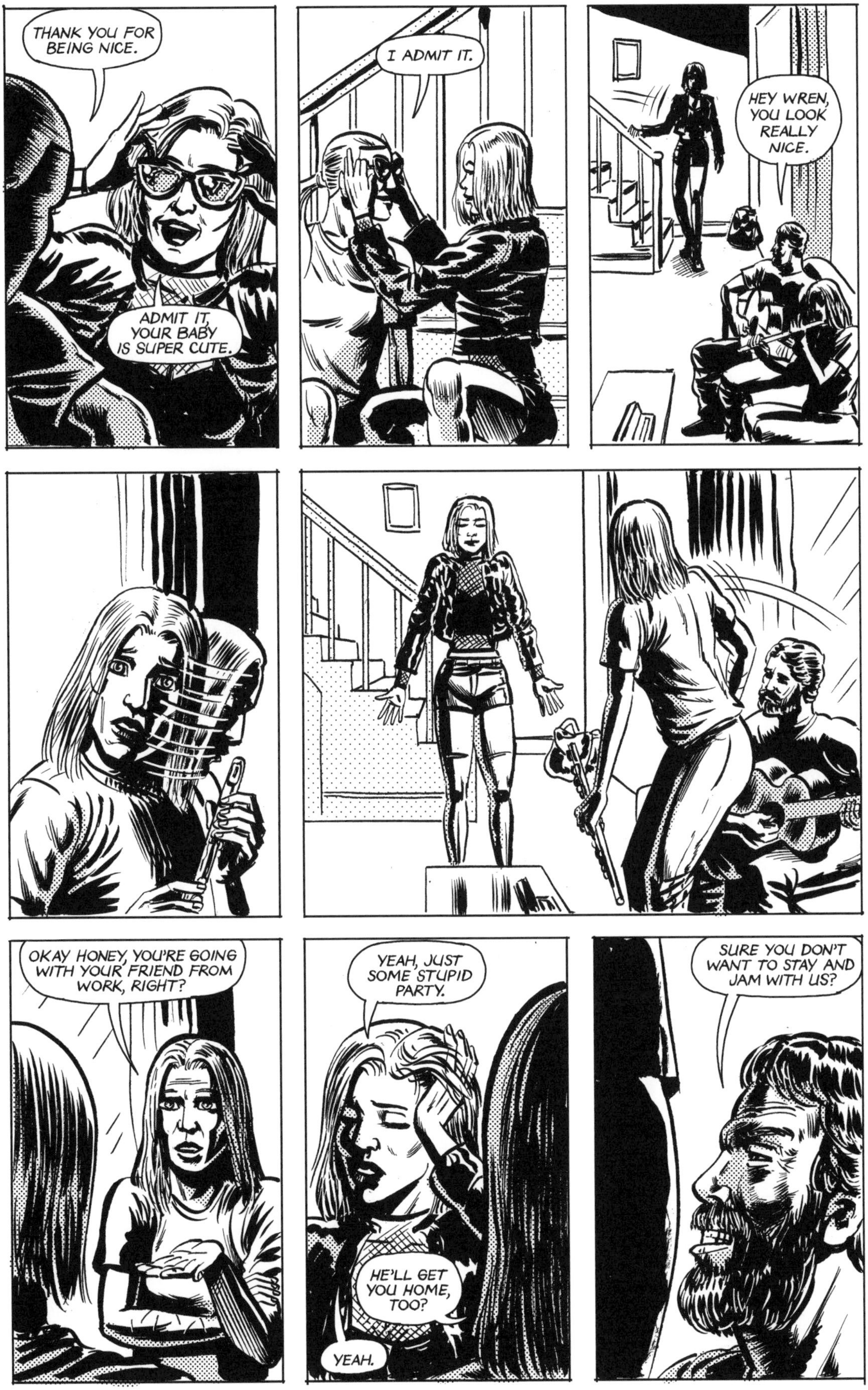
THANK YOU FOR BEING NICE.
ADMIT IT, YOUR BABY IS SUPER CUTE.
I ADMIT IT.
HEY WREN, YOU LOOK REALLY NICE.
OKAY HONEY, YOU'RE GOING WITH YOUR FRIEND FROM WORK, RIGHT?
YEAH, JUST SOME STUPID PARTY.
HE'LL GET YOU HOME, TOO?
YEAH.
SURE YOU DON'T WANT TO STAY AND JAM WITH US?

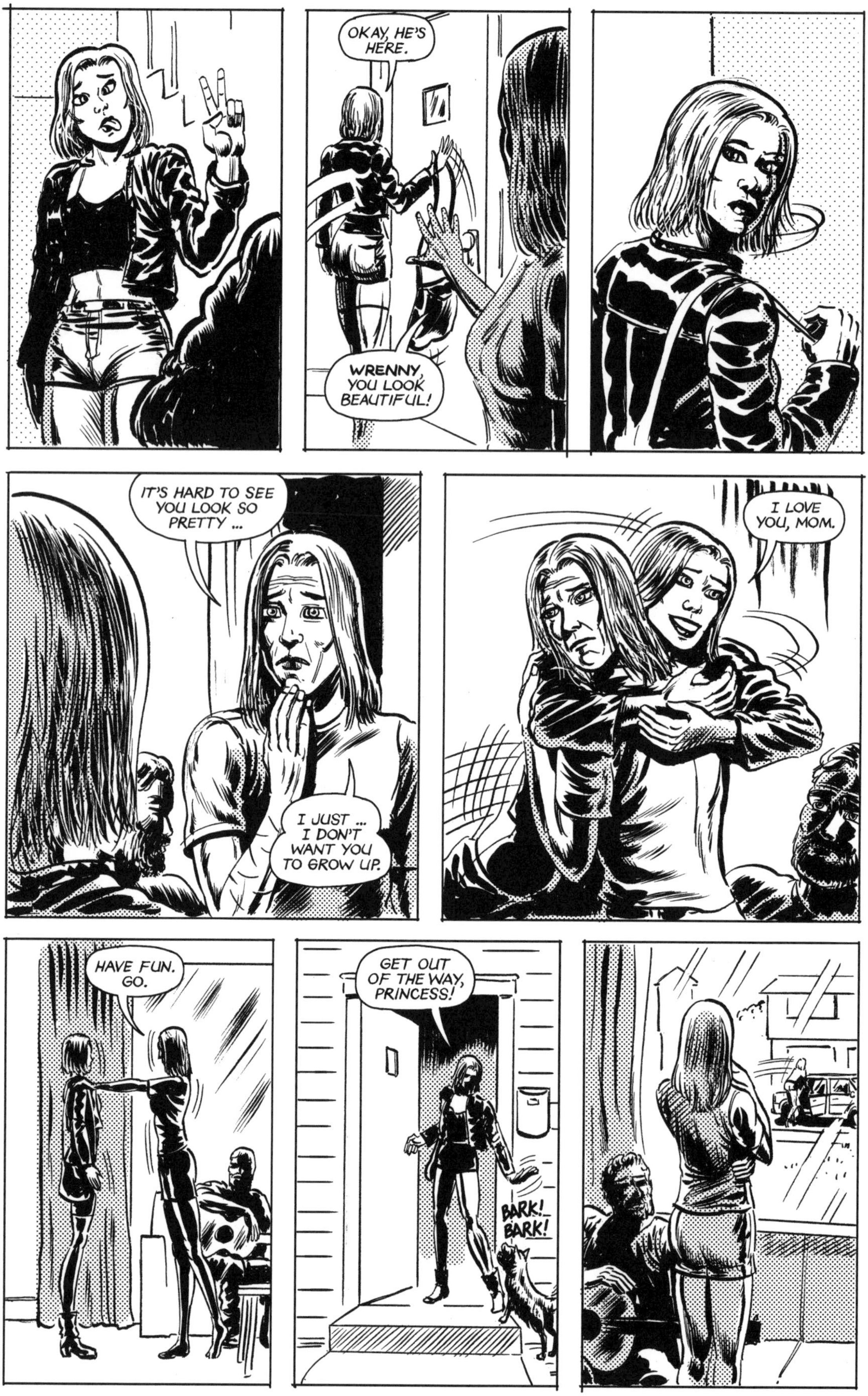
OKAY, HE'S HERE.
WRENNY, YOU LOOK BEAUTIFUL!
IT'S HARD TO SEE YOU LOOK SO PRETTY ...
I JUST ... I DON'T WANT YOU TO GROW UP.
I LOVE YOU, MOM.
HAVE FUN. GO.
GET OUT OF THE WAY, PRINCESS!
BARK! BARK!

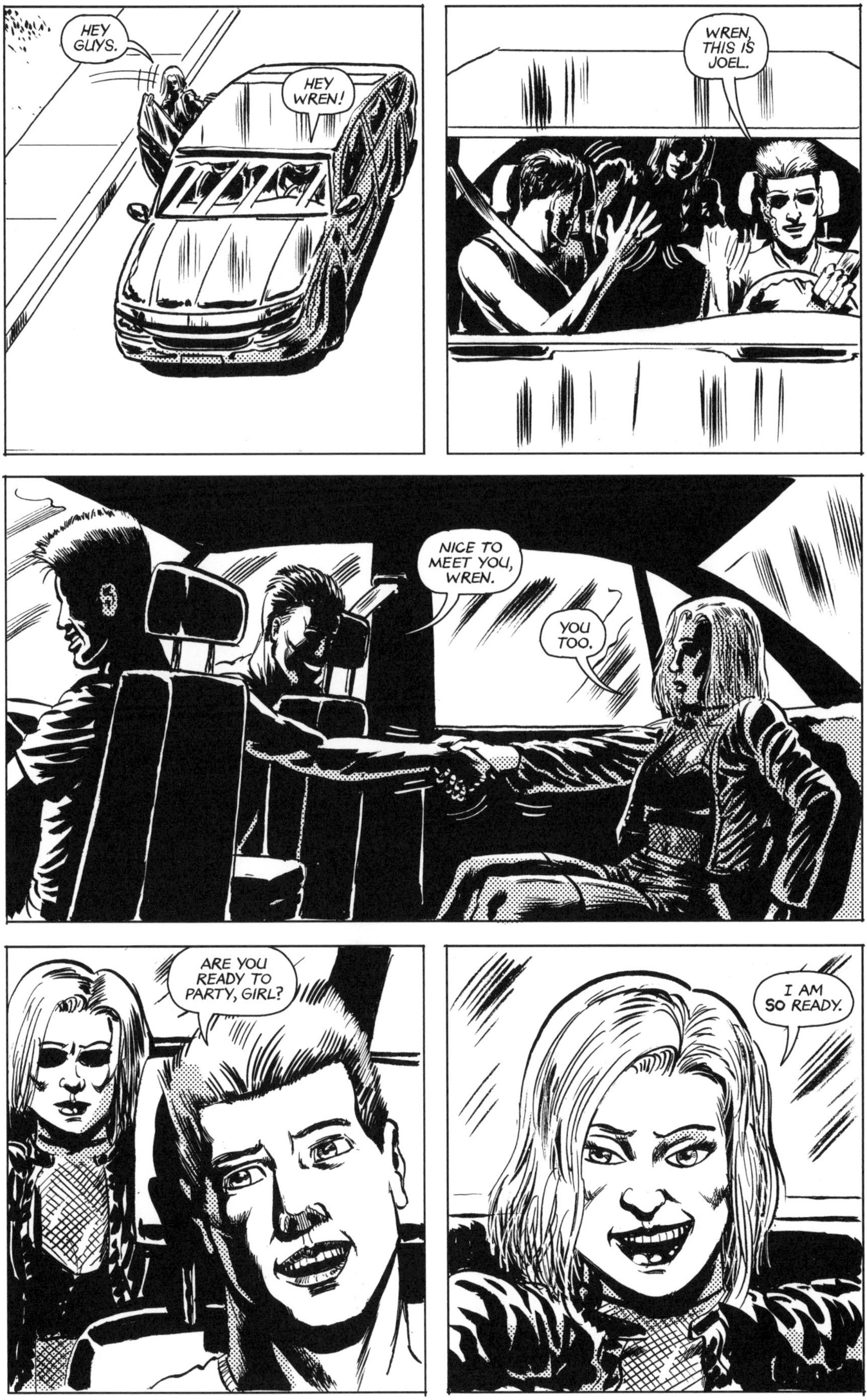
HEY GUYS.
HEY WREN!
WREN, THIS IS JOEL.
NICE TO MEET YOU, WREN.
YOU TOO.
ARE YOU READY TO PARTY, GIRL?
I AM SO READY.

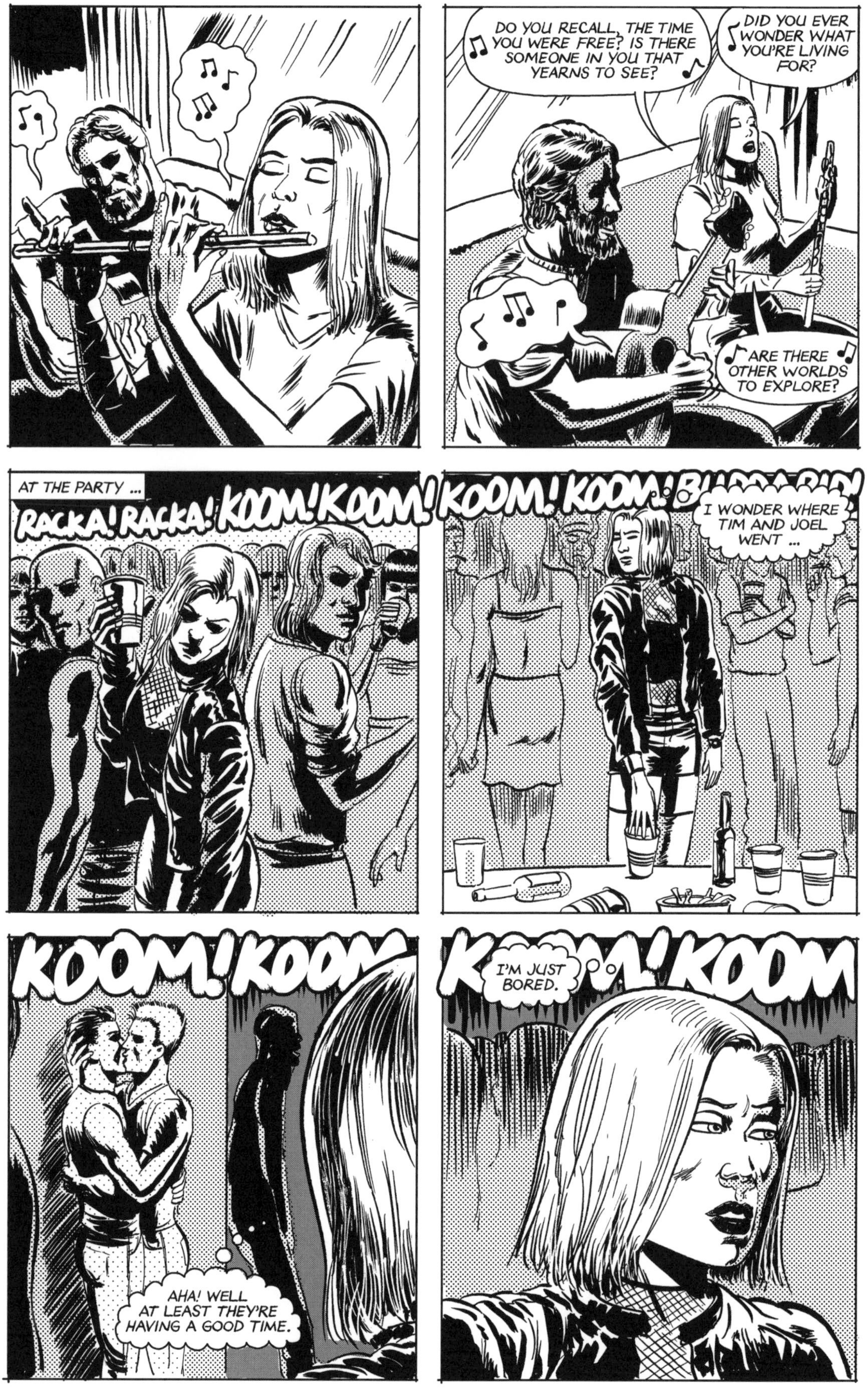
DO YOU RECALL, THE TIME YOU WERE FREE? IS THERE SOMEONE IN YOU THAT YEARNS TO SEE?
DID YOU EVER WONDER WHAT YOU'RE LIVING FOR?
ARE THERE OTHER WORLDS TO EXPLORE?
AT THE PARTY ...
RACKA! RACKA! KOOM! KOOM! KOOM! KOOM!
I WONDER WHERE TIM AND JOEL WENT ...
KOOM! KOOM
AHA! WELL AT LEAST THEY'RE HAVING A GOOD TIME.
I'M JUST BORED.
KOOM

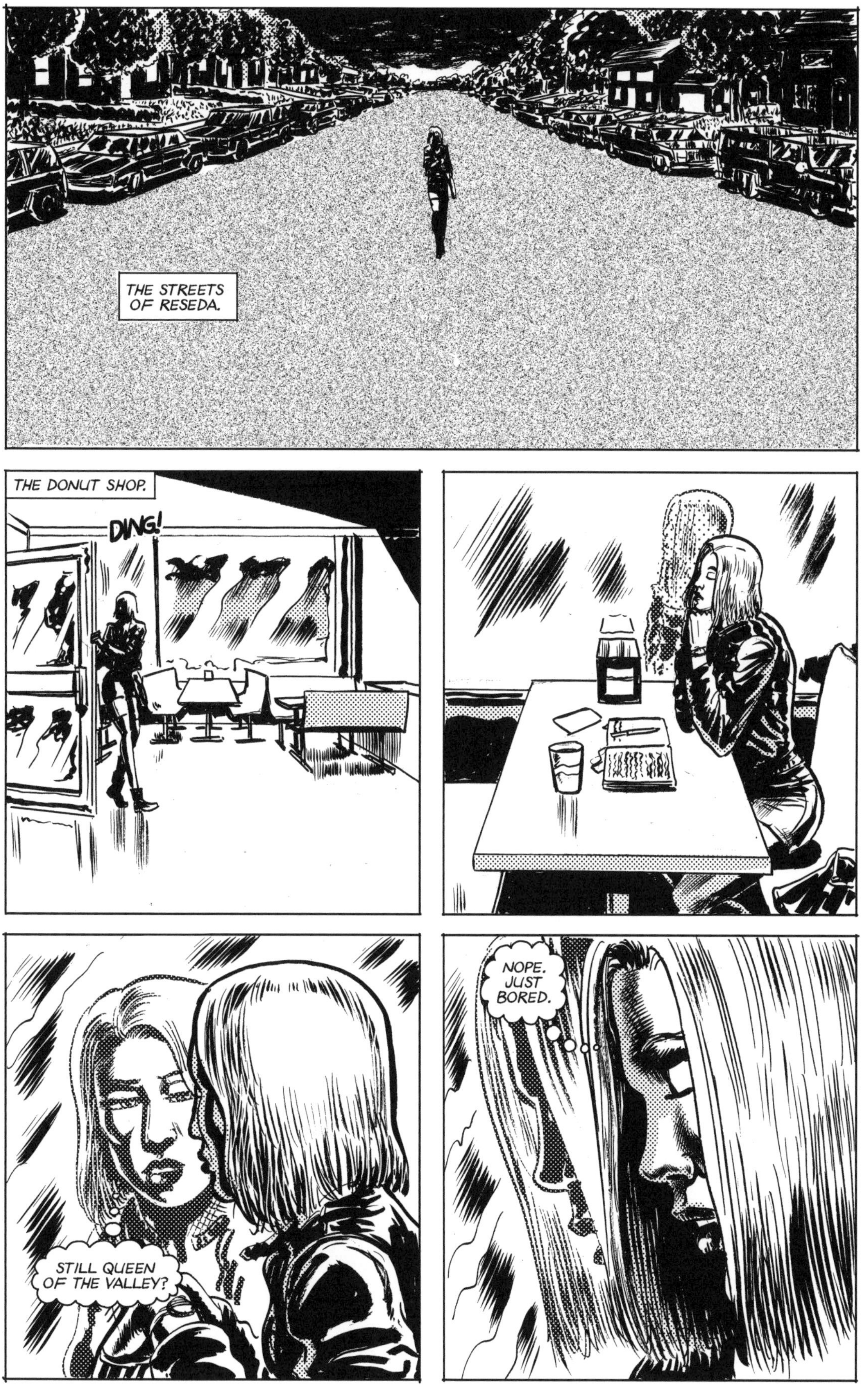
THE STREETS OF RESEDA.
THE DONUT SHOP.
DING!
STILL QUEEN OF THE VALLEY?
NOPE. JUST BORED.

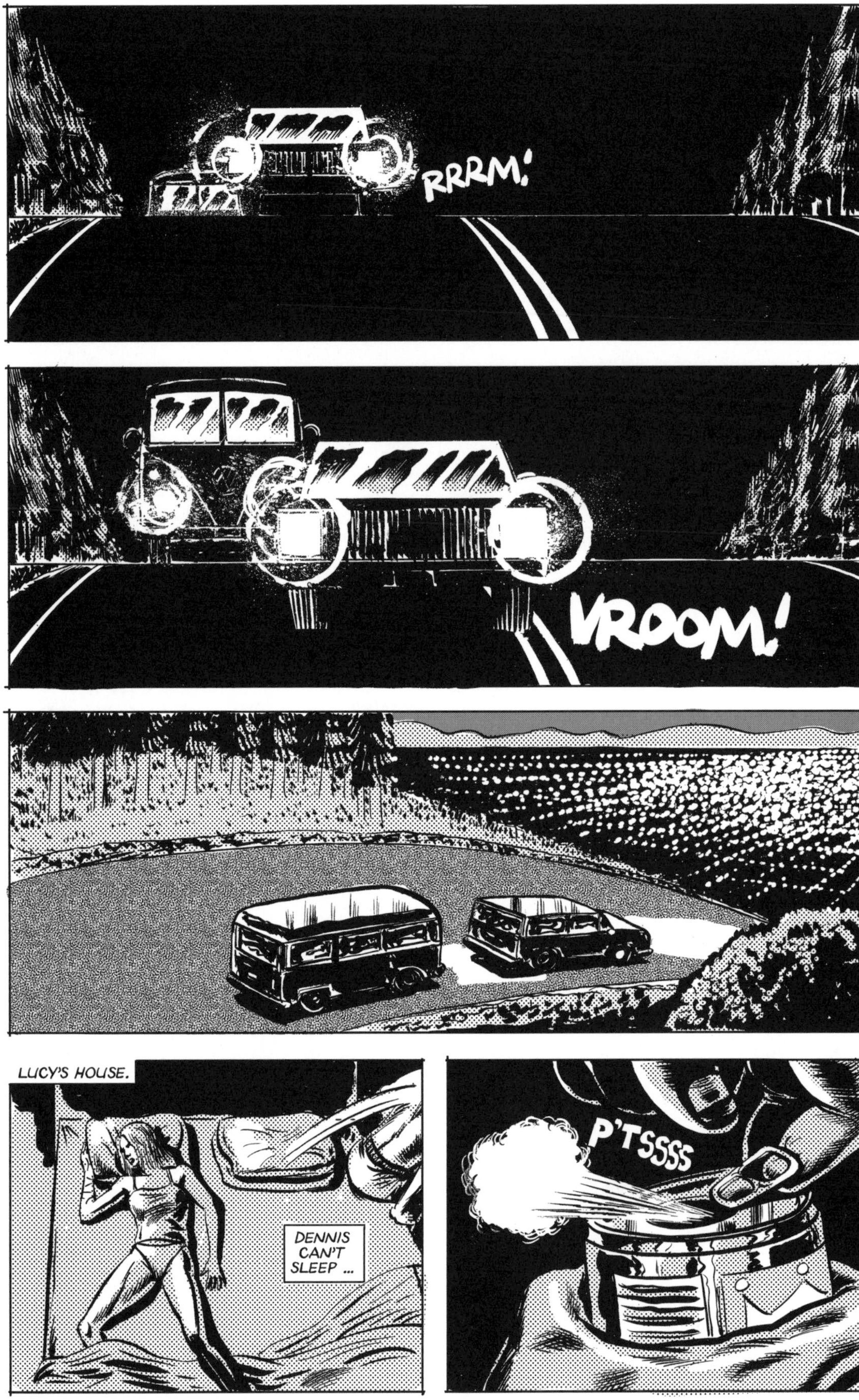
RRRM!
VROOM!
LUCY'S HOUSE.
DENNIS CAN'T SLEEP ...
P'TSSSS

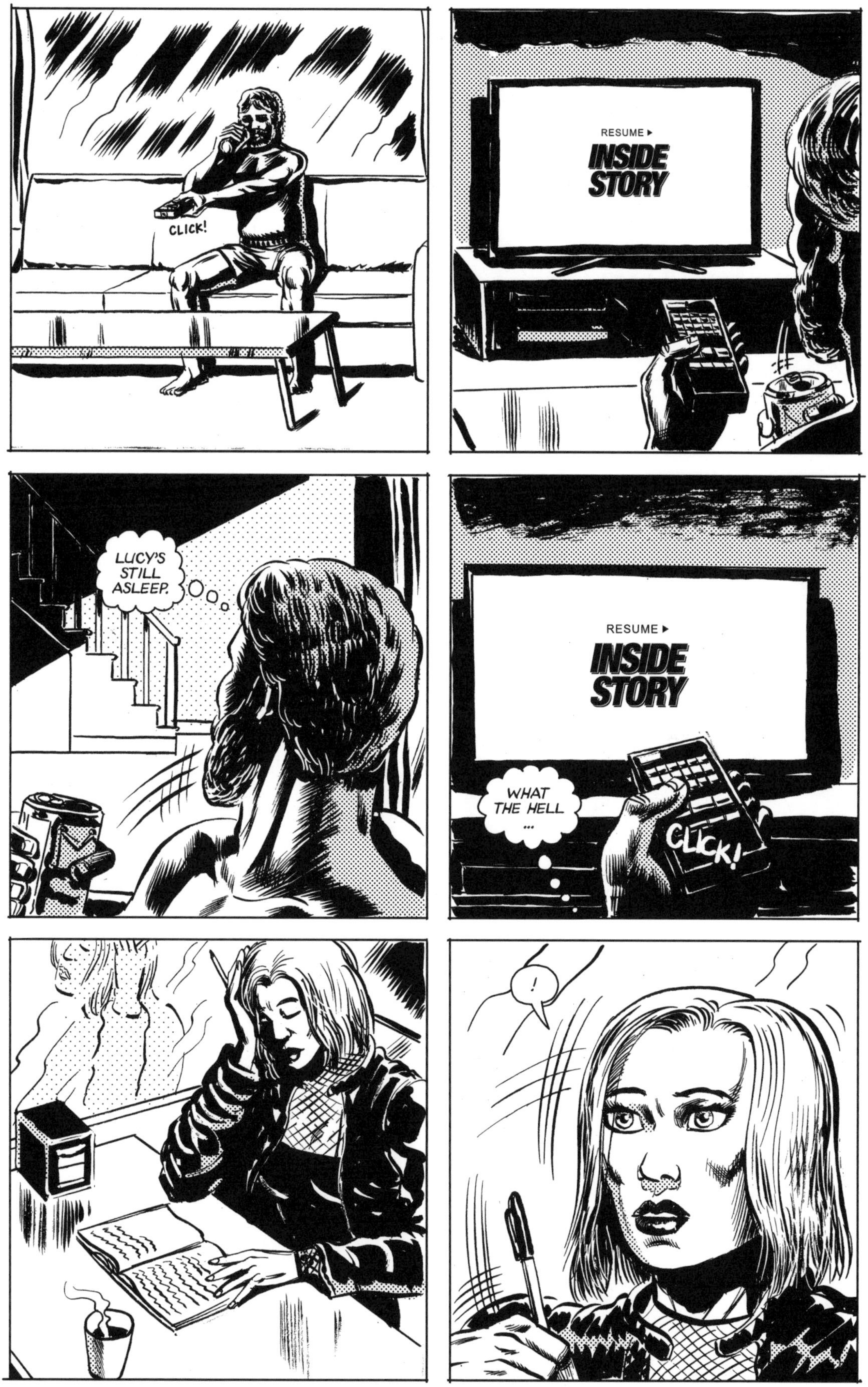
CLICK!
RESUME ▶
INSIDE STORY
LUCY'S STILL ASLEEP.
RESUME ▶
INSIDE STORY
WHAT THE HELL ...
CLICK!
!

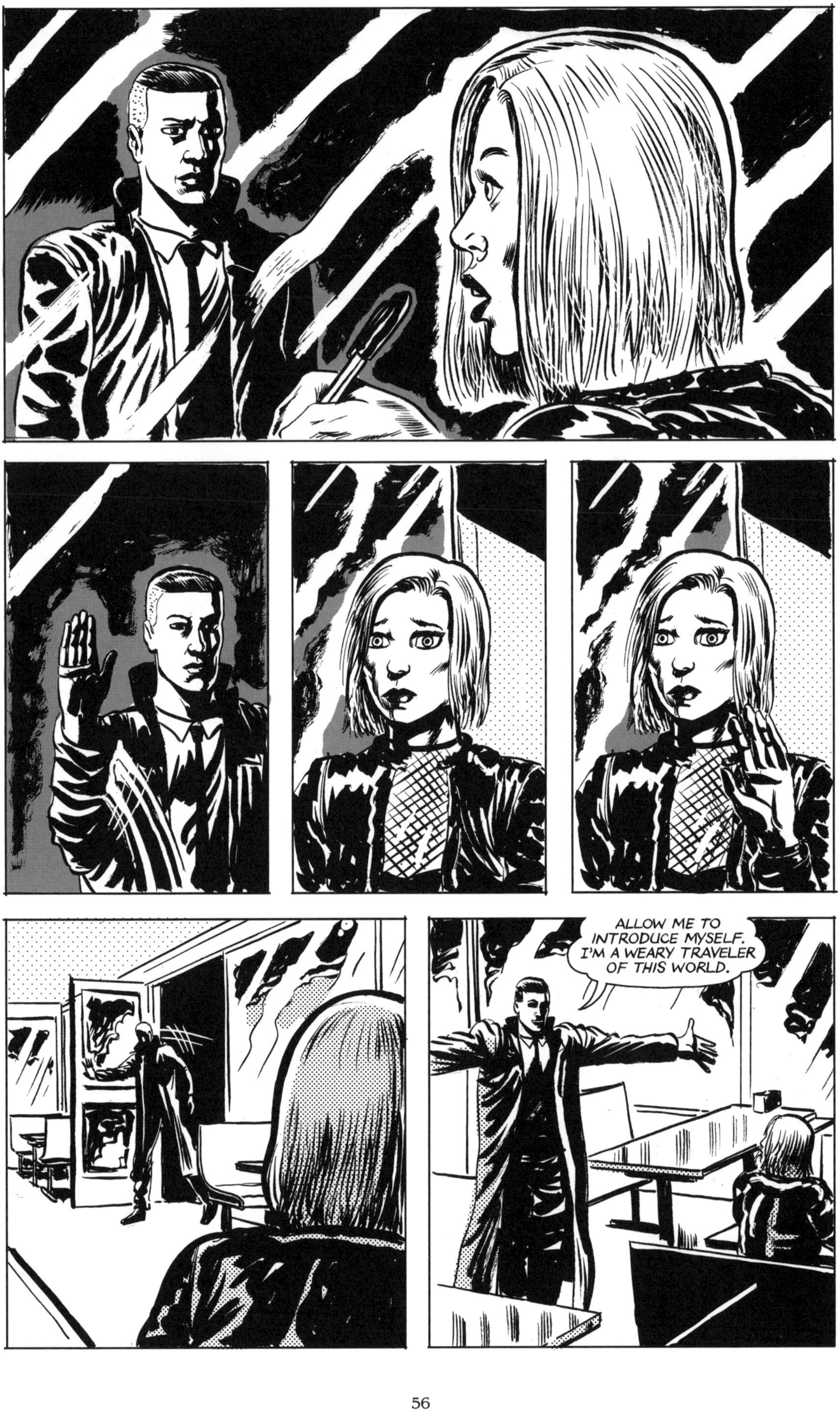
ALLOW ME TO INTRODUCE MYSELF. I'M A WEARY TRAVELER OF THIS WORLD.

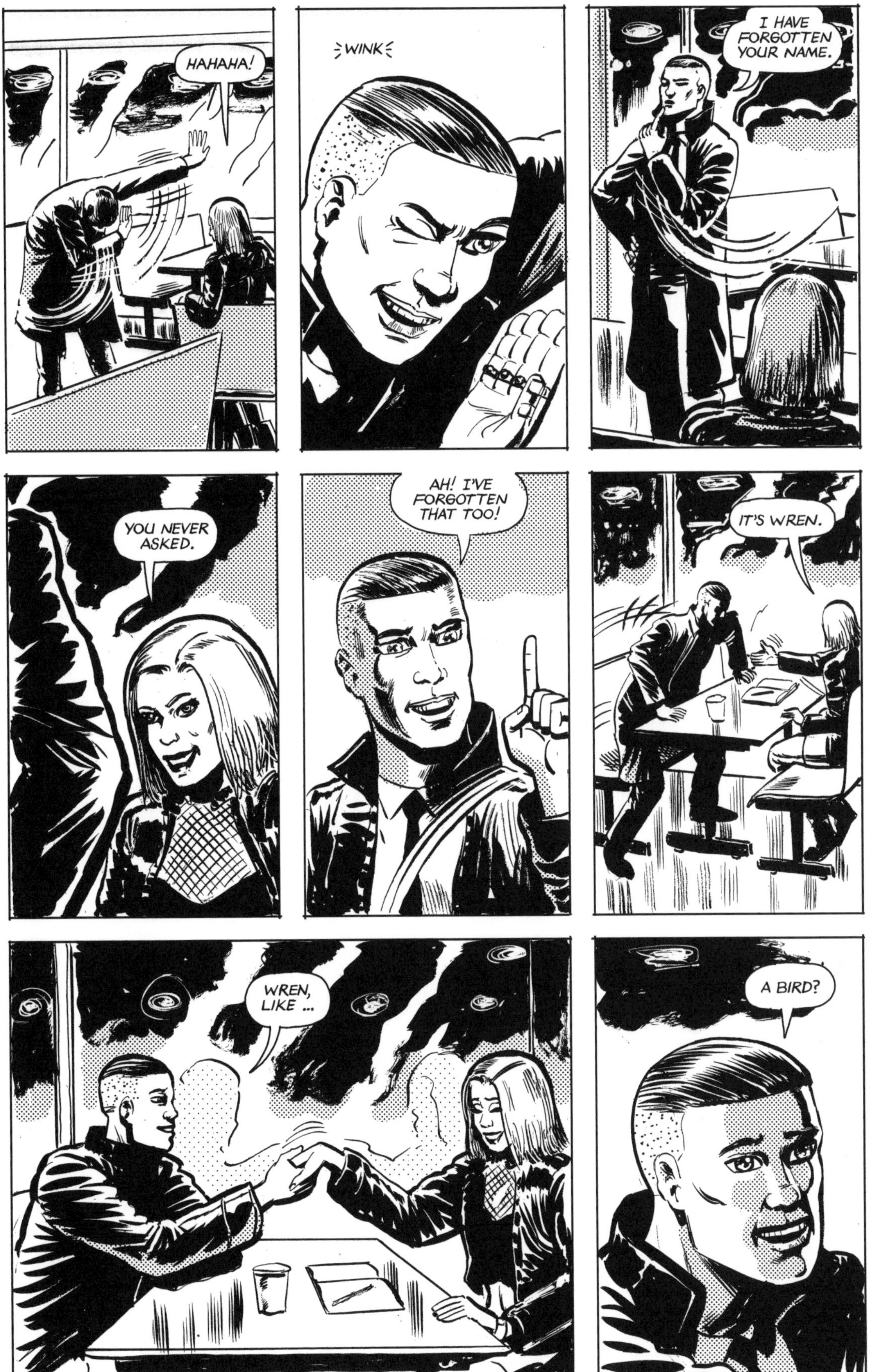
HAHAHA!
WINK
I HAVE FORGOTTEN YOUR NAME.
YOU NEVER ASKED.
AH! I'VE FORGOTTEN THAT TOO!
IT'S WREN.
WREN, LIKE ...
A BIRD?

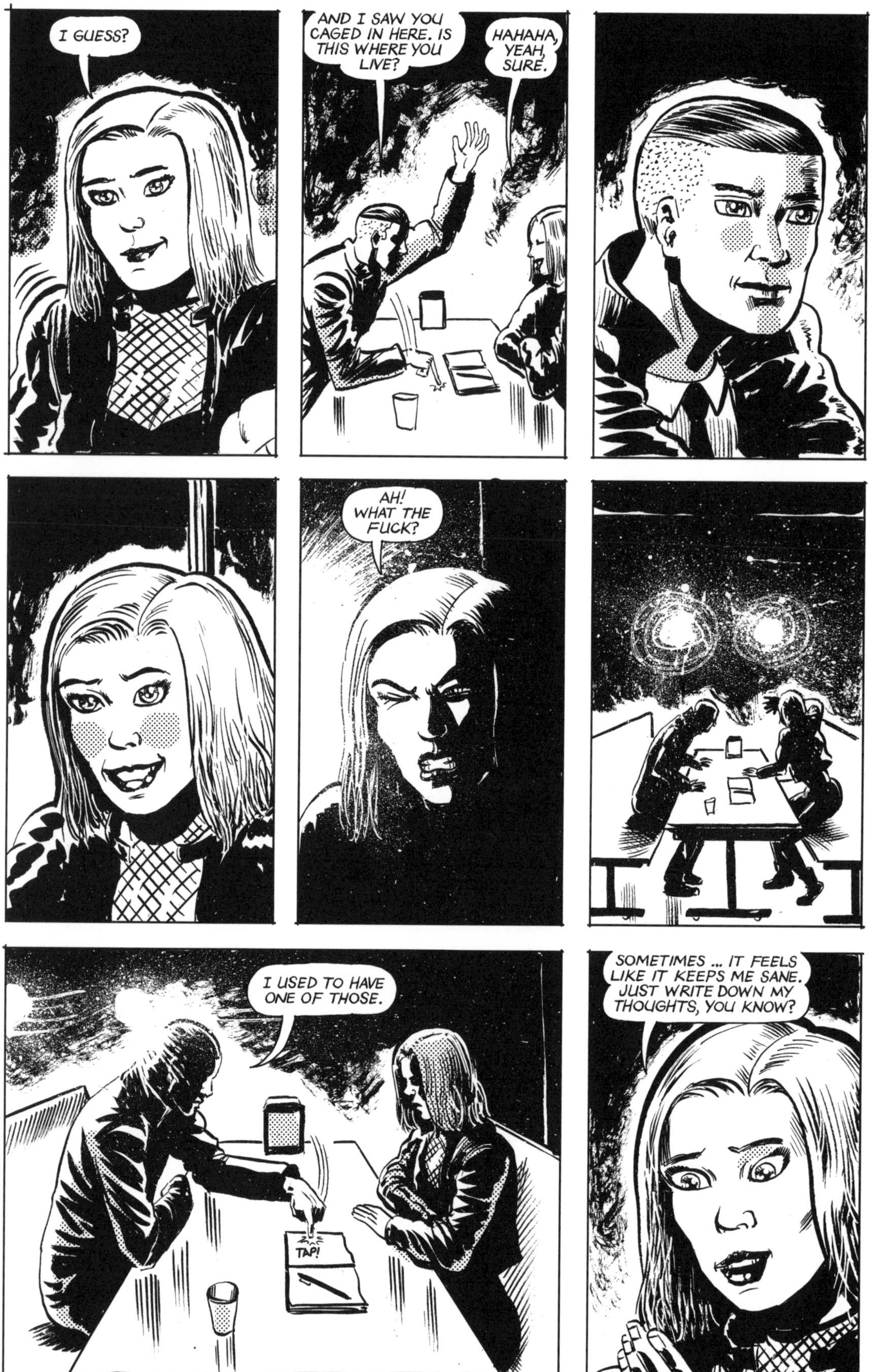
I GUESS?
AND I SAW YOU CAGED IN HERE. IS THIS WHERE YOU LIVE?
HAHAHA, YEAH, SURE.
AH! WHAT THE FUCK?
I USED TO HAVE ONE OF THOSE.
TAP!
SOMETIMES ... IT FEELS LIKE IT KEEPS ME SANE. JUST WRITE DOWN MY THOUGHTS, YOU KNOW?

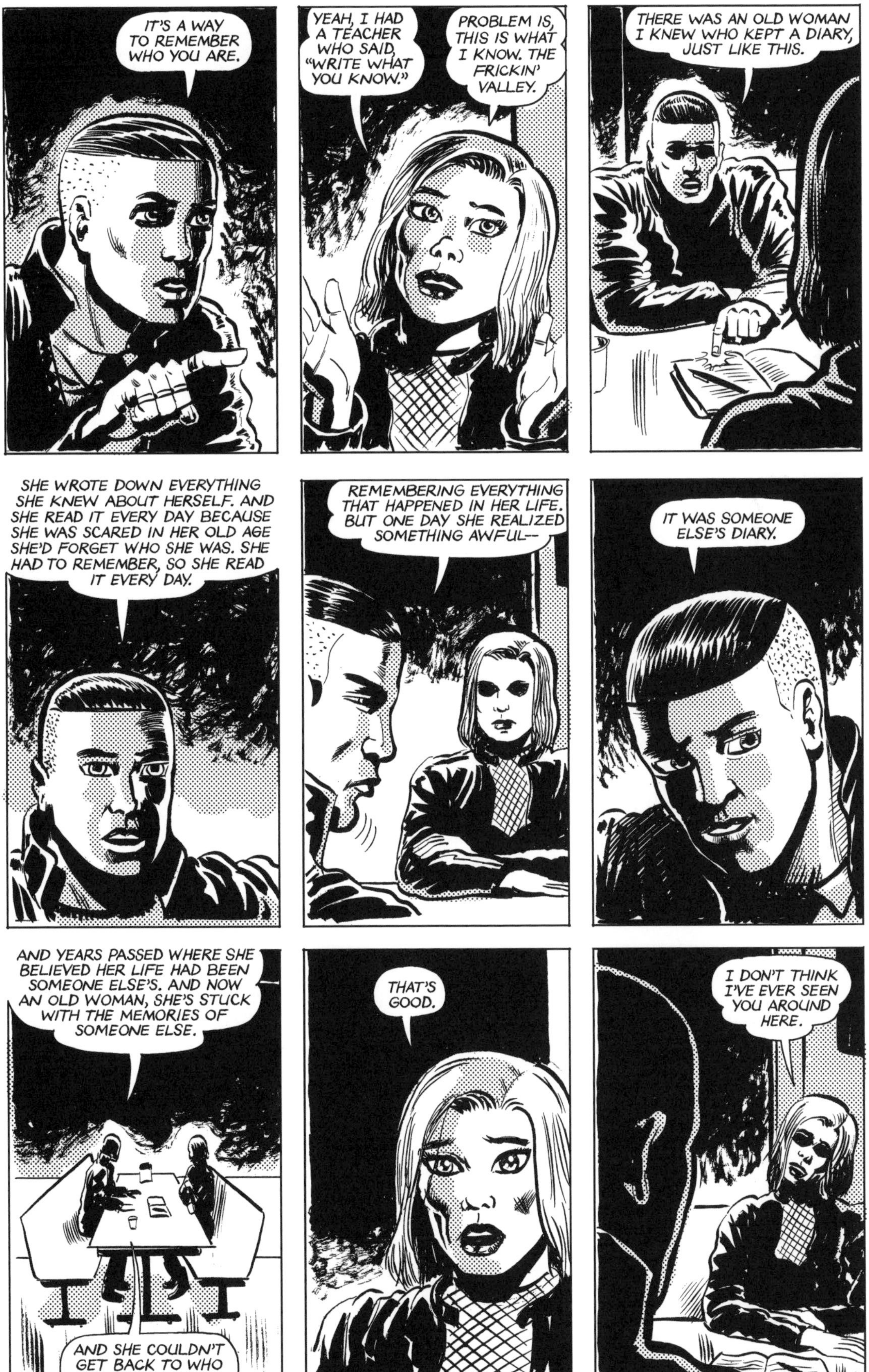
IT'S A WAY TO REMEMBER WHO YOU ARE.
YEAH, I HAD A TEACHER WHO SAID, "WRITE WHAT YOU KNOW."
PROBLEM IS, THIS IS WHAT I KNOW. THE FRICKIN' VALLEY.
THERE WAS AN OLD WOMAN I KNEW WHO KEPT A DIARY, JUST LIKE THIS.
SHE WROTE DOWN EVERYTHING SHE KNEW ABOUT HERSELF. AND SHE READ IT EVERY DAY BECAUSE SHE WAS SCARED IN HER OLD AGE SHE'D FORGET WHO SHE WAS. SHE HAD TO REMEMBER, SO SHE READ IT EVERY DAY.
REMEMBERING EVERYTHING THAT HAPPENED IN HER LIFE. BUT ONE DAY SHE REALIZED SOMETHING AWFUL--
IT WAS SOMEONE ELSE'S DIARY.
AND YEARS PASSED WHERE SHE BELIEVED HER LIFE HAD BEEN SOMEONE ELSE'S. AND NOW AN OLD WOMAN, SHE'S STUCK WITH THE MEMORIES OF SOMEONE ELSE.
AND SHE COULDN'T GET BACK TO WHO SHE REALLY WAS.
THAT'S GOOD.
I DON'T THINK I'VE EVER SEEN YOU AROUND HERE.

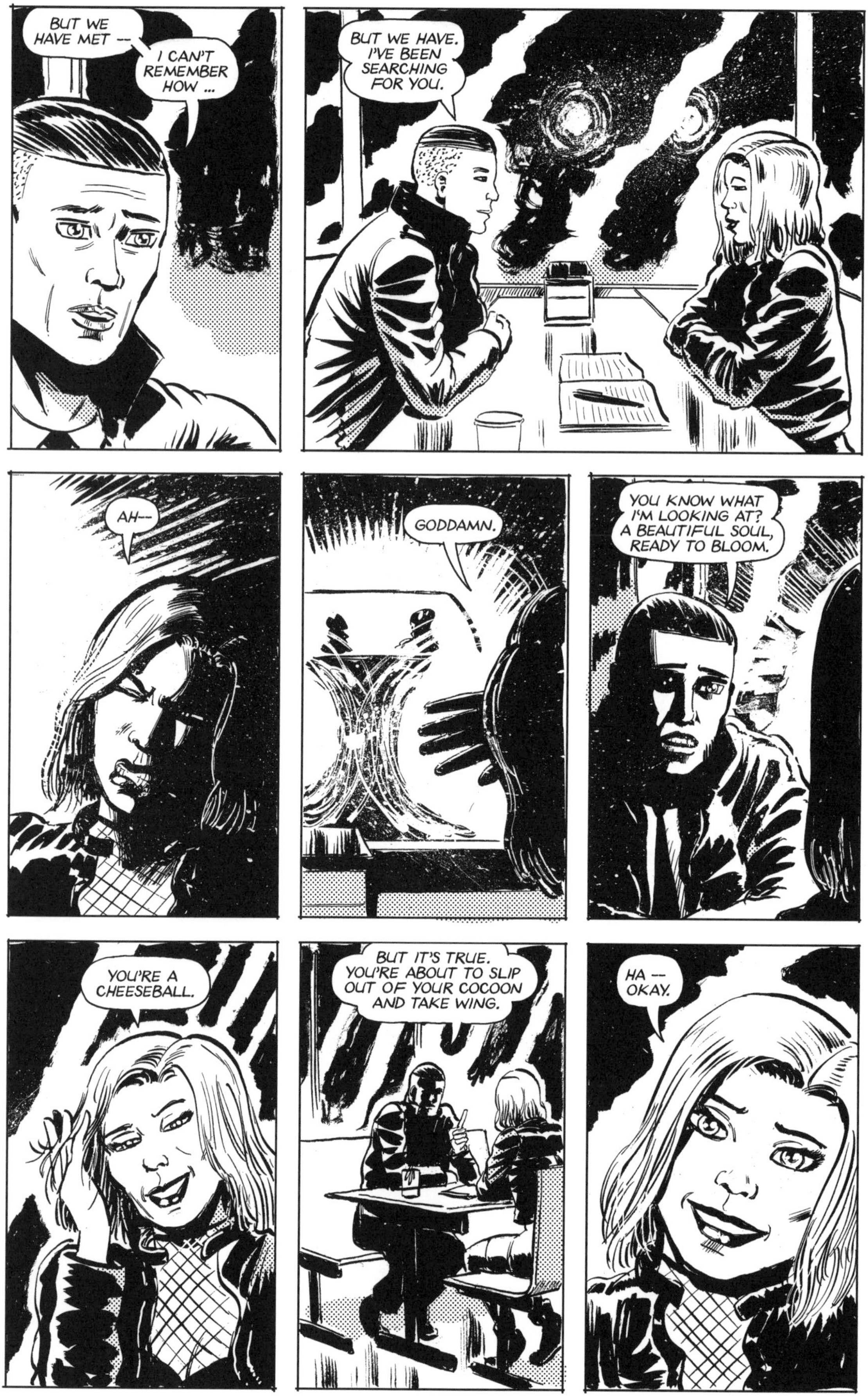
BUT WE HAVE MET --
I CAN'T REMEMBER HOW ...
BUT WE HAVE. I'VE BEEN SEARCHING FOR YOU.
AH--
GODDAMN.
YOU KNOW WHAT I'M LOOKING AT? A BEAUTIFUL SOUL, READY TO BLOOM.
YOU'RE A CHEESEBALL.
BUT IT'S TRUE. YOU'RE ABOUT TO SLIP OUT OF YOUR COCOON AND TAKE WING.
HA -- OKAY.

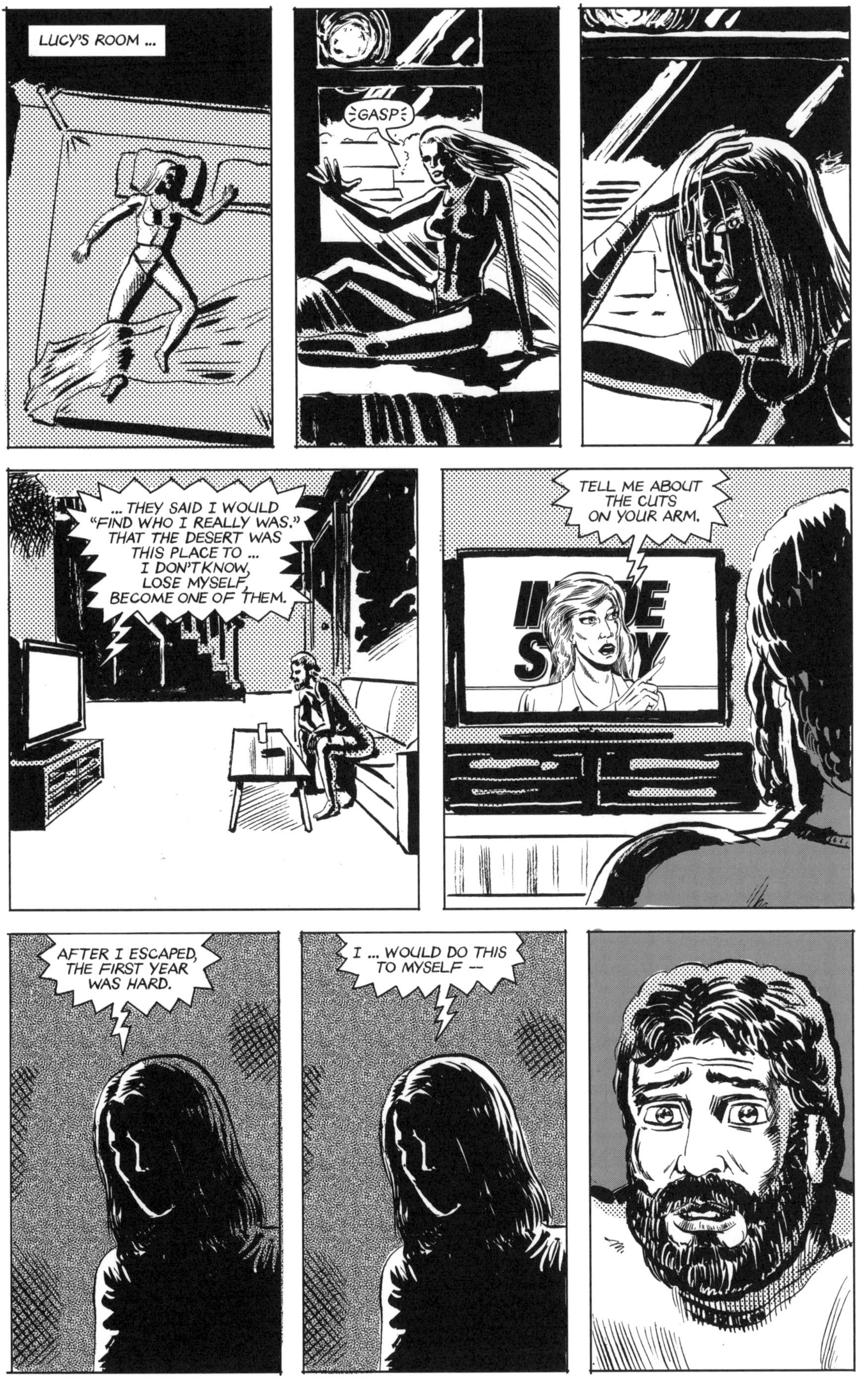
LUCY'S ROOM ...
GASP
... THEY SAID I WOULD "FIND WHO I REALLY WAS." THAT THE DESERT WAS THIS PLACE TO ... I DON'T KNOW, LOSE MYSELF, BECOME ONE OF THEM.
TELL ME ABOUT THE CUTS ON YOUR ARM.
AFTER I ESCAPED, THE FIRST YEAR WAS HARD.
I ... WOULD DO THIS TO MYSELF --

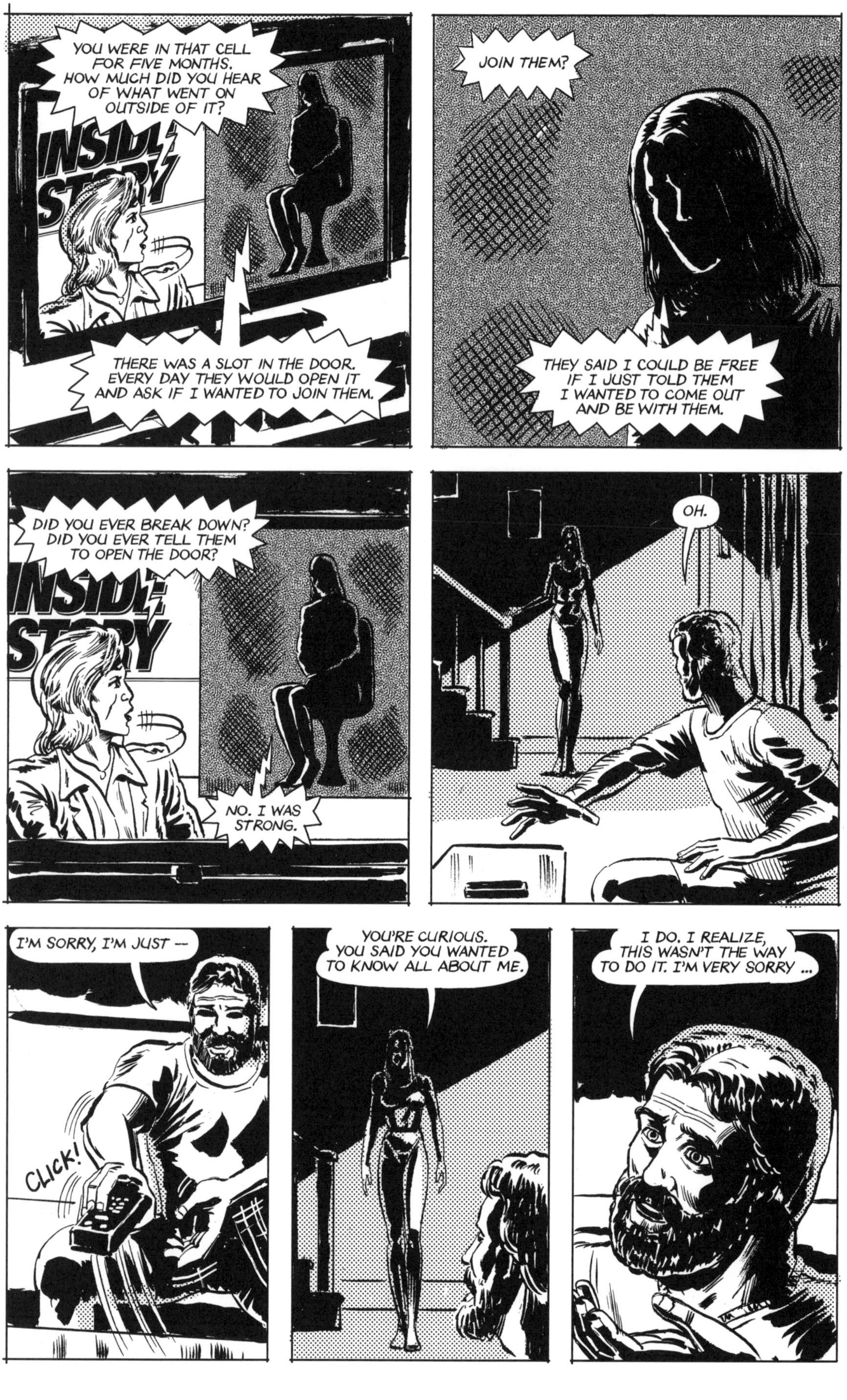
YOU WERE IN THAT CELL FOR FIVE MONTHS. HOW MUCH DID YOU HEAR OF WHAT WENT ON OUTSIDE OF IT?
INSIDE STORY
THERE WAS A SLOT IN THE DOOR. EVERY DAY THEY WOULD OPEN IT AND ASK IF I WANTED TO JOIN THEM.
JOIN THEM?
THEY SAID I COULD BE FREE IF I JUST TOLD THEM I WANTED TO COME OUT AND BE WITH THEM.
DID YOU EVER BREAK DOWN? DID YOU EVER TELL THEM TO OPEN THE DOOR?
INSIDE STORY
NO. I WAS STRONG.
OH.
I'M SORRY, I'M JUST --
CLICK!
YOU'RE CURIOUS. YOU SAID YOU WANTED TO KNOW ALL ABOUT ME.
I DO. I REALIZE, THIS WASN'T THE WAY TO DO IT. I'M VERY SORRY ...

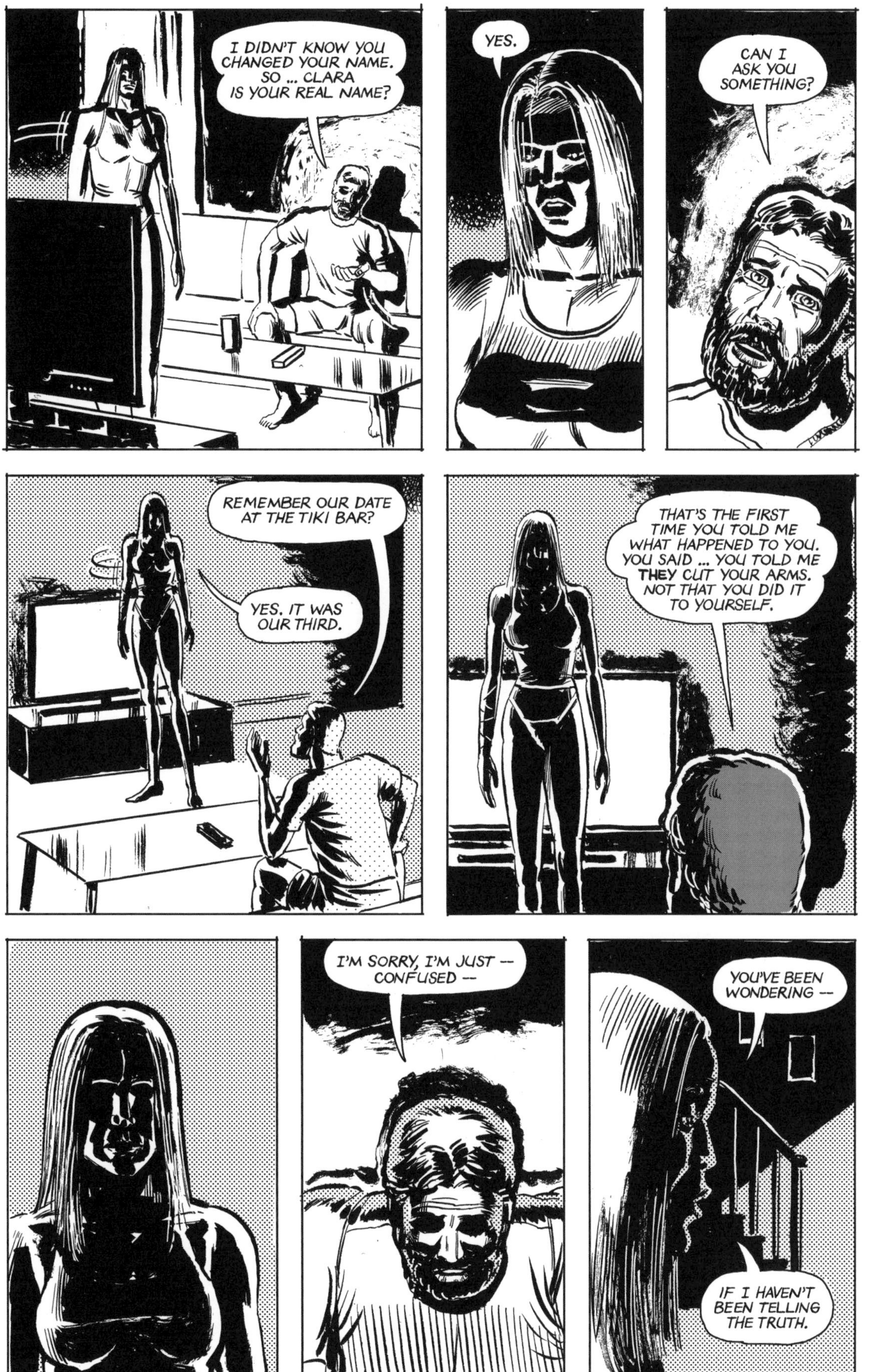

I DIDN'T KNOW YOU CHANGED YOUR NAME. SO ... CLARA IS YOUR REAL NAME?
YES.
CAN I ASK YOU SOMETHING?
REMEMBER OUR DATE AT THE TIKI BAR?
YES. IT WAS OUR THIRD.
THAT'S THE FIRST TIME YOU TOLD ME WHAT HAPPENED TO YOU. YOU SAID ... YOU TOLD ME THEY CUT YOUR ARMS. NOT THAT YOU DID IT TO YOURSELF.
I'M SORRY, I'M JUST -- CONFUSED --
YOU'VE BEEN WONDERING --
IF I HAVEN'T BEEN TELLING THE TRUTH.

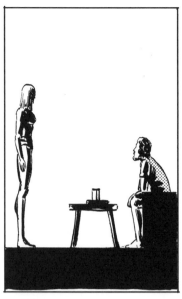

YES. I LIED ABOUT WHAT HAPPENED.

HE WOULD CALL ME "BLUEBERRY" ... SUCH A STUPID NAME.

WHO WOULD CALL YOU THAT?

DO YOU WANT TO HEAR ABOUT IT?

UH, YEAH.

HE WOULD CALL ME THAT WHEN I WAS TRAPPED INSIDE. THE FIRST TIME HE HEARD ME LAUGH AT THE NAME, HE OPENED THE DOOR.

HE OPENED THE DOOR?

HE BEGAN TO LET ME OUT ... JUST TO WATCH. TO TALK ME THROUGH WHAT I WAS FEELING INSIDE.

DO YOU WANT TO KNOW WHAT I WAS FEELING INSIDE?

YES.

THEY WOULD BRING ME INTO A DARK ROOM. THE WINDOWS HAD HEAVY CURTAINS OVER THEM, LIKE CURTAINS IN A MOTEL.

YOU COULDN'T TELL IF IT WAS DAY OR NIGHT. THERE WAS MUSIC PLAYING, THAT HE WOULD MAKE, OR FROM HIS RECORDS ...

OR I WOULD MAKE WITH HIM ...

THEY MADE ME TAKE OFF MY CLOTHES. WE WERE ALL NAKED TOGETHER, IN THE DARK ROOM. AND THEY ... TOUCHED ME. I WAS KISSING MY FRIEND WENDY BEFORE I REALIZED IT WAS HER. DO YOU KNOW HOW I KNEW IT WAS HER?

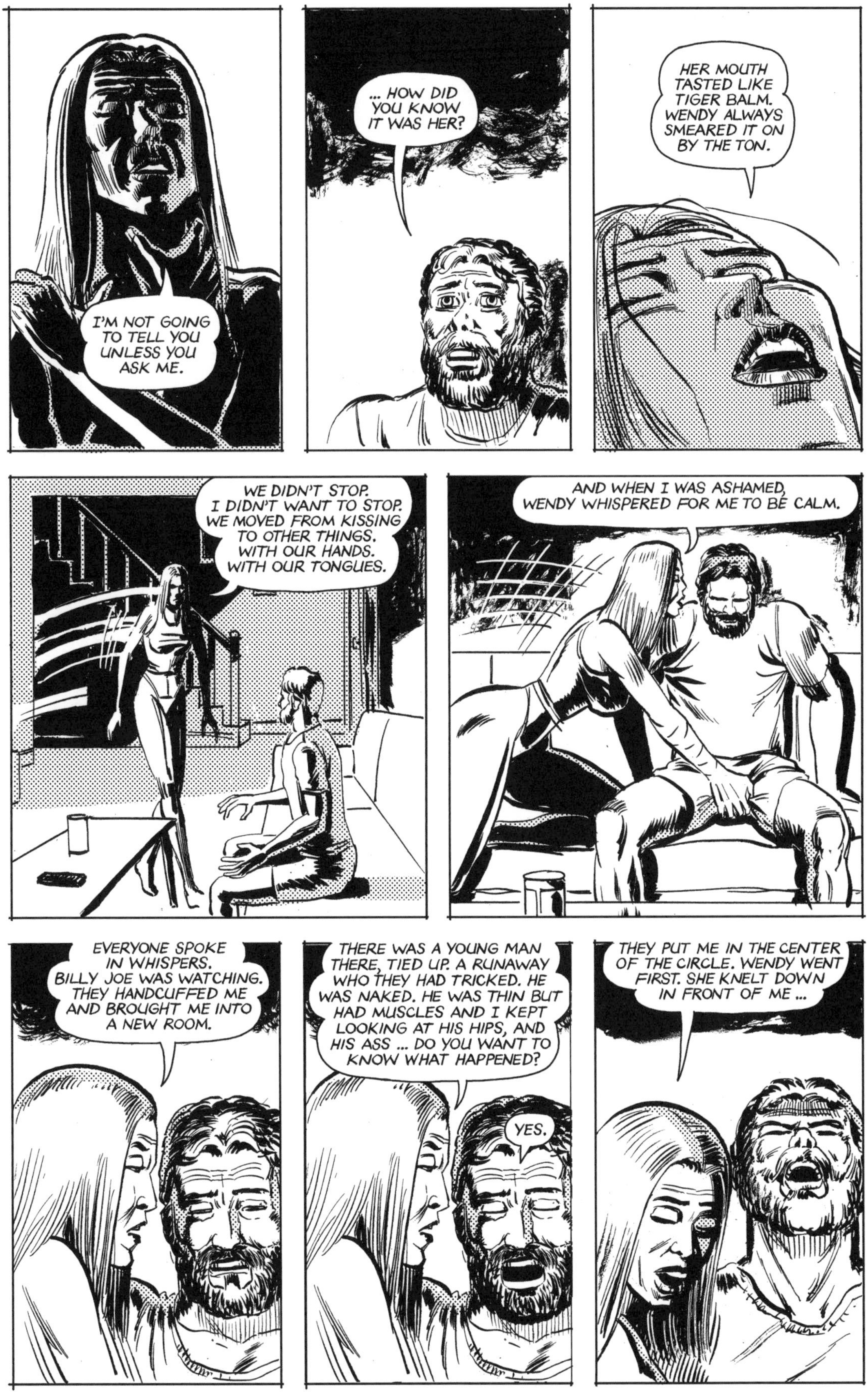
I'M NOT GOING TO TELL YOU UNLESS YOU ASK ME.
... HOW DID YOU KNOW IT WAS HER?
HER MOUTH TASTED LIKE TIGER BALM. WENDY ALWAYS SMEARED IT ON BY THE TON.
WE DIDN'T STOP. I DIDN'T WANT TO STOP. WE MOVED FROM KISSING TO OTHER THINGS. WITH OUR HANDS. WITH OUR TONGUES.
AND WHEN I WAS ASHAMED, WENDY WHISPERED FOR ME TO BE CALM.
EVERYONE SPOKE IN WHISPERS. BILLY JOE WAS WATCHING. THEY HANDCUFFED ME AND BROUGHT ME INTO A NEW ROOM.
THERE WAS A YOUNG MAN THERE, TIED UP. A RUNAWAY WHO THEY HAD TRICKED. HE WAS NAKED. HE WAS THIN BUT HAD MUSCLES AND I KEPT LOOKING AT HIS HIPS, AND HIS ASS ... DO YOU WANT TO KNOW WHAT HAPPENED?
YES.
THEY PUT ME IN THE CENTER OF THE CIRCLE. WENDY WENT FIRST. SHE KNELT DOWN IN FRONT OF ME ...

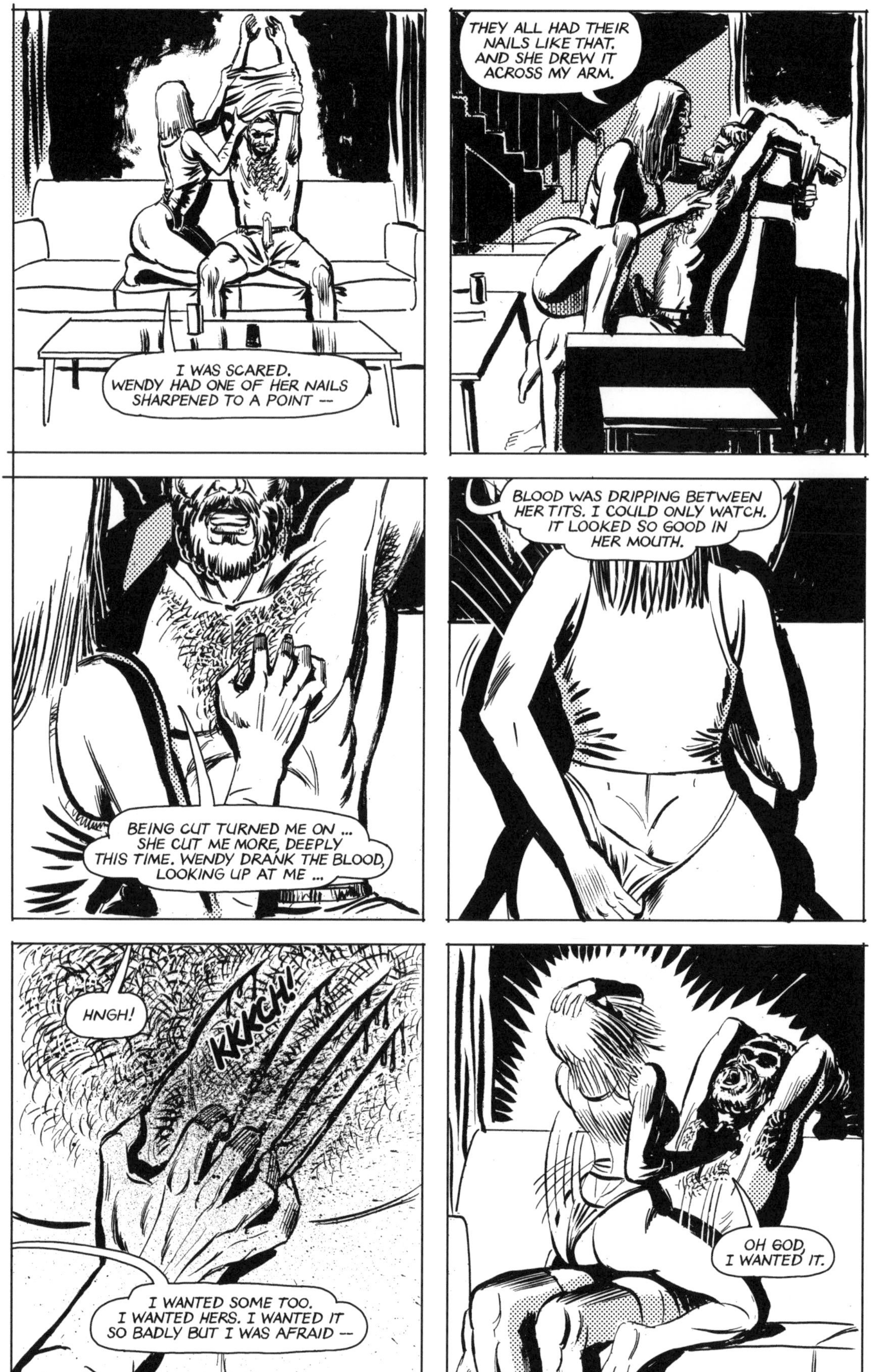
I WAS SCARED. WENDY HAD ONE OF HER NAILS SHARPENED TO A POINT --
THEY ALL HAD THEIR NAILS LIKE THAT. AND SHE DREW IT ACROSS MY ARM.
BEING CUT TURNED ME ON ... SHE CUT ME MORE, DEEPLY THIS TIME. WENDY DRANK THE BLOOD, LOOKING UP AT ME ...
BLOOD WAS DRIPPING BETWEEN HER TITS. I COULD ONLY WATCH. IT LOOKED SO GOOD IN HER MOUTH.
HNGH!
KKKCH!
I WANTED SOME TOO. I WANTED HERS. I WANTED IT SO BADLY BUT I WAS AFRAID --
OH GOD, I WANTED IT.

UHN, OH GOD ...
UH, YES.
UGHN, AH!
OH FUCK!
AAAHHH!
PANT, PANT
I NEVER GOT TO TASTE IT ... I RAN AWAY BEFORE I DID. I NEVER GOT TO TASTE IT. I WANTED TO BE ONE OF THEM SO BAD.
THERE'S A DINER NEAR MY HOUSE THAT HAS OLD PICTURES THAT SHOW HOW THIS USED TO BE ORCHARDS.
THERE ARE STILL ROCKS AND CAVES. THEY'VE BEEN HERE FOREVER. THEY WOULD SHOOT MOVIES WITH COWBOYS AND INDIANS IN THEM.
I'VE SLEPT IN THOSE CAVES ... I'VE SLEPT EVERYWHERE.

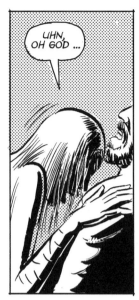

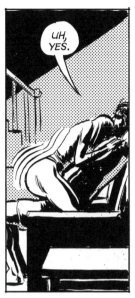

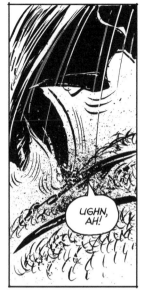

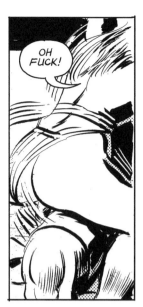

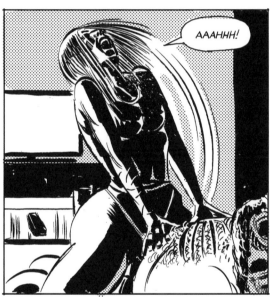

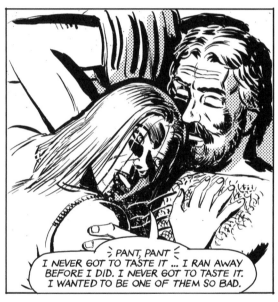

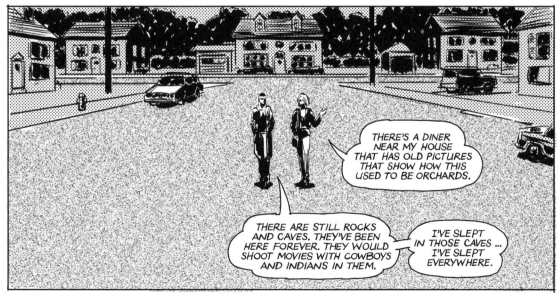

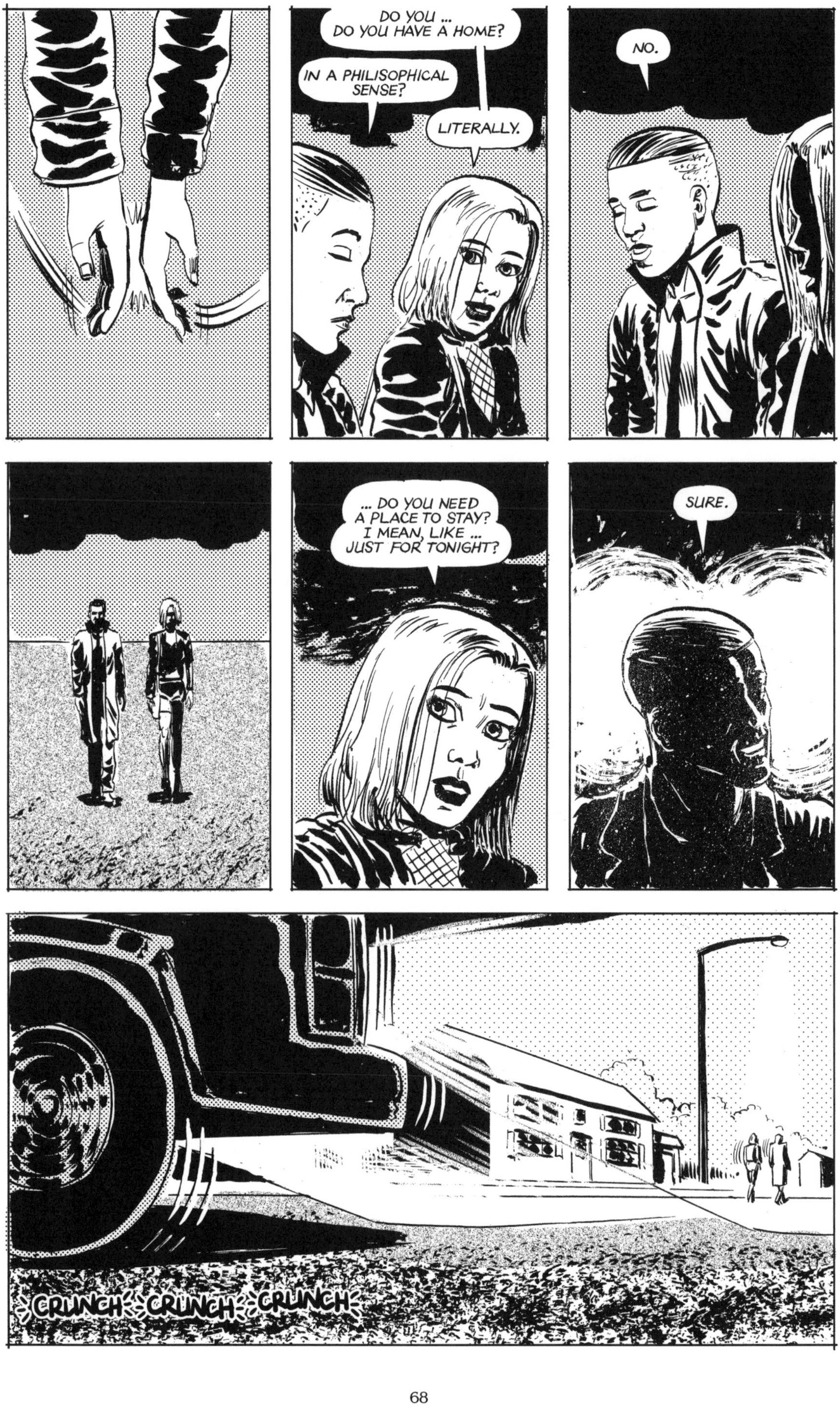
DO YOU ... DO YOU HAVE A HOME?
IN A PHILISOPHICAL SENSE?
LITERALLY.
NO.
... DO YOU NEED A PLACE TO STAY? I MEAN, LIKE ... JUST FOR TONIGHT?
SURE.
CRUNCH CRUNCH CRUNCH

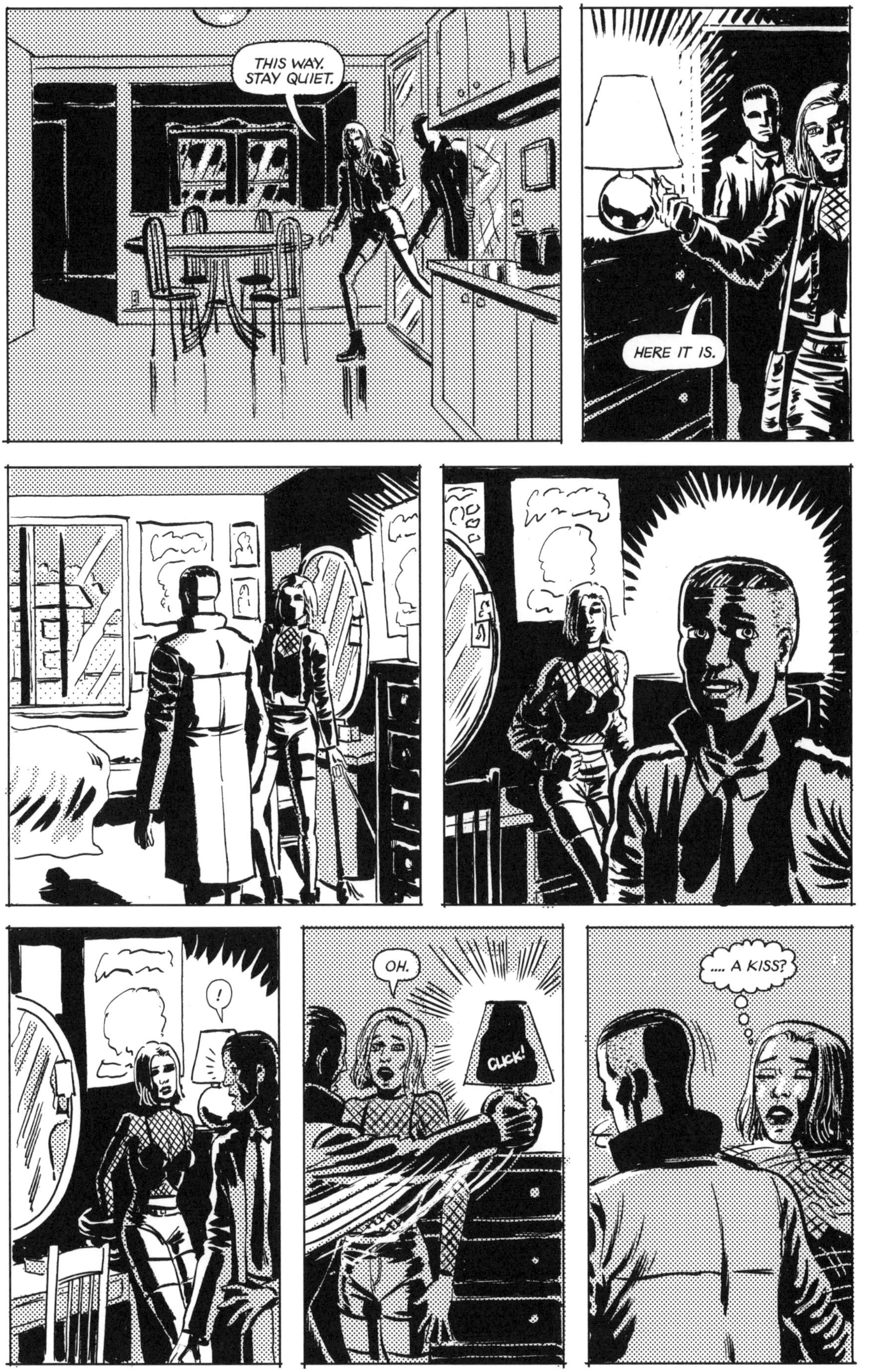
THIS WAY. STAY QUIET.
HERE IT IS.
!
OH.
CLICK!
.... A KISS?

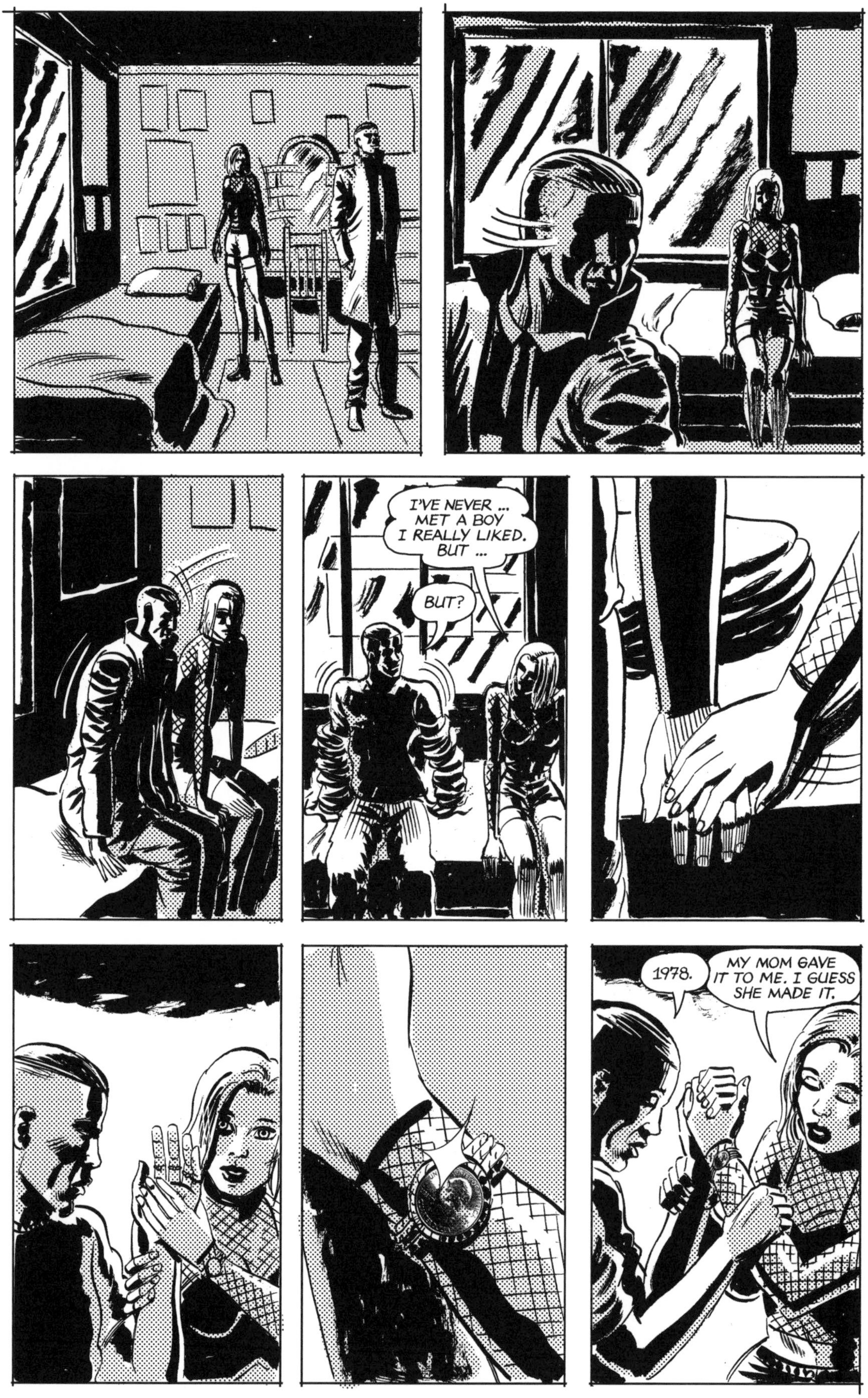
I'VE NEVER ... MET A BOY I REALLY LIKED. BUT ...
BUT?
1978.
MY MOM GAVE IT TO ME. I GUESS SHE MADE IT.

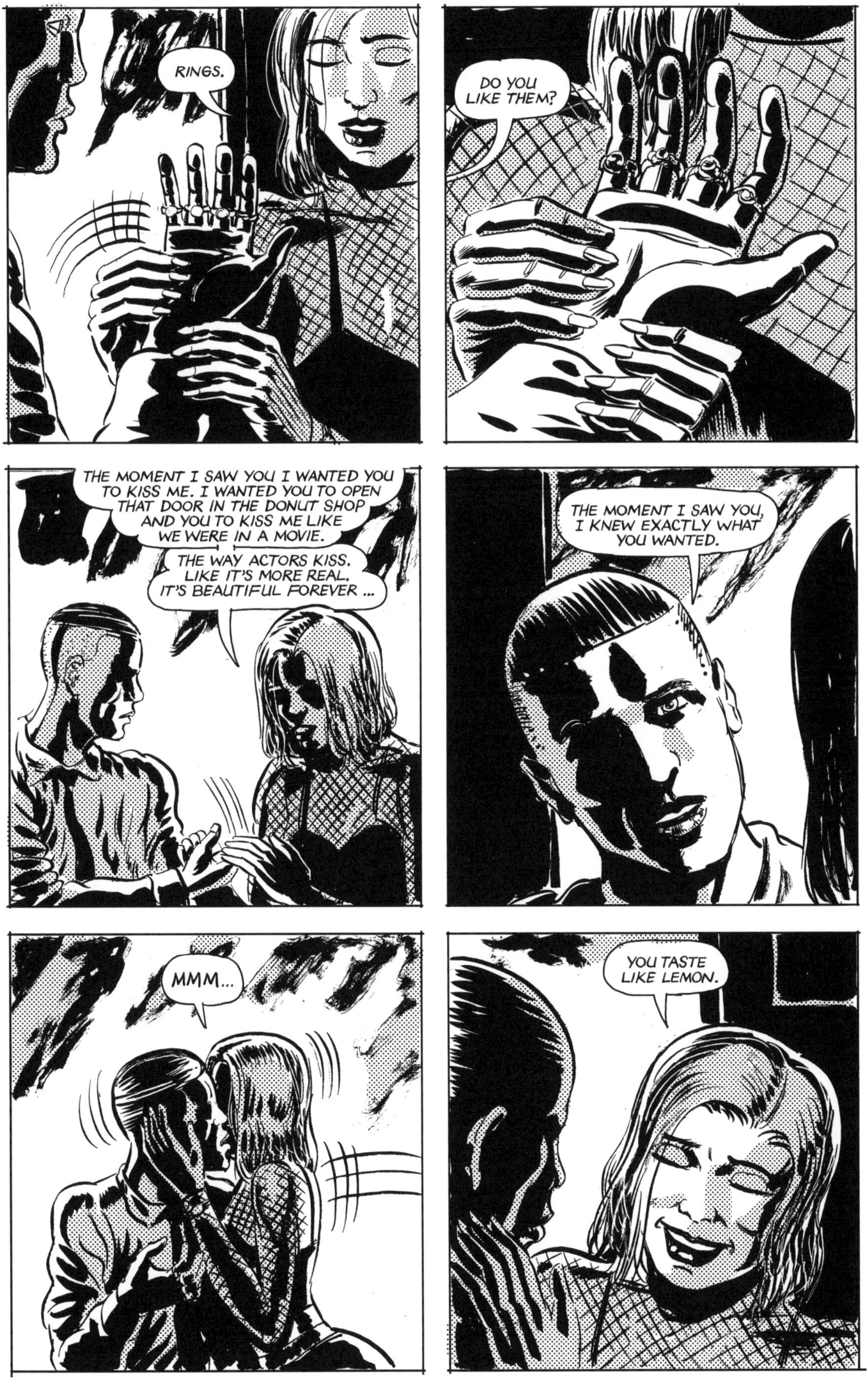
RINGS.
DO YOU LIKE THEM?
THE MOMENT I SAW YOU I WANTED YOU TO KISS ME. I WANTED YOU TO OPEN THAT DOOR IN THE DONUT SHOP AND YOU TO KISS ME LIKE WE WERE IN A MOVIE.
THE WAY ACTORS KISS. LIKE IT'S MORE REAL. IT'S BEAUTIFUL FOREVER ...
THE MOMENT I SAW YOU, I KNEW EXACTLY WHAT YOU WANTED.
MMM...
YOU TASTE LIKE LEMON.

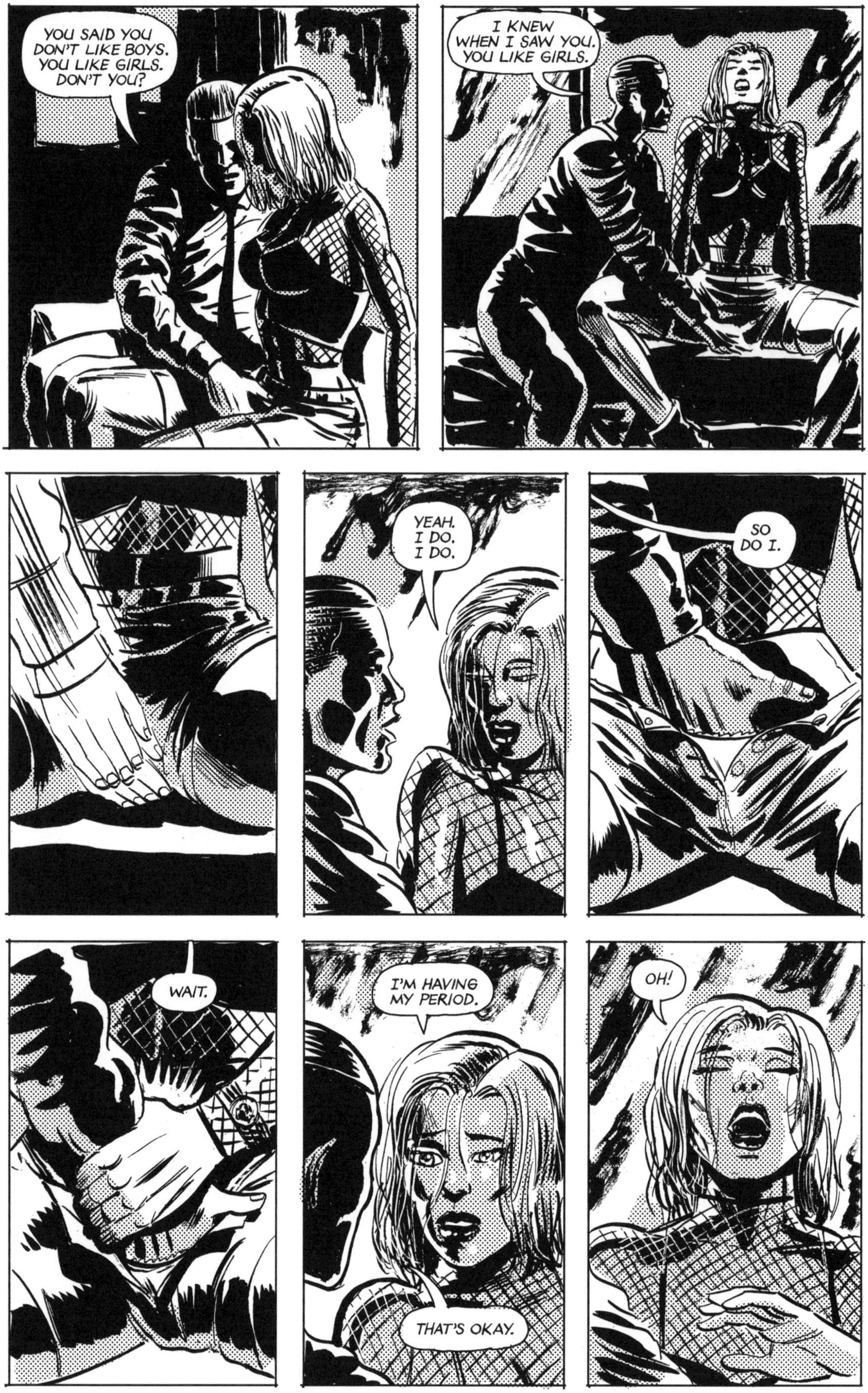
YOU SAID YOU DON'T LIKE BOYS. YOU LIKE GIRLS. DON'T YOU?
I KNEW WHEN I SAW YOU. YOU LIKE GIRLS.
YEAH. I DO. I DO.
SO DO I.
WAIT.
I'M HAVING MY PERIOD.
THAT'S OKAY.
OH!

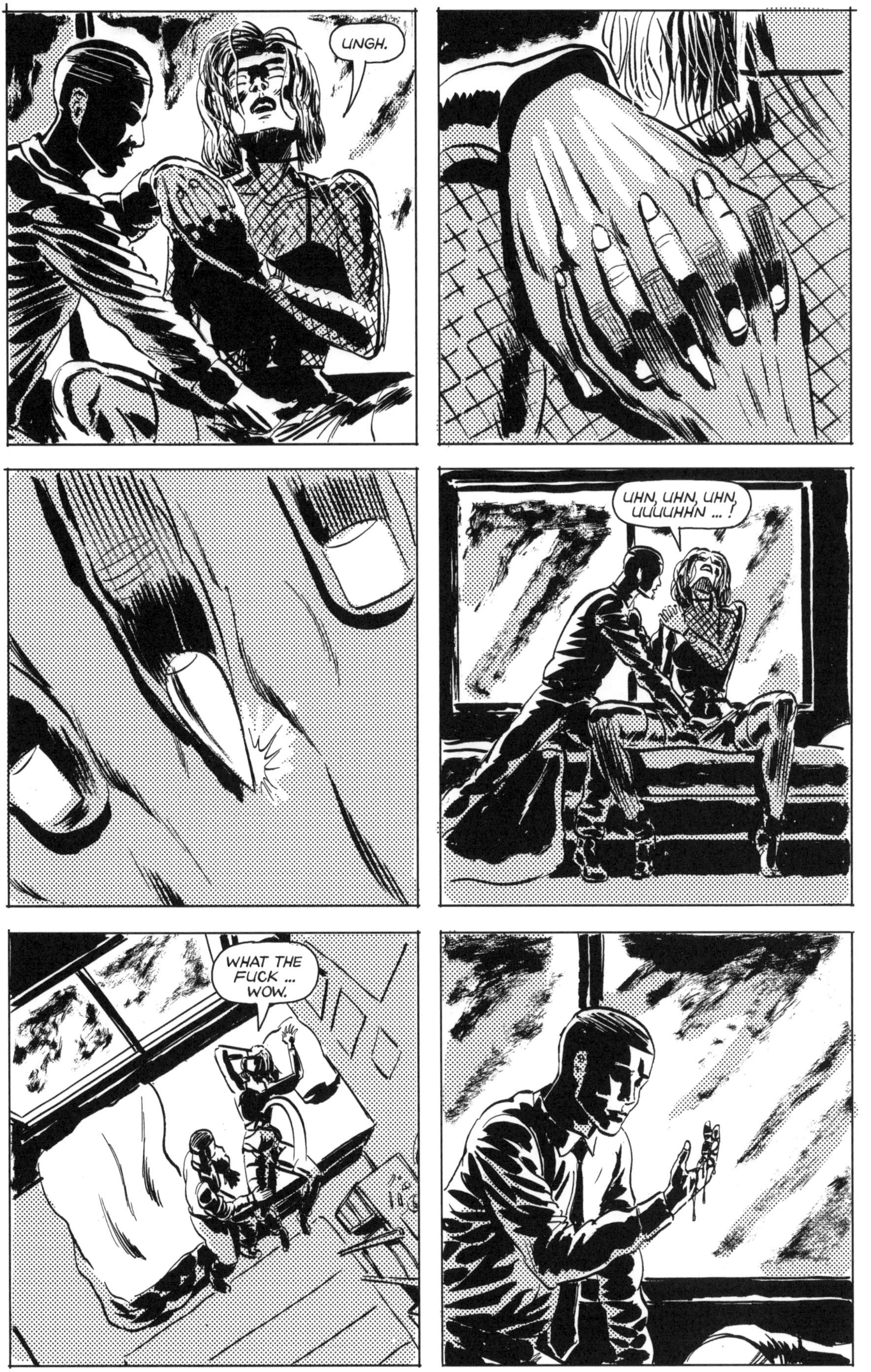
UNGH.
UHN, UHN, UHN, UUUUHHN ... !
WHAT THE FUCK ... WOW.

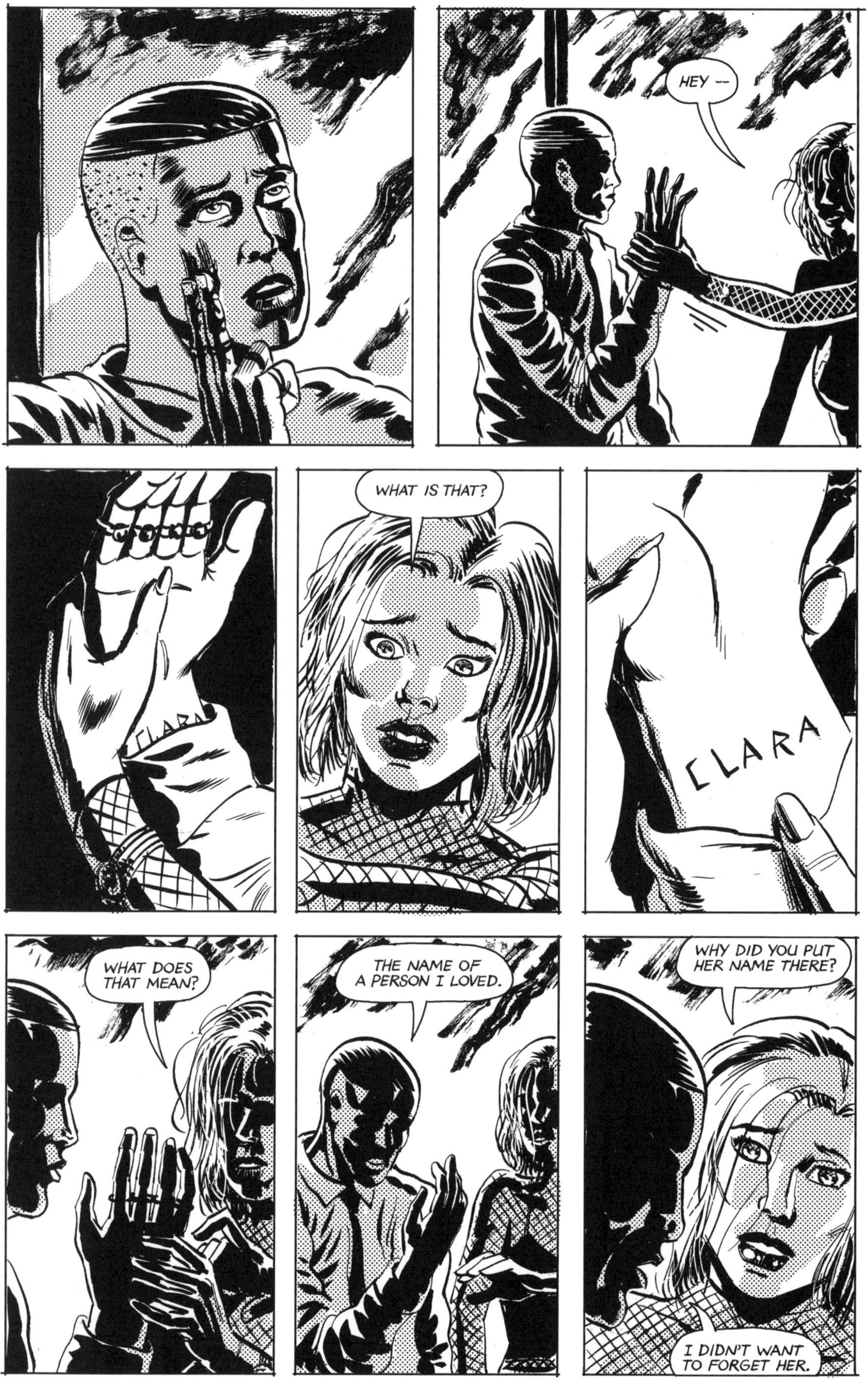
HEY --
WHAT IS THAT?
CLARA
CLARA
WHAT DOES THAT MEAN?
THE NAME OF A PERSON I LOVED.
WHY DID YOU PUT HER NAME THERE?
I DIDN'T WANT TO FORGET HER.

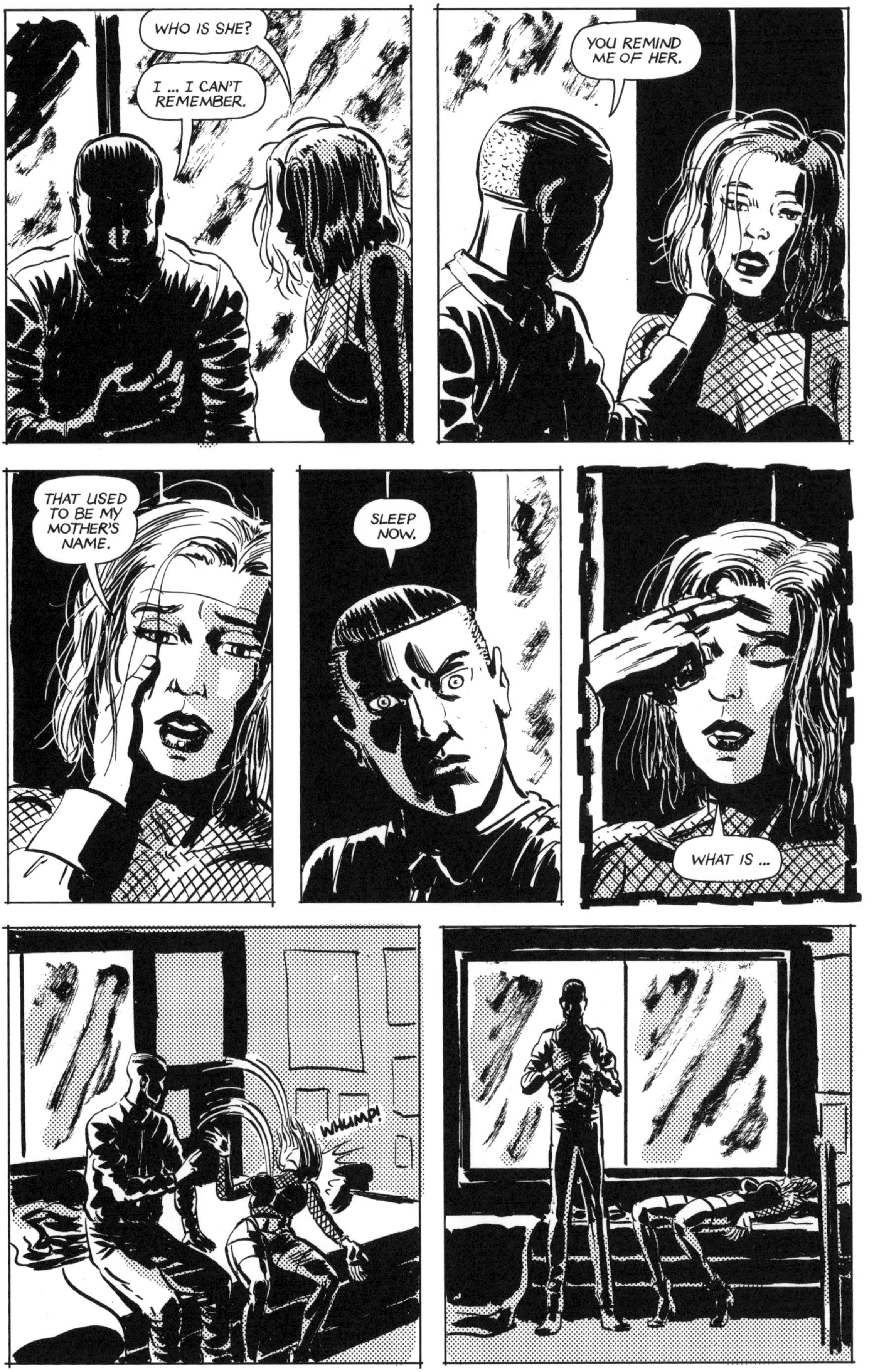
WHO IS SHE?
I ... I CAN'T REMEMBER.
YOU REMIND ME OF HER.
THAT USED TO BE MY MOTHER'S NAME.
SLEEP NOW.
WHAT IS ...
WHUMP!

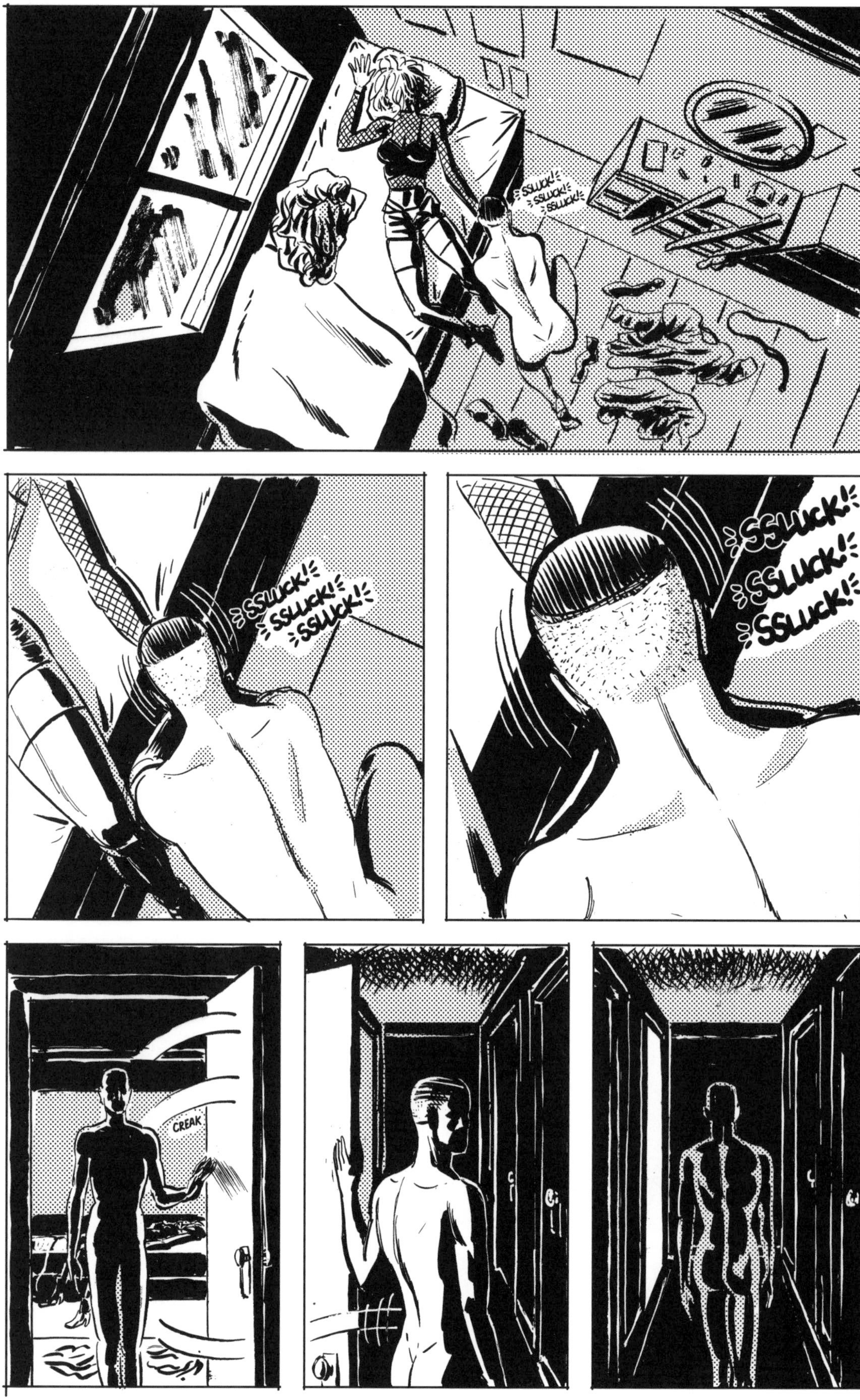
SSLUCK!
SSLUCK!
SSLUCK!
SSLUCK!
SSLUCK!
SSLUCK!
SSLUCK!
SSLUCK!
SSLUCK!
CREAK

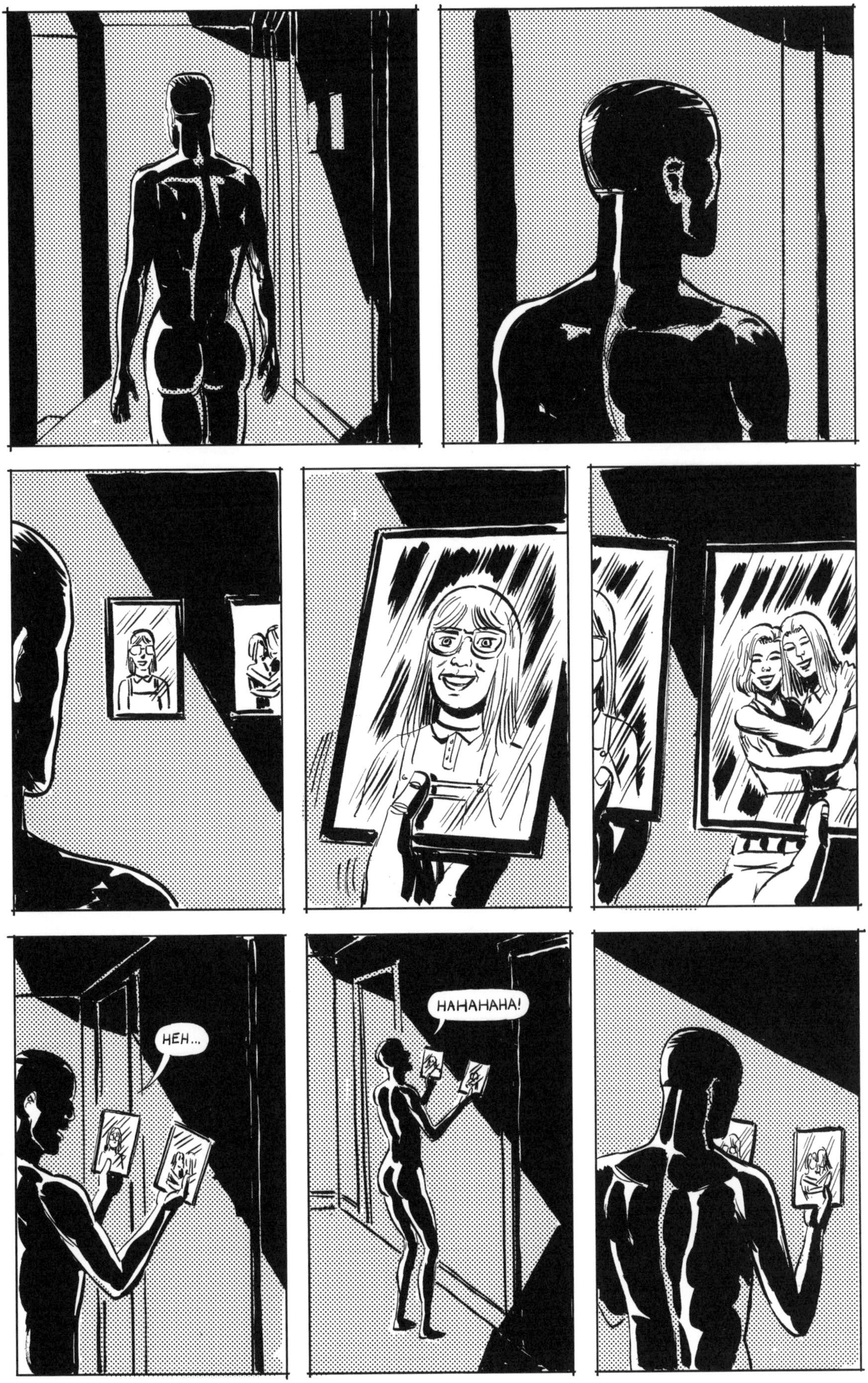
HEH...
HAHAHAHA!

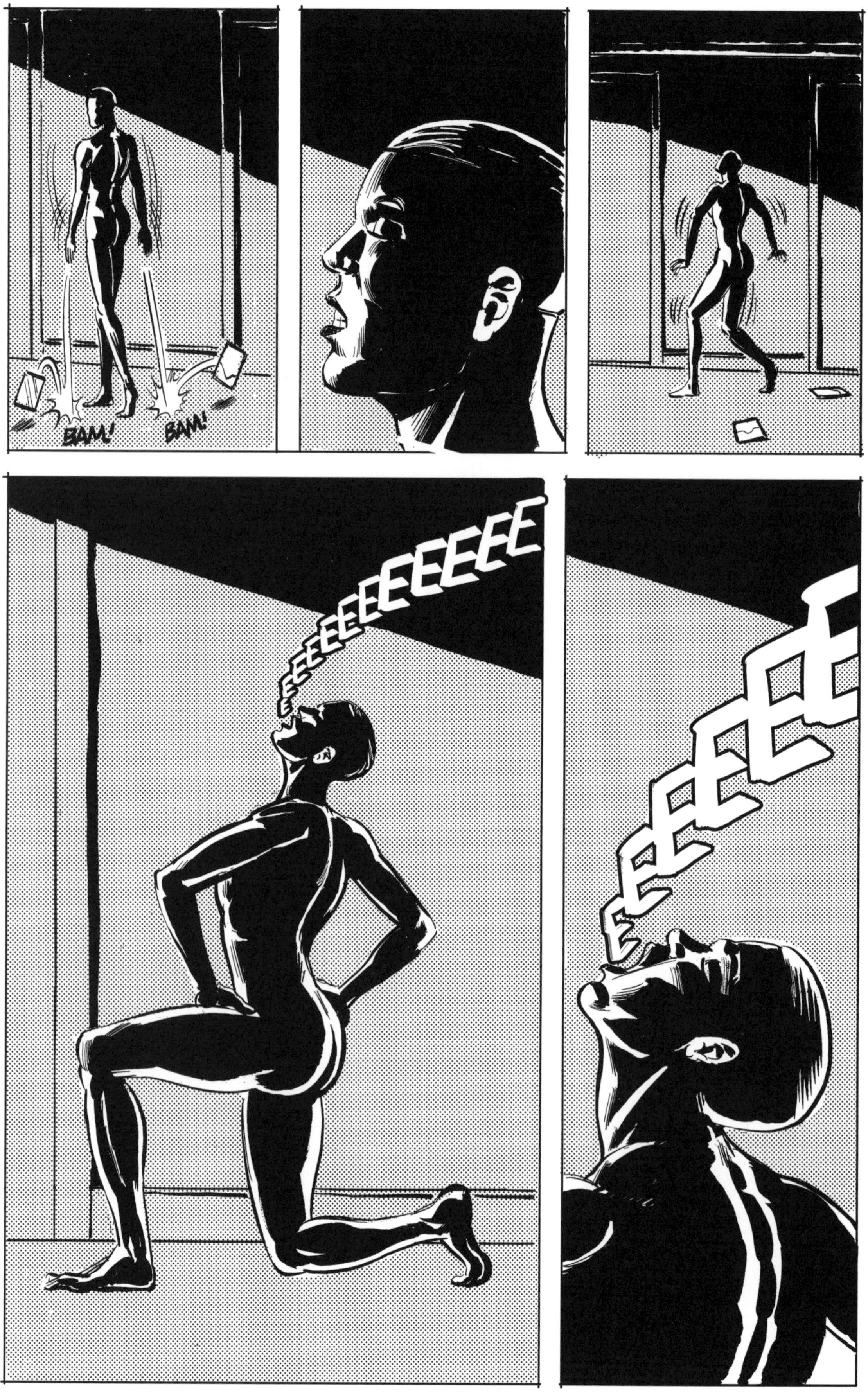
BAM!
BAM!
EEEEEEEEEEEEE
EEEEEEE

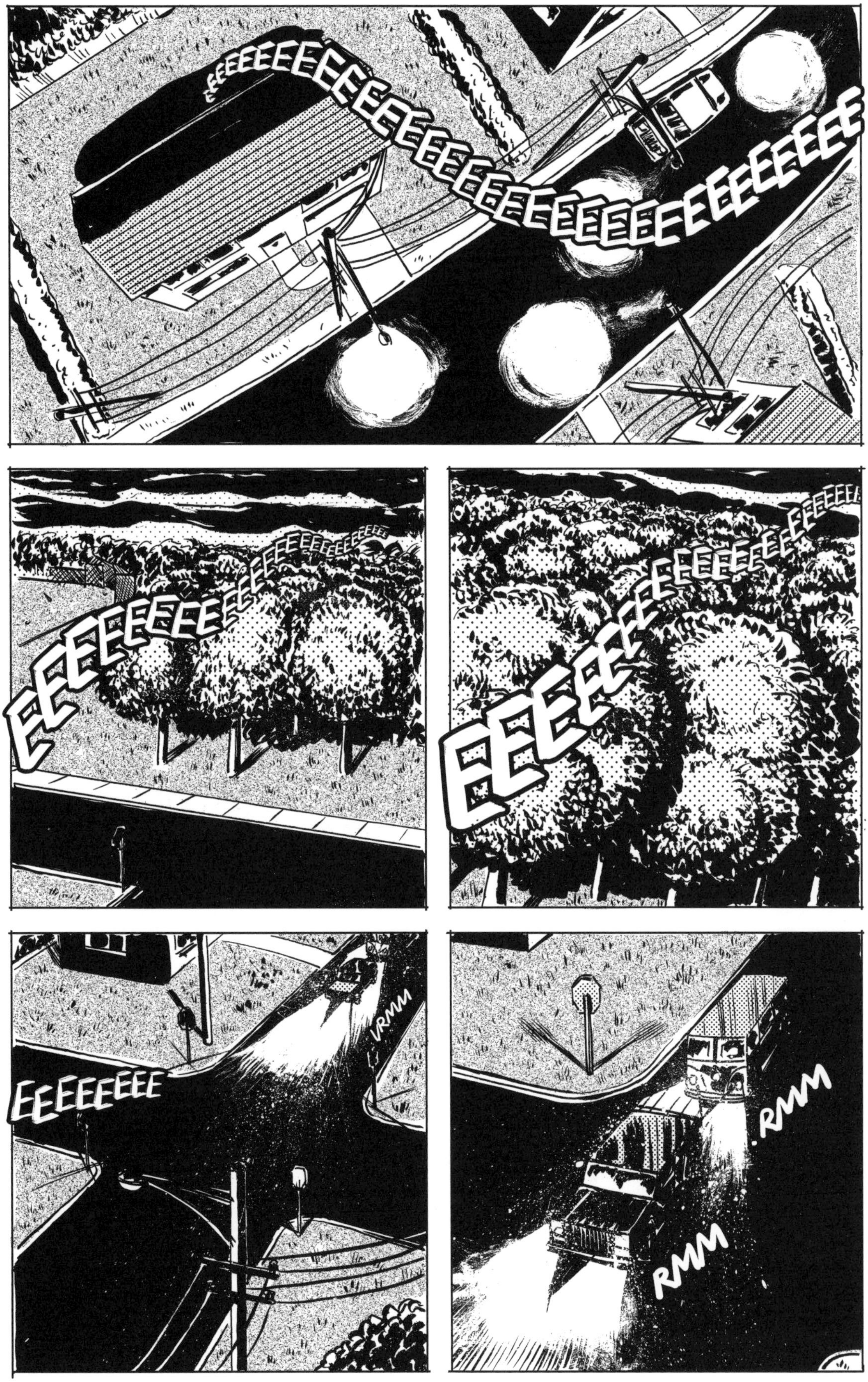
EEEEEEE
VRMM
RMM
RMM

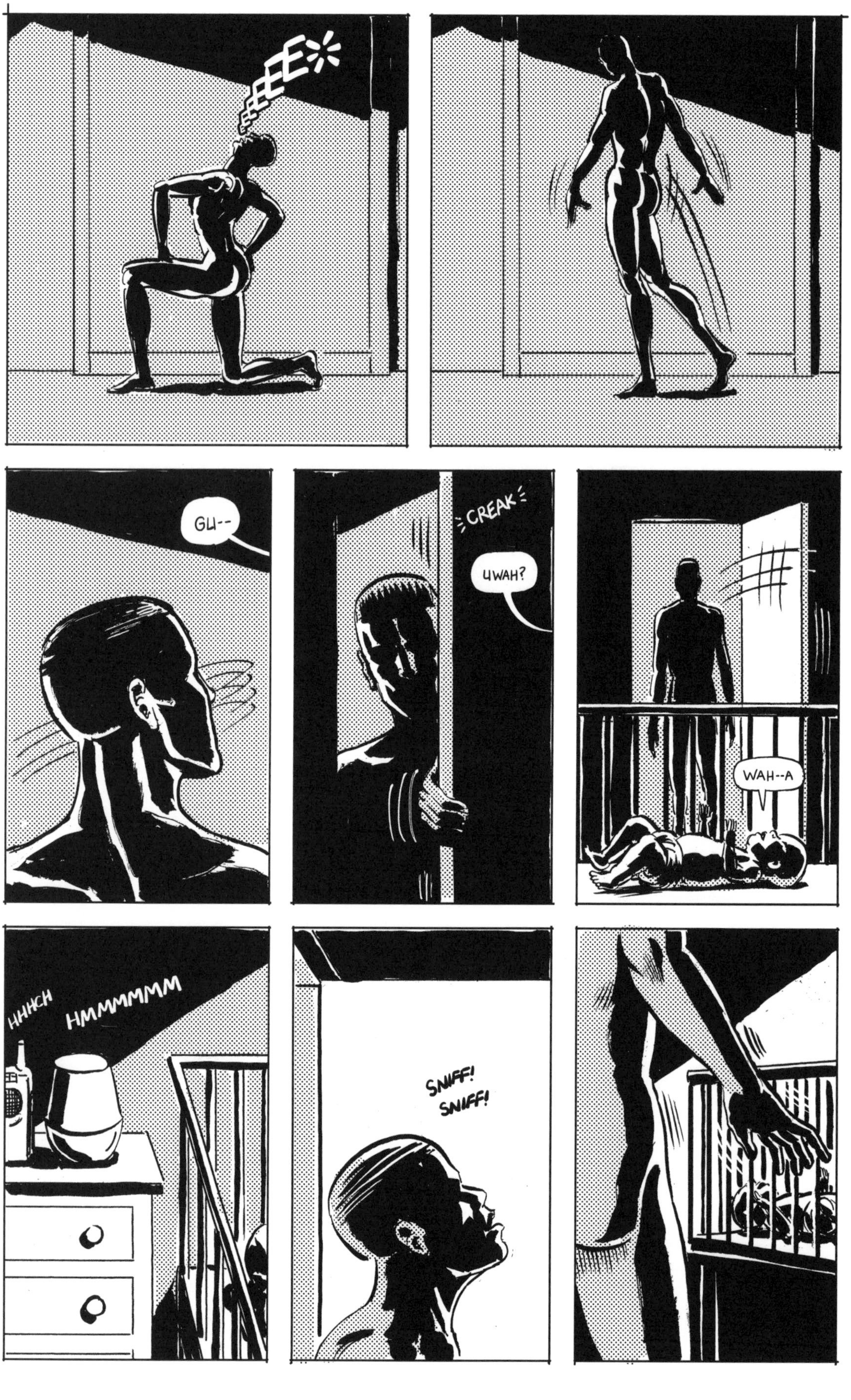
EEEEEE
GU--
CREAK
UWAH?
WAH--A
HHHCH
HMMMMMM
SNIFF!
SNIFF!

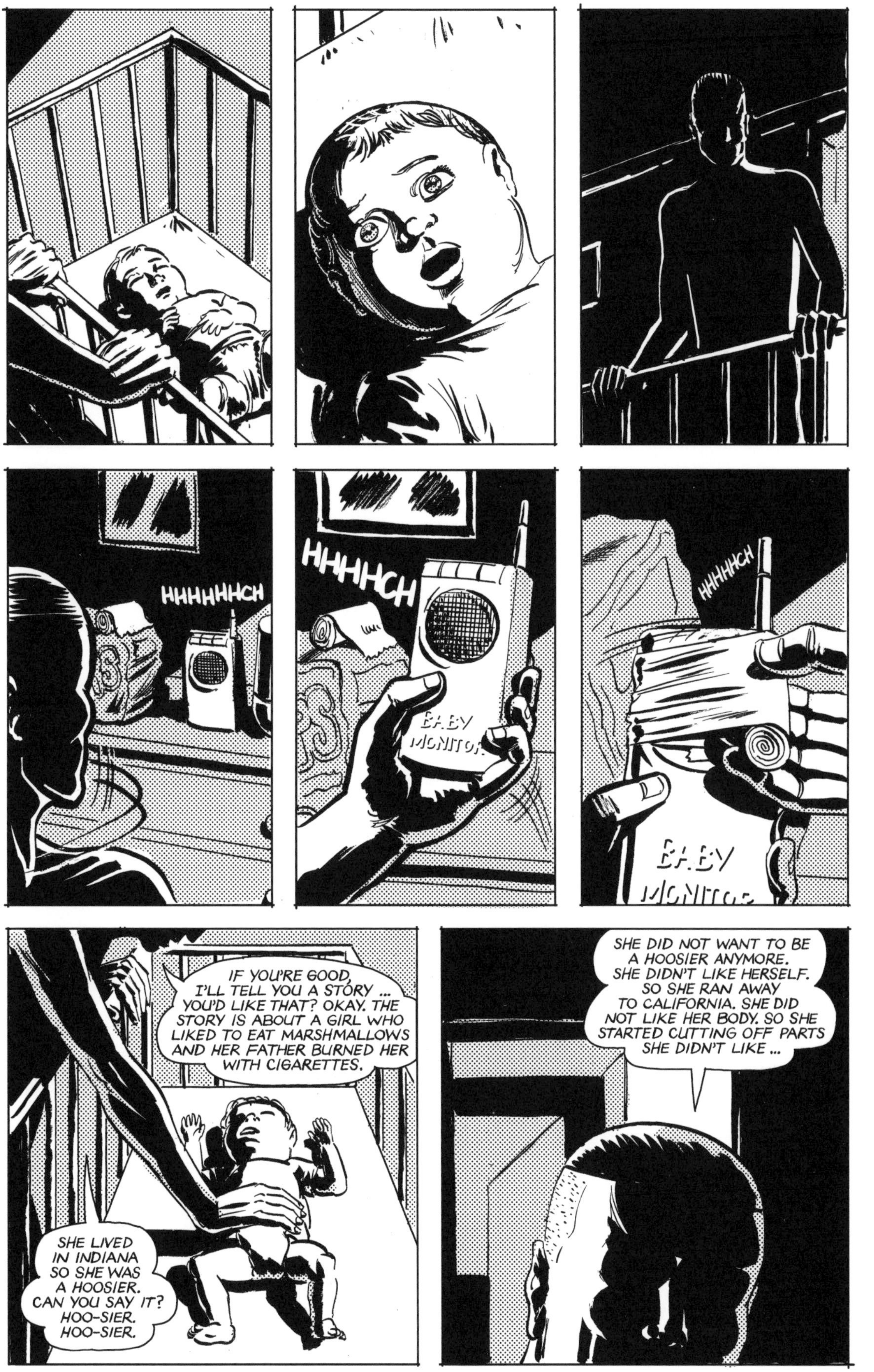
HHHHHHCH
HHHHCH
BABY MONITOR
HHHHHCH
BABY MONITOR
IF YOU'RE GOOD, I'LL TELL YOU A STORY ... YOU'D LIKE THAT? OKAY. THE STORY IS ABOUT A GIRL WHO LIKED TO EAT MARSHMALLOWS AND HER FATHER BURNED HER WITH CIGARETTES.
SHE LIVED IN INDIANA SO SHE WAS A HOOSIER. CAN YOU SAY IT? HOO-SIER. HOO-SIER.
SHE DID NOT WANT TO BE A HOOSIER ANYMORE. SHE DIDN'T LIKE HERSELF. SO SHE RAN AWAY TO CALIFORNIA. SHE DID NOT LIKE HER BODY. SO SHE STARTED CUTTING OFF PARTS SHE DIDN'T LIKE ...

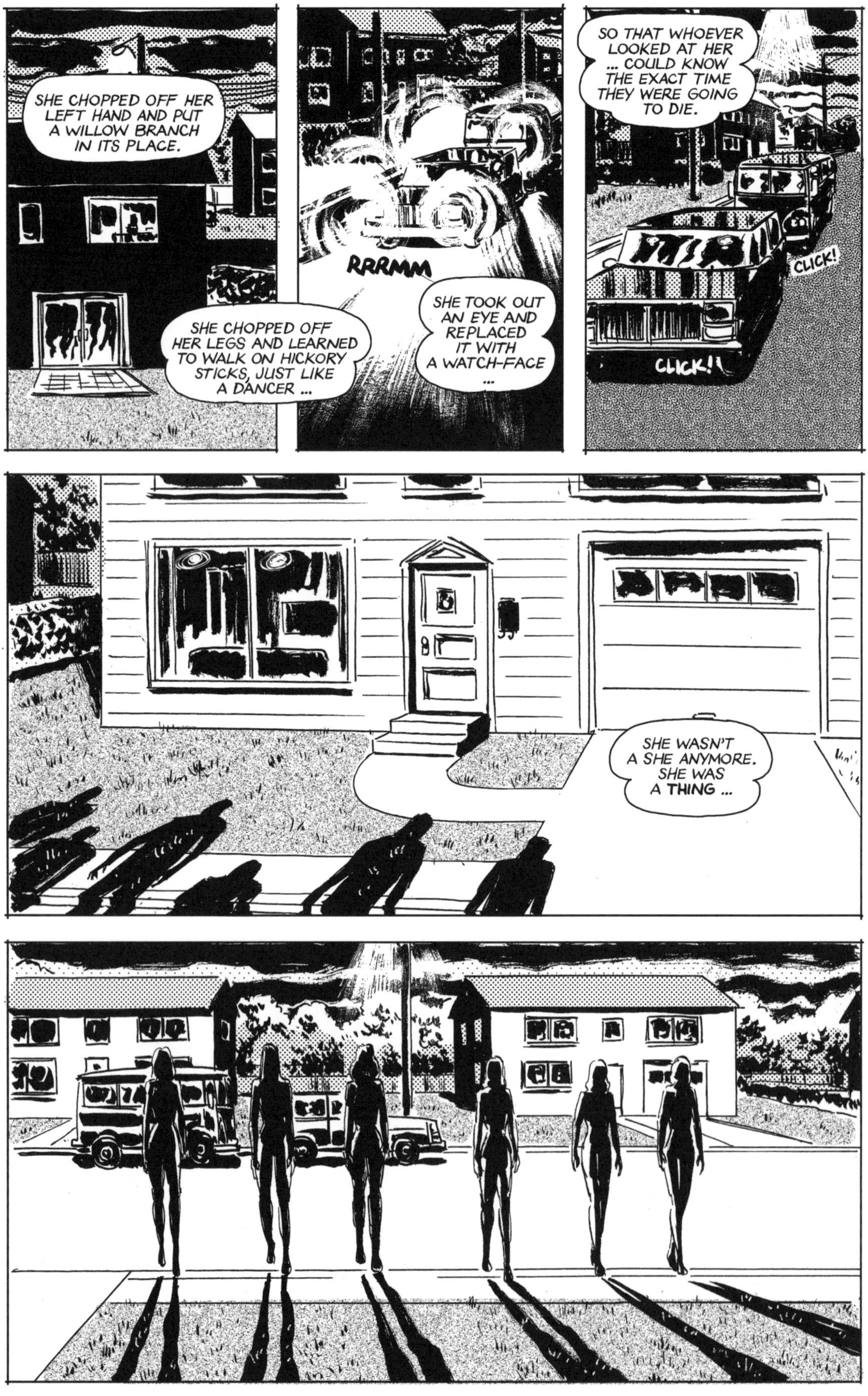
SHE CHOPPED OFF HER LEFT HAND AND PUT A WILLOW BRANCH IN ITS PLACE.
SHE CHOPPED OFF HER LEGS AND LEARNED TO WALK ON HICKORY STICKS, JUST LIKE A DANCER ...
RRRMM
SHE TOOK OUT AN EYE AND REPLACED IT WITH A WATCH-FACE ...
SO THAT WHOEVER LOOKED AT HER ... COULD KNOW THE EXACT TIME THEY WERE GOING TO DIE.
CLICK!
CLICK!
SHE WASN'T A SHE ANYMORE. SHE WAS A THING ...

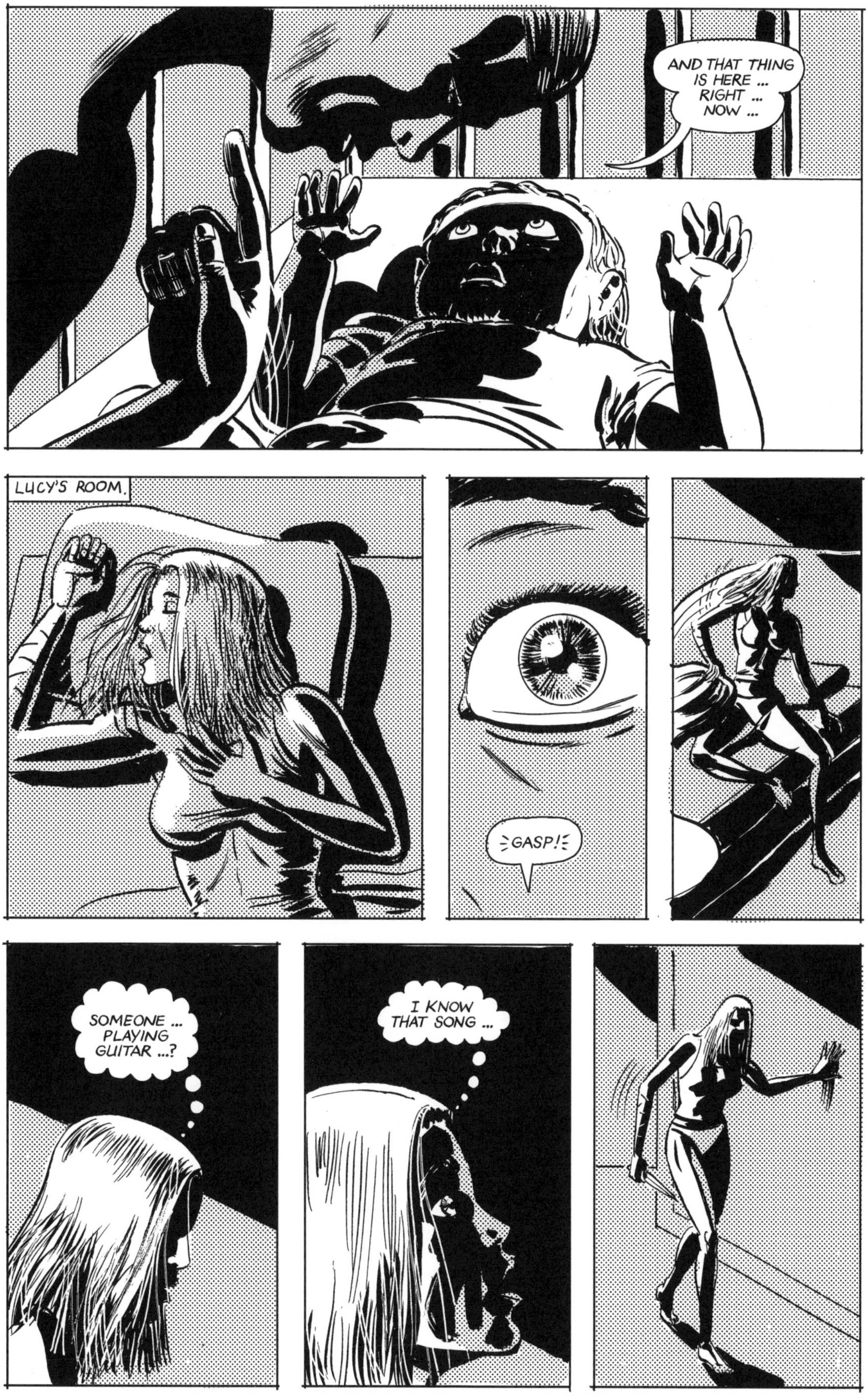
AND THAT THING IS HERE ... RIGHT ... NOW ...
LUCY'S ROOM.
GASP!
SOMEONE ... PLAYING GUITAR ...?
I KNOW THAT SONG ...

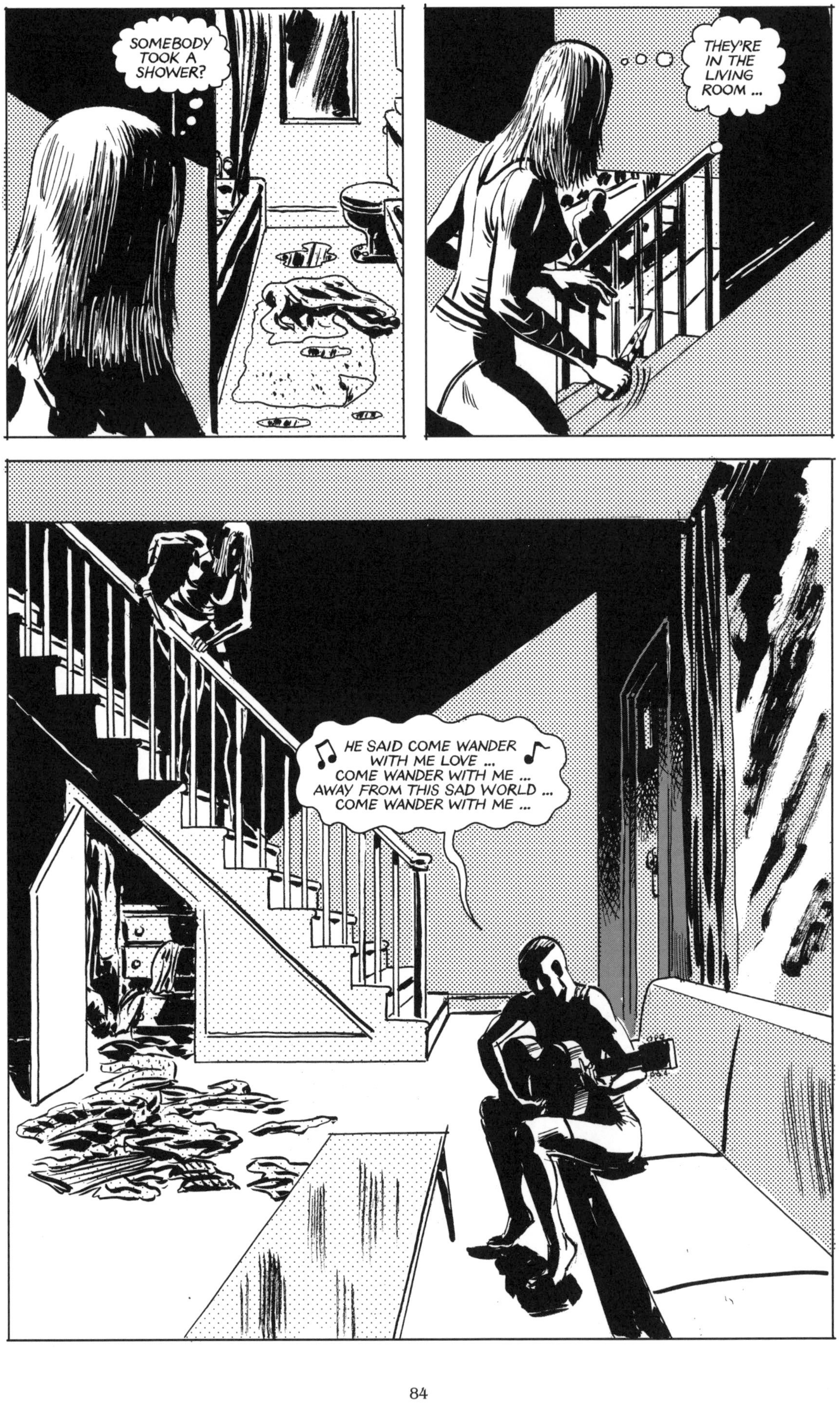
SOMEBODY TOOK A SHOWER?
THEY'RE IN THE LIVING ROOM ...
HE SAID COME WANDER WITH ME LOVE ... COME WANDER WITH ME ... AWAY FROM THIS SAD WORLD ... COME WANDER WITH ME ...

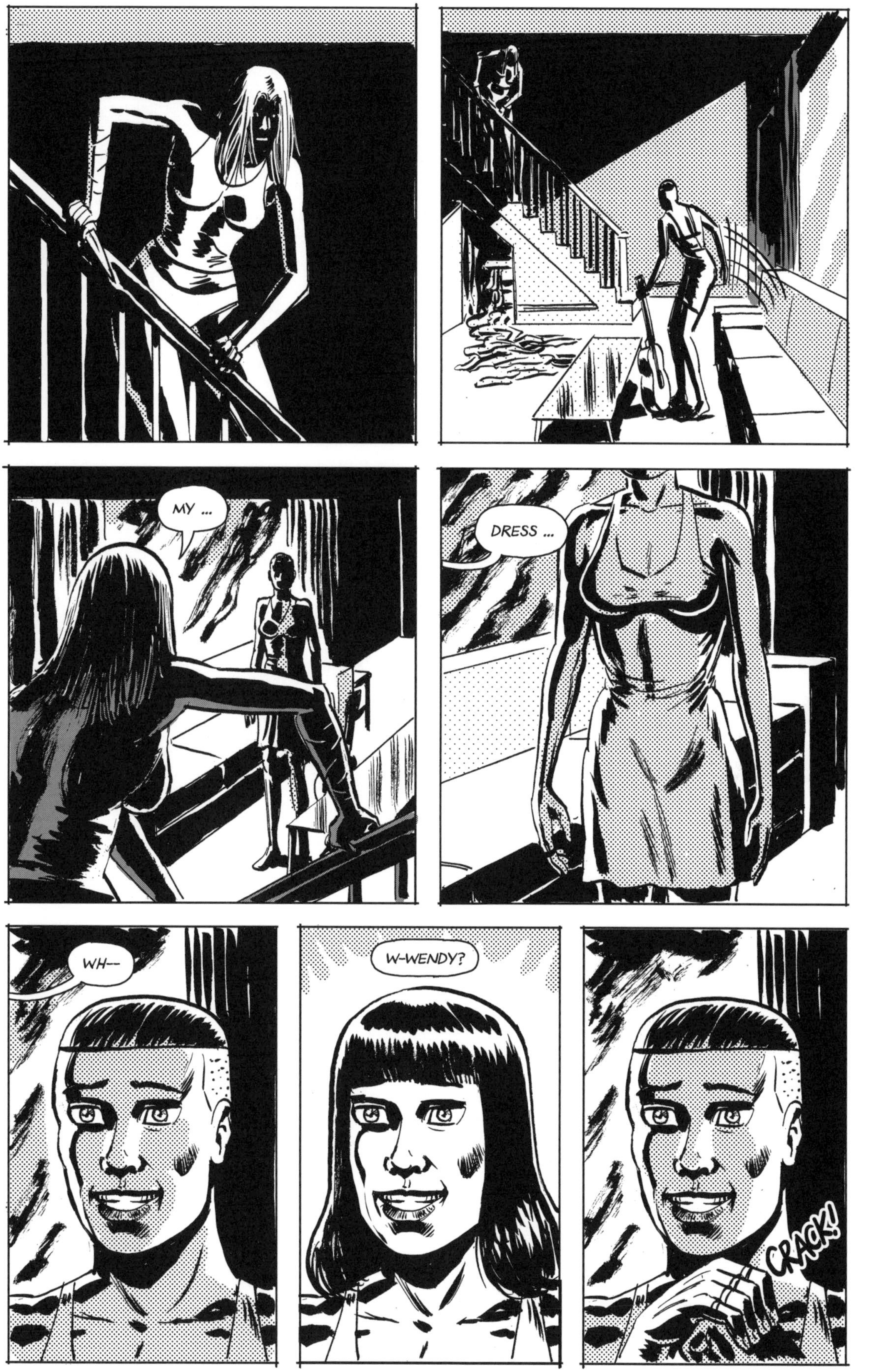
MY ...
DRESS ...
WH--
W-WENDY?
CRACK!

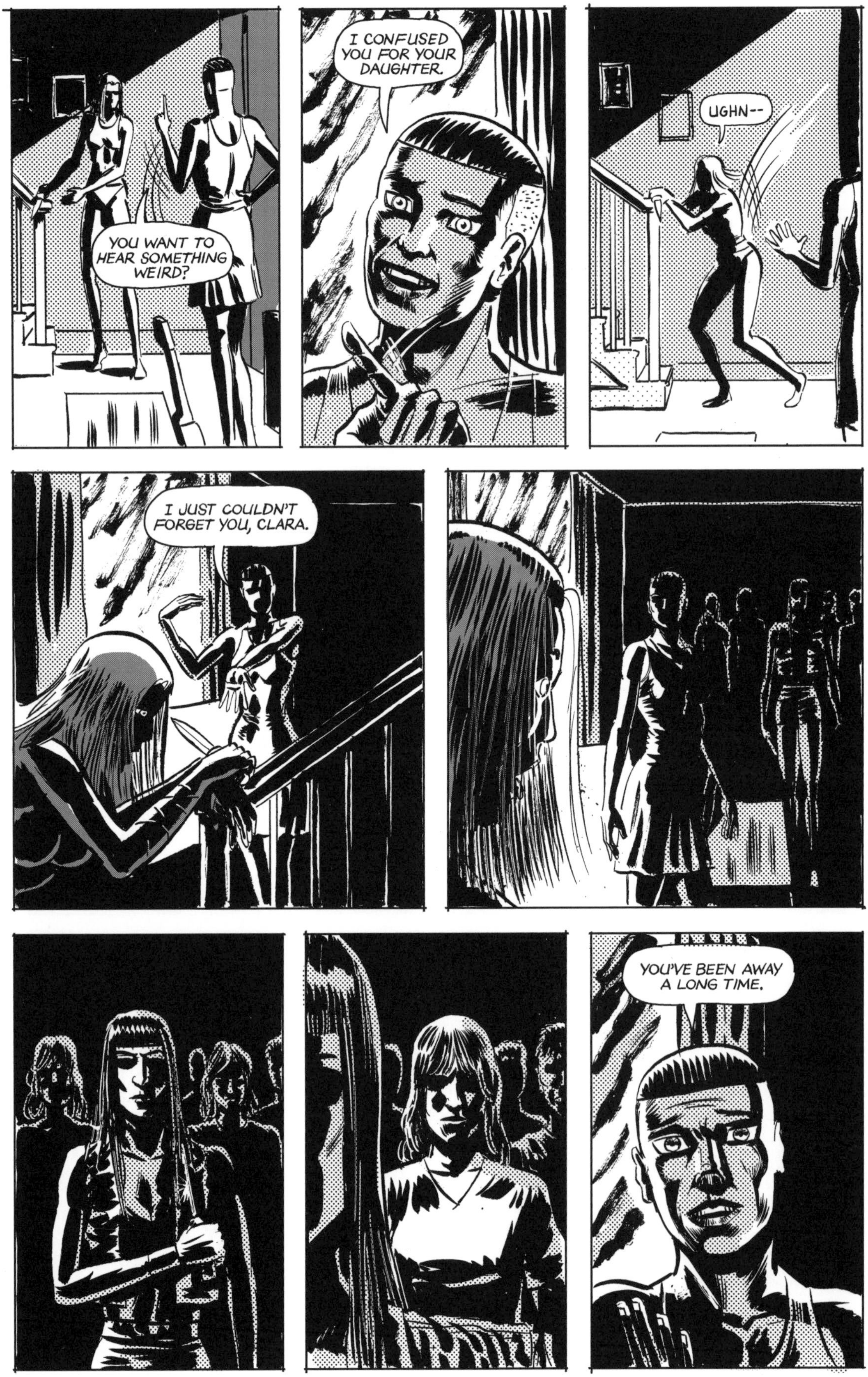
YOU WANT TO HEAR SOMETHING WEIRD?
I CONFUSED YOU FOR YOUR DAUGHTER.
UGHN--
I JUST COULDN'T FORGET YOU, CLARA.
YOU'VE BEEN AWAY A LONG TIME.

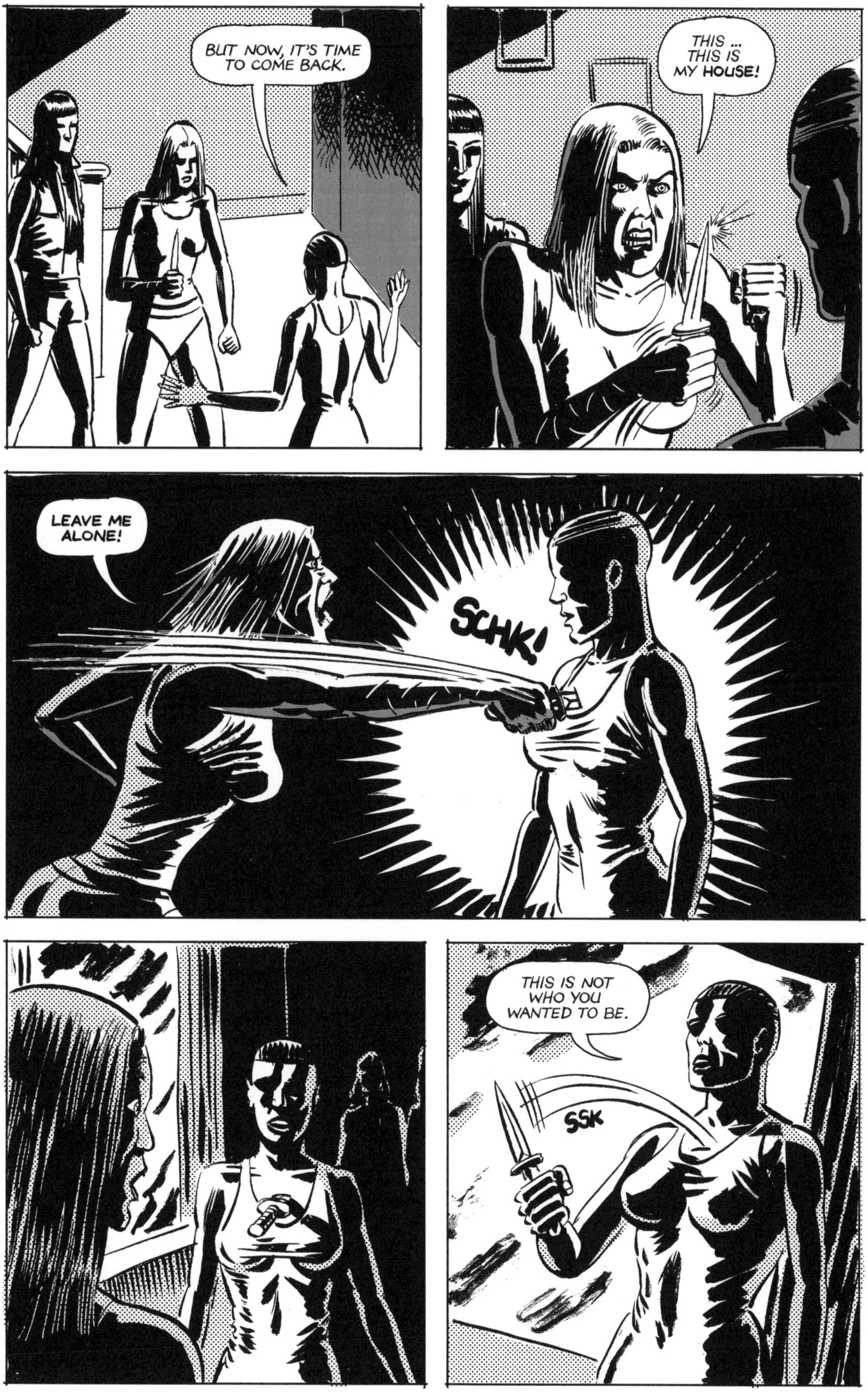
BUT NOW, IT'S TIME TO COME BACK.
THIS ... THIS IS MY HOUSE!
LEAVE ME ALONE!
SCHK!
THIS IS NOT WHO YOU WANTED TO BE.
SSK

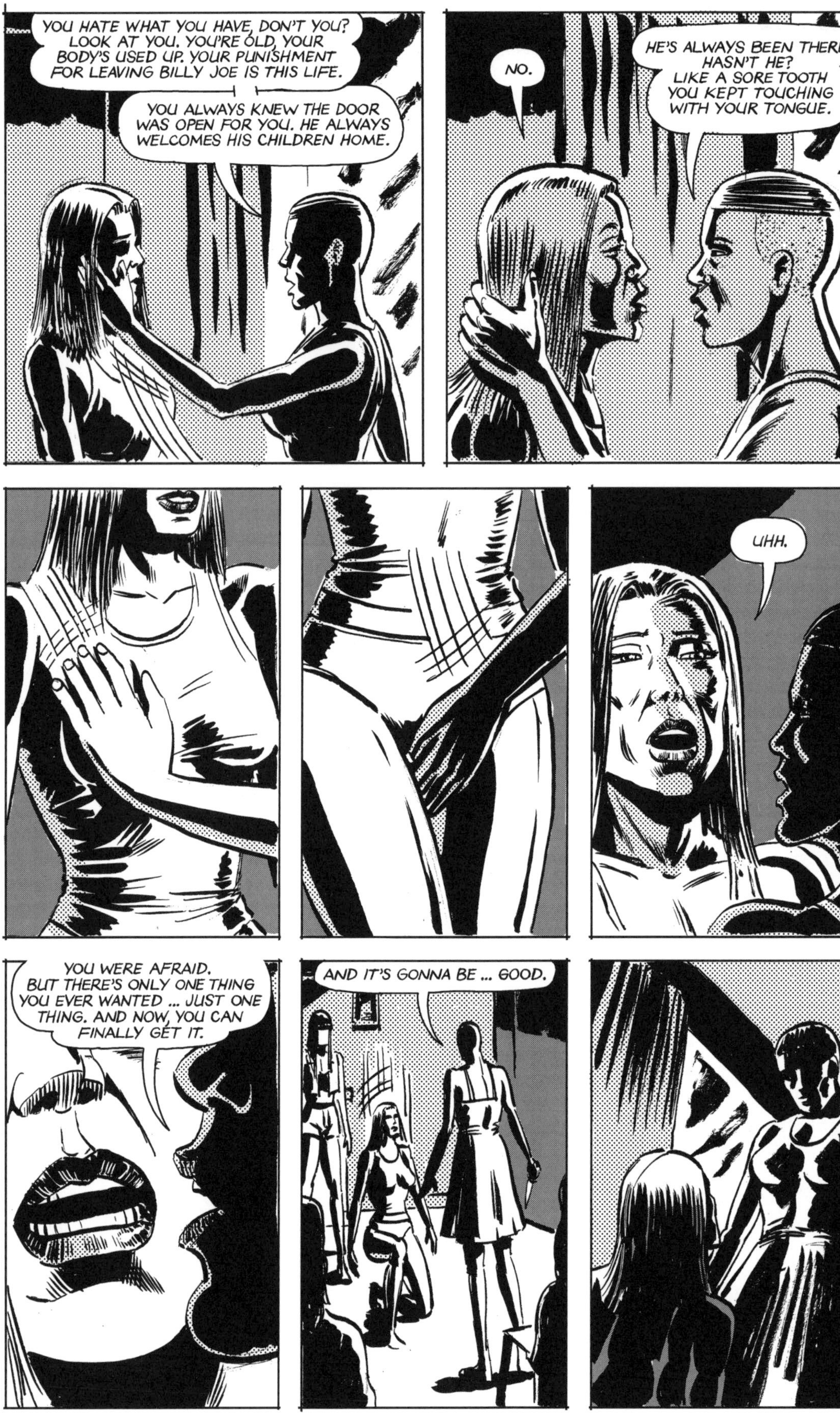
YOU HATE WHAT YOU HAVE, DON'T YOU? LOOK AT YOU. YOU'RE OLD, YOUR BODY'S USED UP. YOUR PUNISHMENT FOR LEAVING BILLY JOE IS THIS LIFE.
YOU ALWAYS KNEW THE DOOR WAS OPEN FOR YOU. HE ALWAYS WELCOMES HIS CHILDREN HOME.
NO.
HE'S ALWAYS BEEN THERE, HASN'T HE? LIKE A SORE TOOTH YOU KEPT TOUCHING WITH YOUR TONGUE.
UHH.
YOU WERE AFRAID. BUT THERE'S ONLY ONE THING YOU EVER WANTED ... JUST ONE THING. AND NOW, YOU CAN FINALLY GET IT.
AND IT'S GONNA BE ... GOOD.

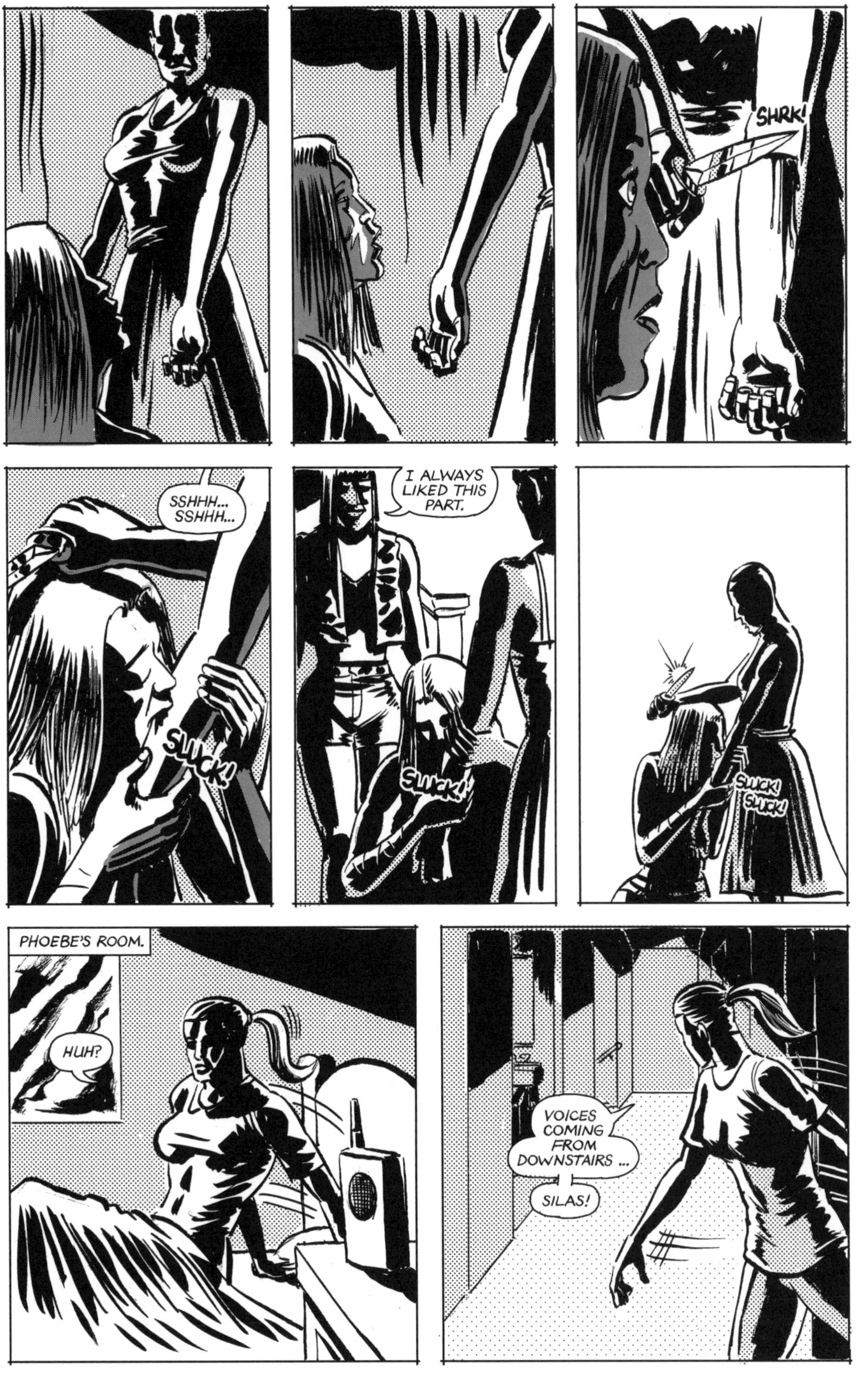
SHRK!
SSHHH... SSHHH...
SLUCK!
I ALWAYS LIKED THIS PART.
SLUCK!
SLUCK! SLUCK!
PHOEBE'S ROOM.
HUH?
VOICES COMING FROM DOWNSTAIRS ...
SILAS!

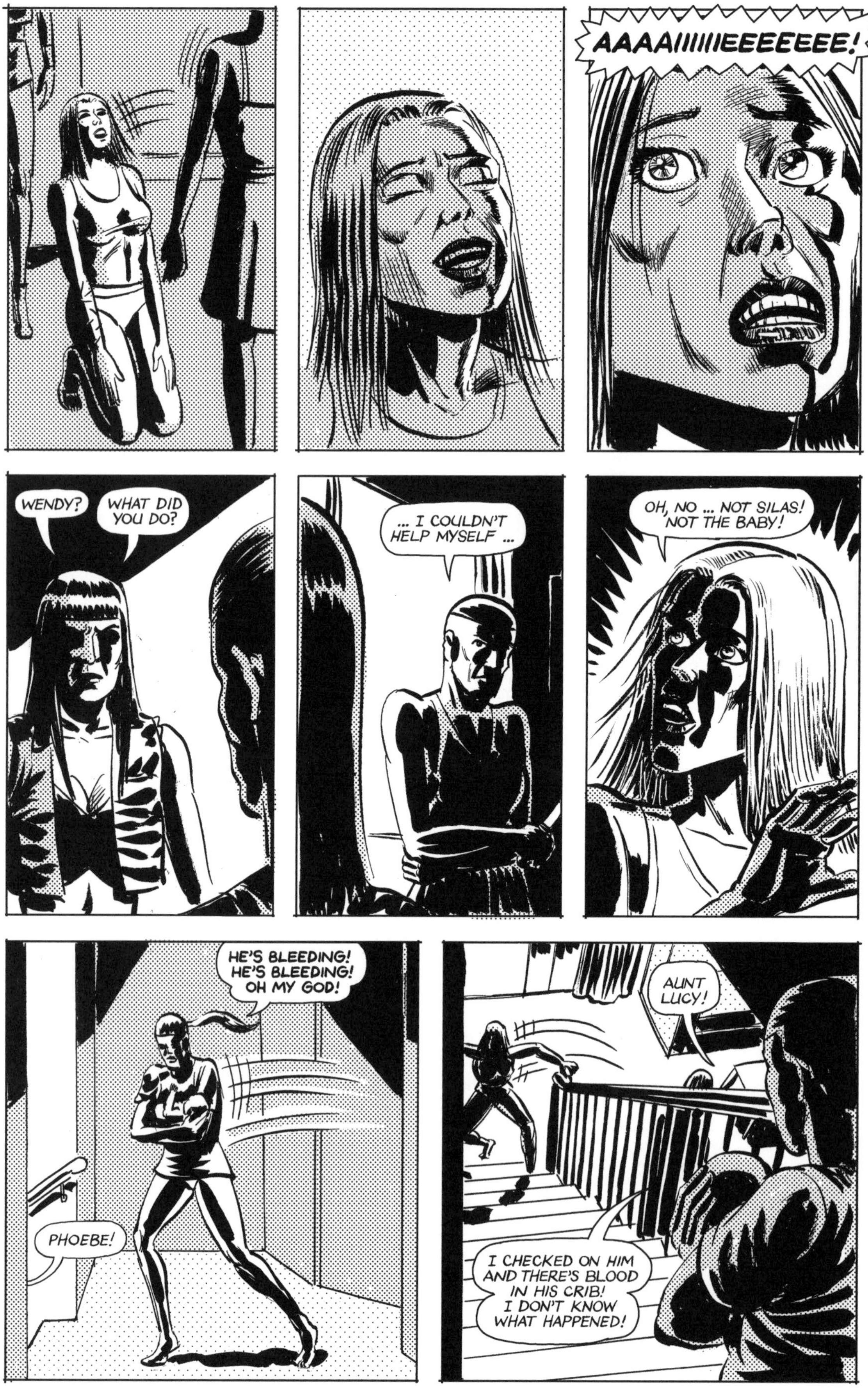
AAAAIIIIIIEEEEEEE!
WENDY?
WHAT DID YOU DO?
... I COULDN'T HELP MYSELF ...
OH, NO ... NOT SILAS! NOT THE BABY!
HE'S BLEEDING! HE'S BLEEDING! OH MY GOD!
PHOEBE!
AUNT LUCY!
I CHECKED ON HIM AND THERE'S BLOOD IN HIS CRIB! I DON'T KNOW WHAT HAPPENED!

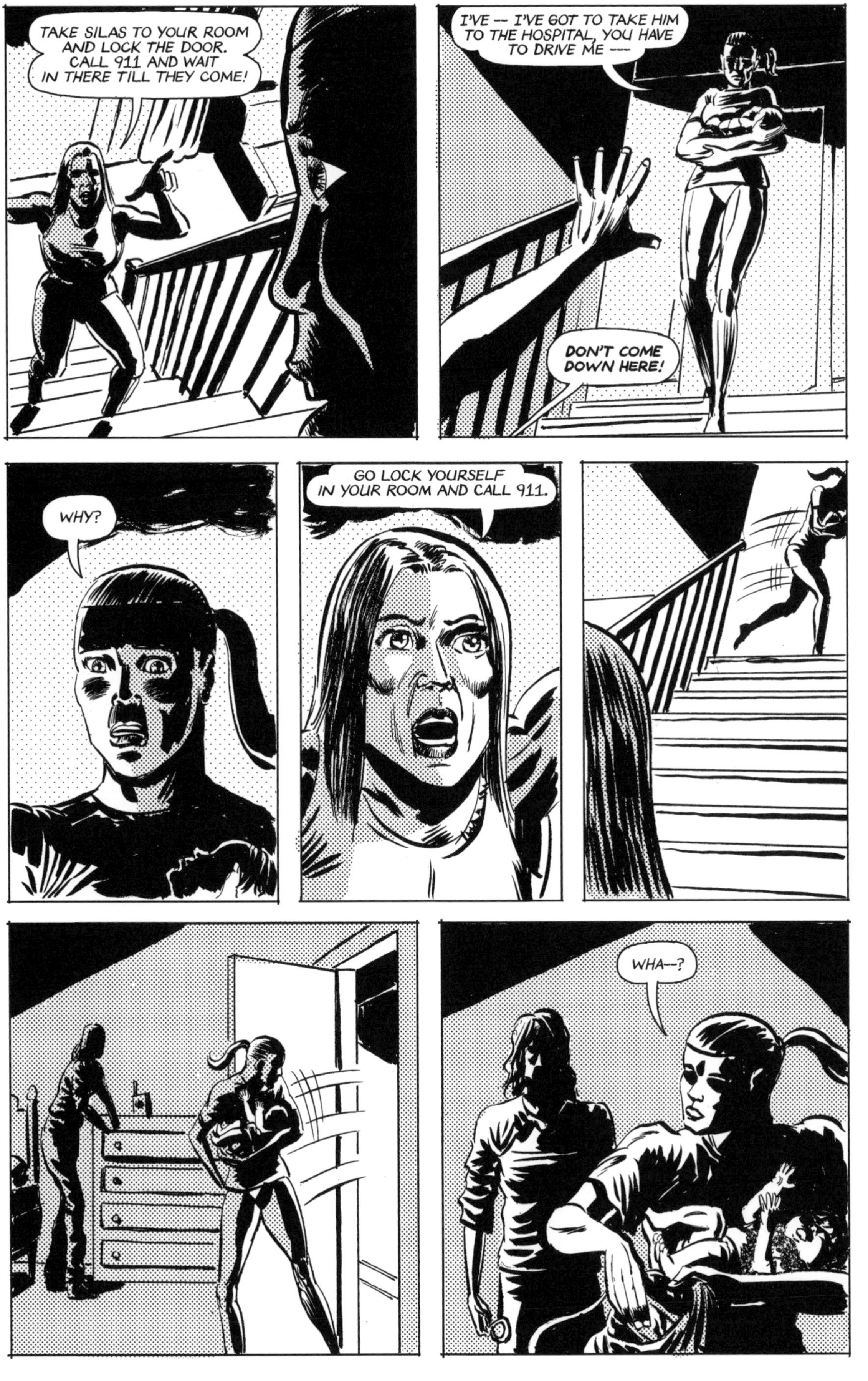
TAKE SILAS TO YOUR ROOM AND LOCK THE DOOR. CALL 911 AND WAIT IN THERE TILL THEY COME!
I'VE -- I'VE GOT TO TAKE HIM TO THE HOSPITAL, YOU HAVE TO DRIVE ME ---
DON'T COME DOWN HERE!
WHY?
GO LOCK YOURSELF IN YOUR ROOM AND CALL 911.
WHA--?

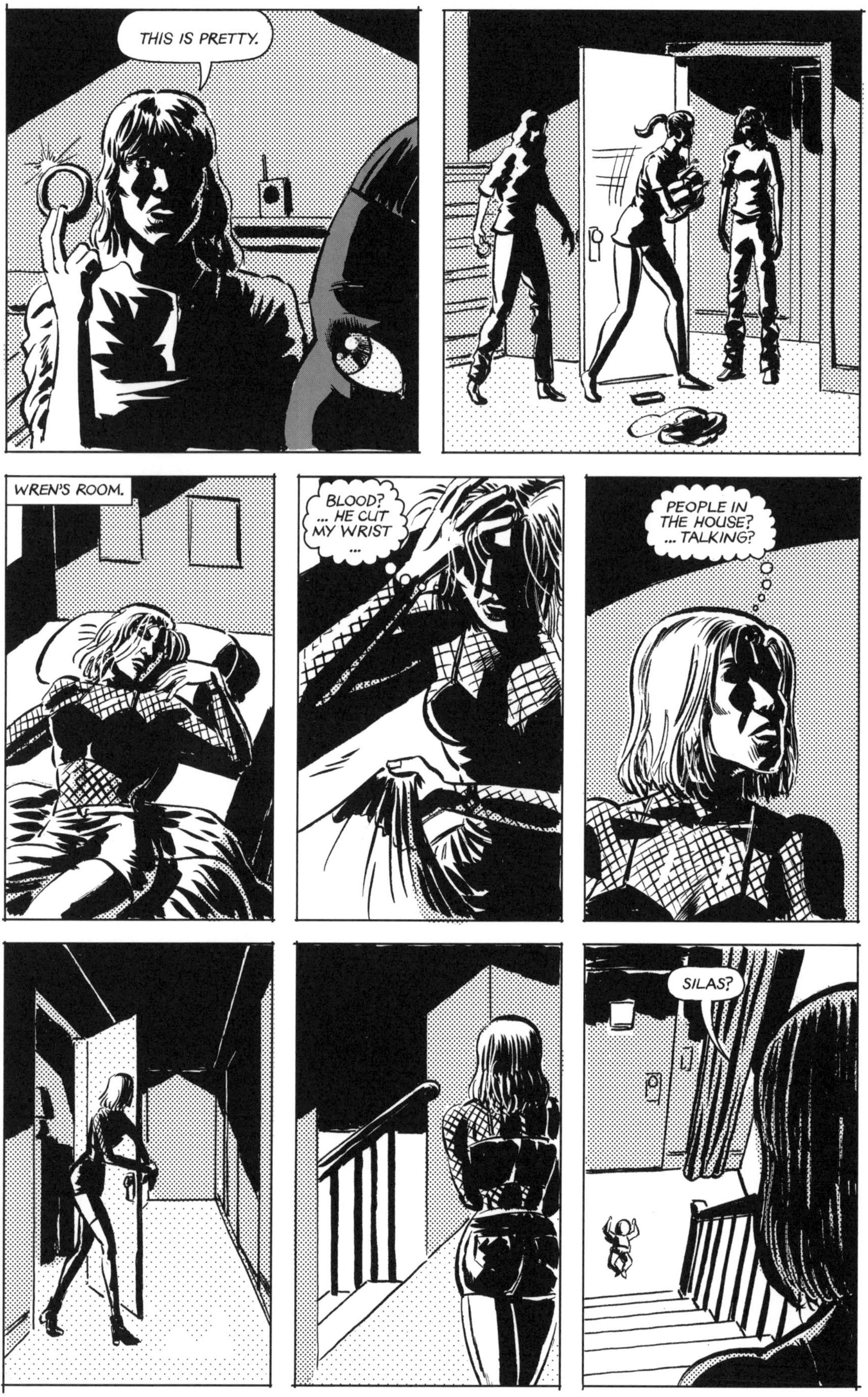
THIS IS PRETTY.
WREN'S ROOM.
BLOOD? ... HE CUT MY WRIST ...
PEOPLE IN THE HOUSE? ...TALKING?
SILAS?

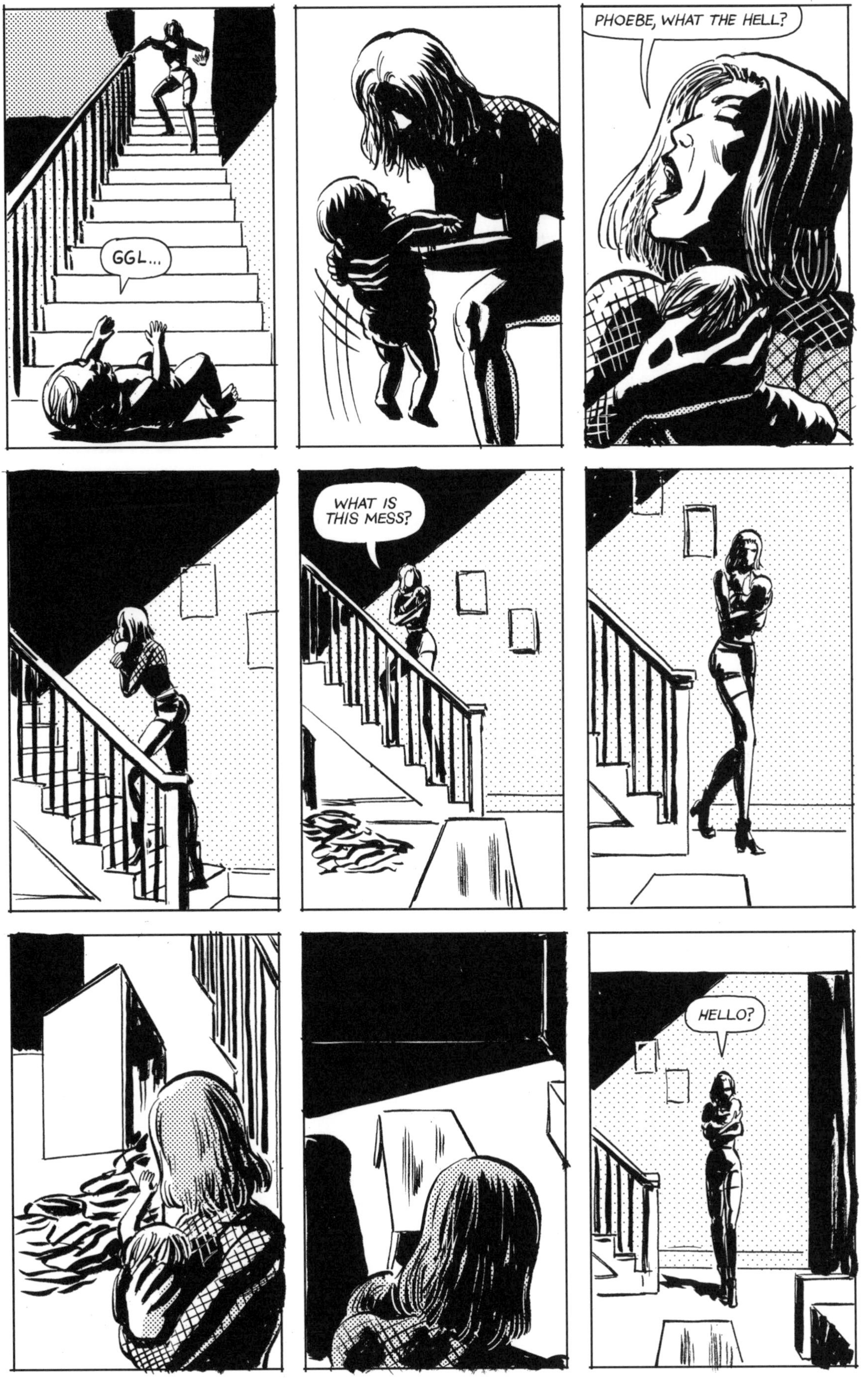
GGL...
PHOEBE, WHAT THE HELL?
WHAT IS THIS MESS?
HELLO?

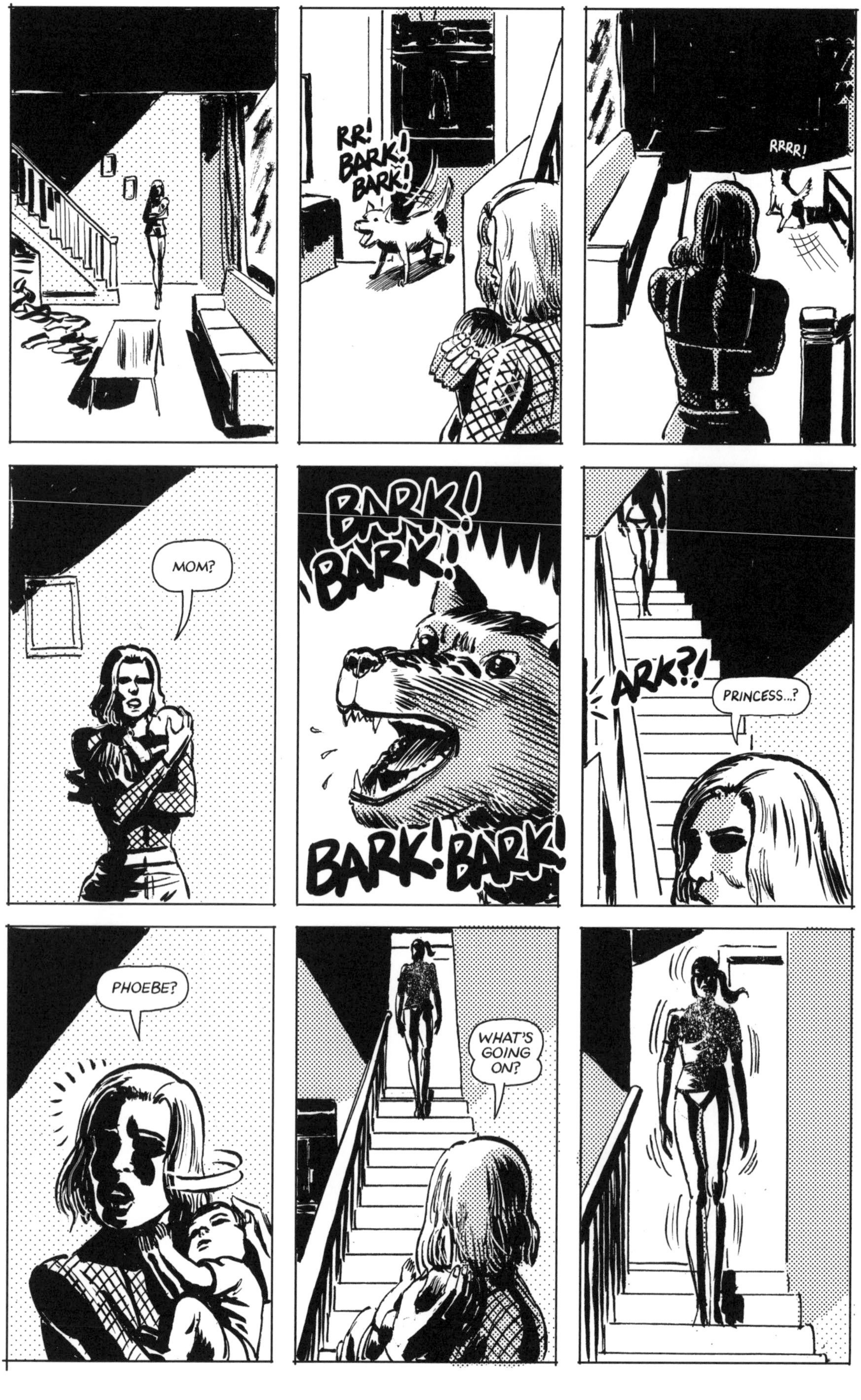
RR!
BARK!
BARK!
RRRR!
MOM?
BARK!
BARK!
BARK! BARK!
ARK?!
PRINCESS...?
PHOEBE?
WHAT'S GOING ON?

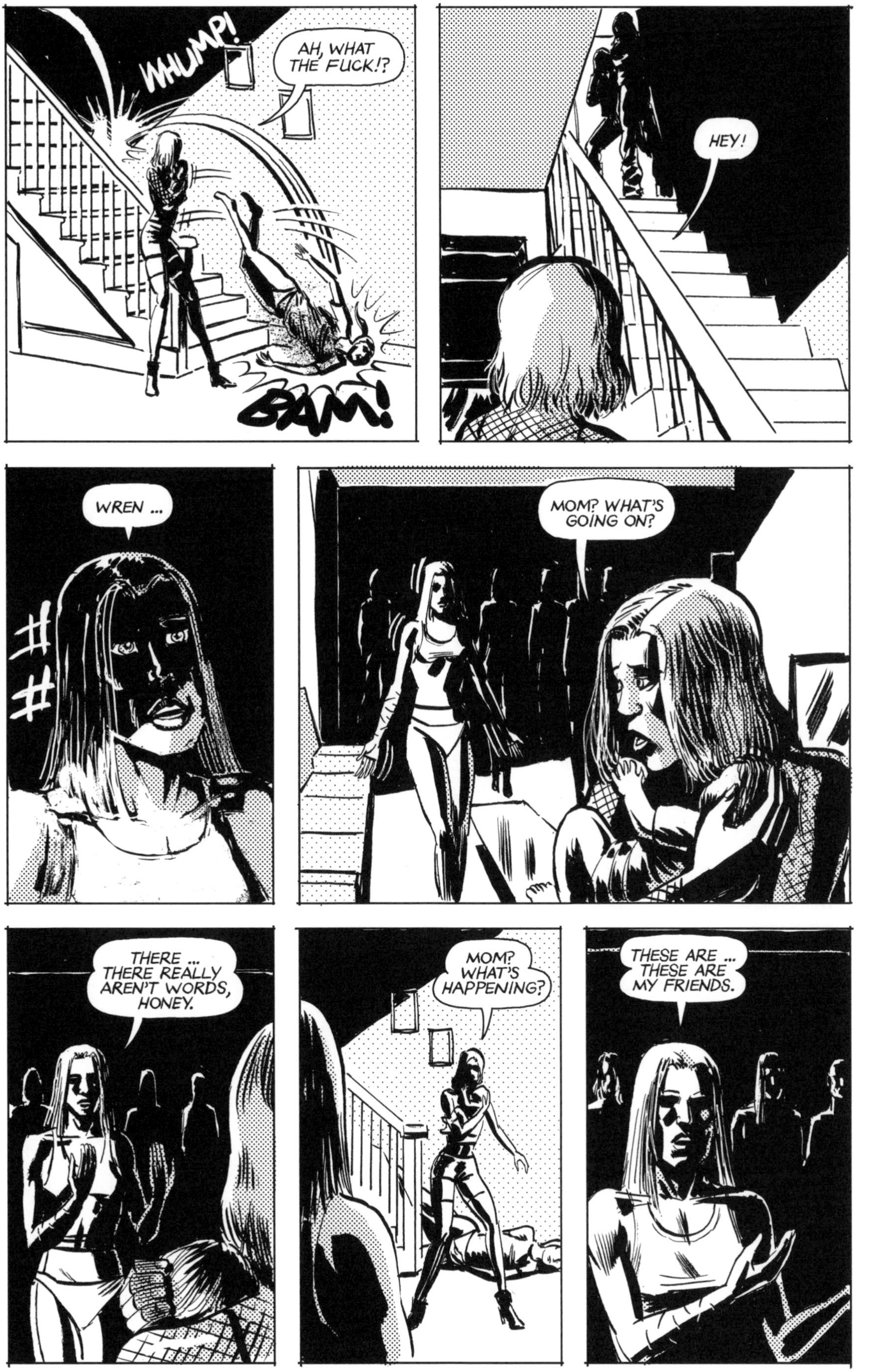
WHUMP!
AH, WHAT THE FUCK!?
BAM!
HEY!
WREN ...
MOM? WHAT'S GOING ON?
THERE ... THERE REALLY AREN'T WORDS, HONEY.
MOM? WHAT'S HAPPENING?
THESE ARE ... THESE ARE MY FRIENDS.

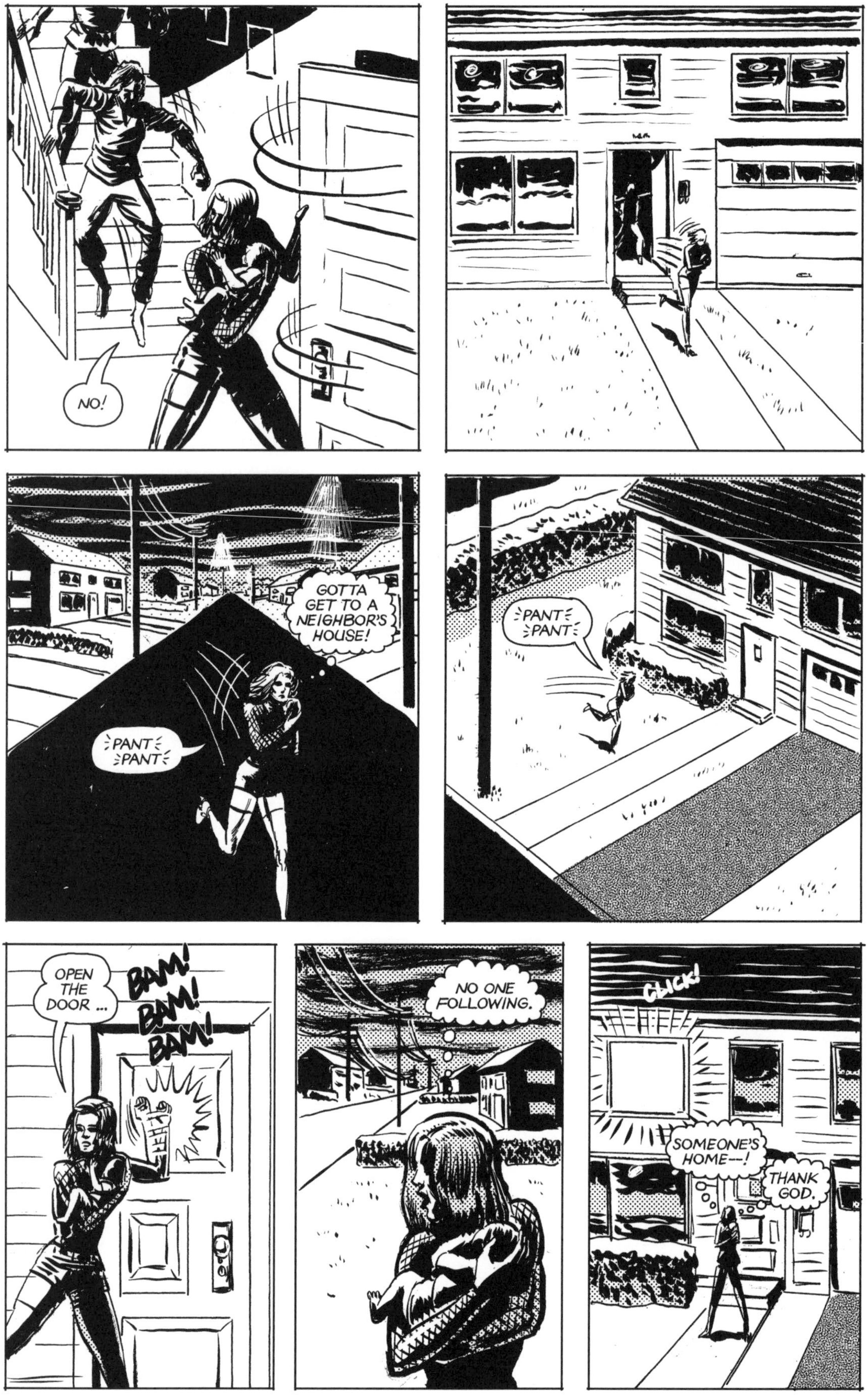
NO!
GOTTA GET TO A NEIGHBOR'S HOUSE!
PANT PANT
PANT PANT
OPEN THE DOOR ...
BAM! BAM! BAM!
NO ONE FOLLOWING.
CLICK!
SOMEONE'S HOME--!
THANK GOD.

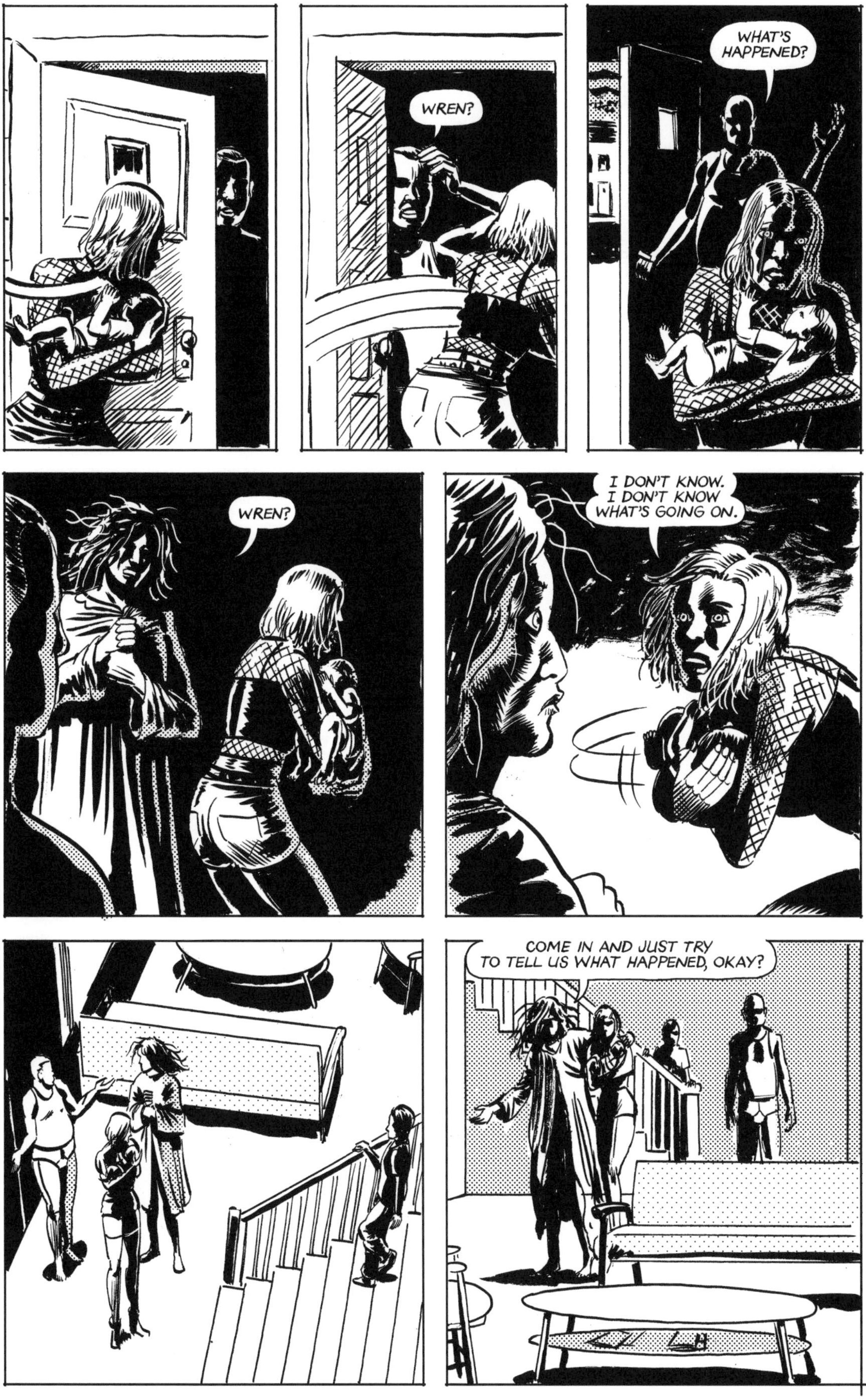
WREN?
WHAT'S HAPPENED?
WREN?
I DON'T KNOW. I DON'T KNOW WHAT'S GOING ON.
COME IN AND JUST TRY TO TELL US WHAT HAPPENED, OKAY?

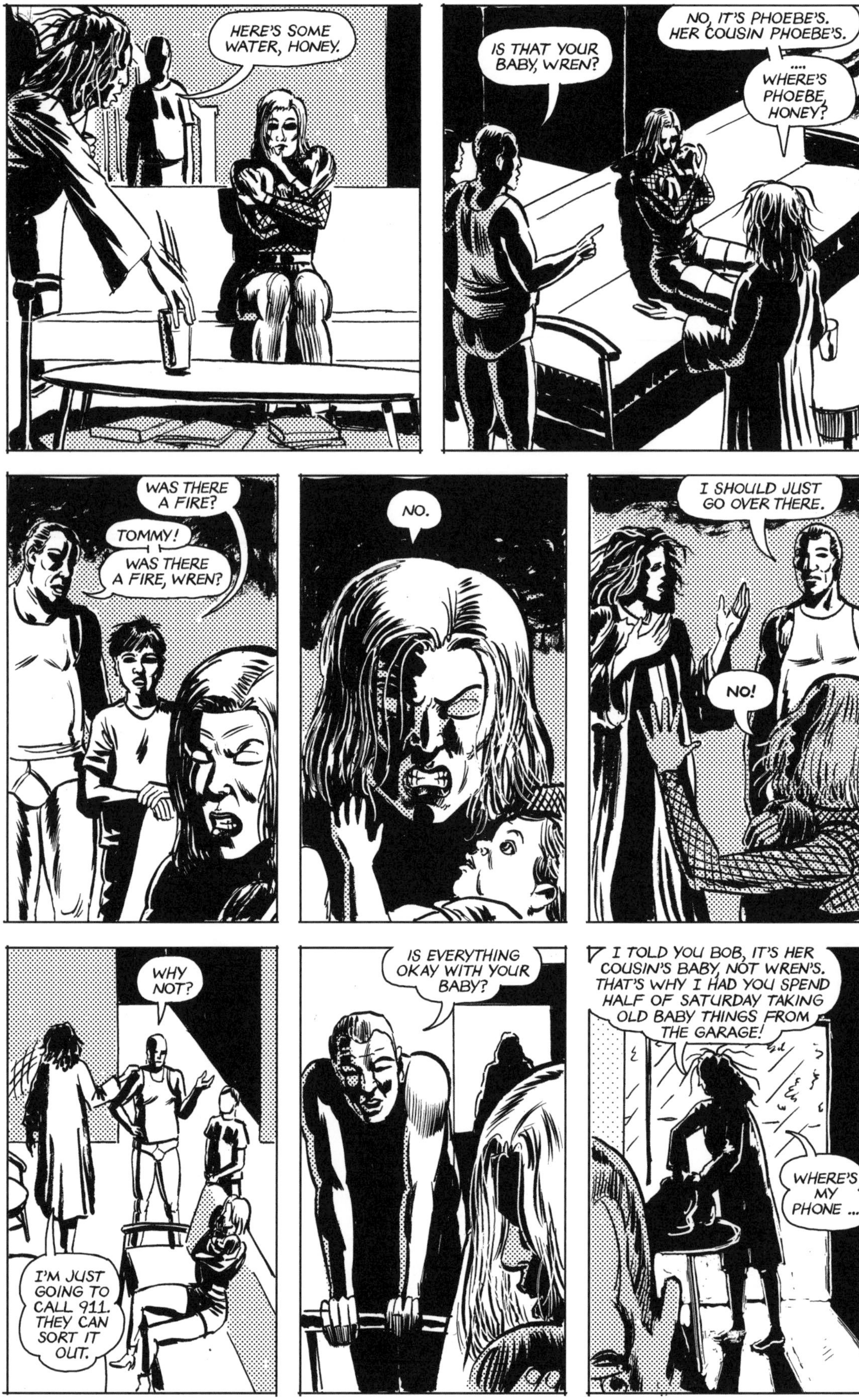
HERE'S SOME WATER, HONEY.
IS THAT YOUR BABY, WREN?
NO, IT'S PHOEBE'S. HER COUSIN PHOEBE'S.
.... WHERE'S PHOEBE, HONEY?
WAS THERE A FIRE?
TOMMY!
WAS THERE A FIRE, WREN?
NO.
I SHOULD JUST GO OVER THERE.
NO!
WHY NOT?
I'M JUST GOING TO CALL 911. THEY CAN SORT IT OUT.
IS EVERYTHING OKAY WITH YOUR BABY?
I TOLD YOU BOB, IT'S HER COUSIN'S BABY, NOT WREN'S. THAT'S WHY I HAD YOU SPEND HALF OF SATURDAY TAKING OLD BABY THINGS FROM THE GARAGE!
WHERE'S MY PHONE ...

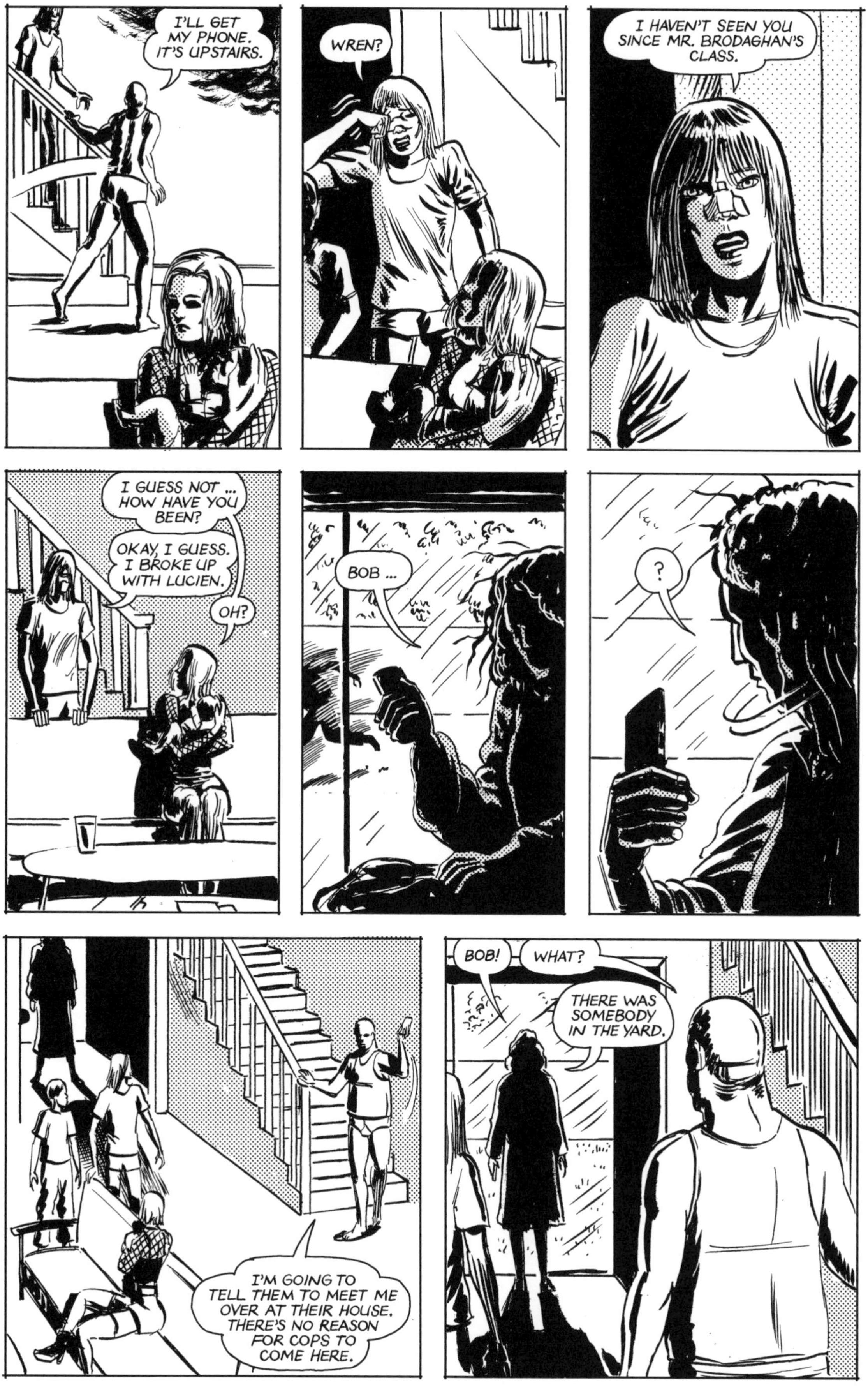
I'LL GET MY PHONE. IT'S UPSTAIRS.
WREN?
I HAVEN'T SEEN YOU SINCE MR. BRODAGHAN'S CLASS.
I GUESS NOT ... HOW HAVE YOU BEEN?
OKAY, I GUESS. I BROKE UP WITH LUCIEN.
OH?
BOB ...
?
I'M GOING TO TELL THEM TO MEET ME OVER AT THEIR HOUSE. THERE'S NO REASON FOR COPS TO COME HERE.
BOB!
WHAT?
THERE WAS SOMEBODY IN THE YARD.

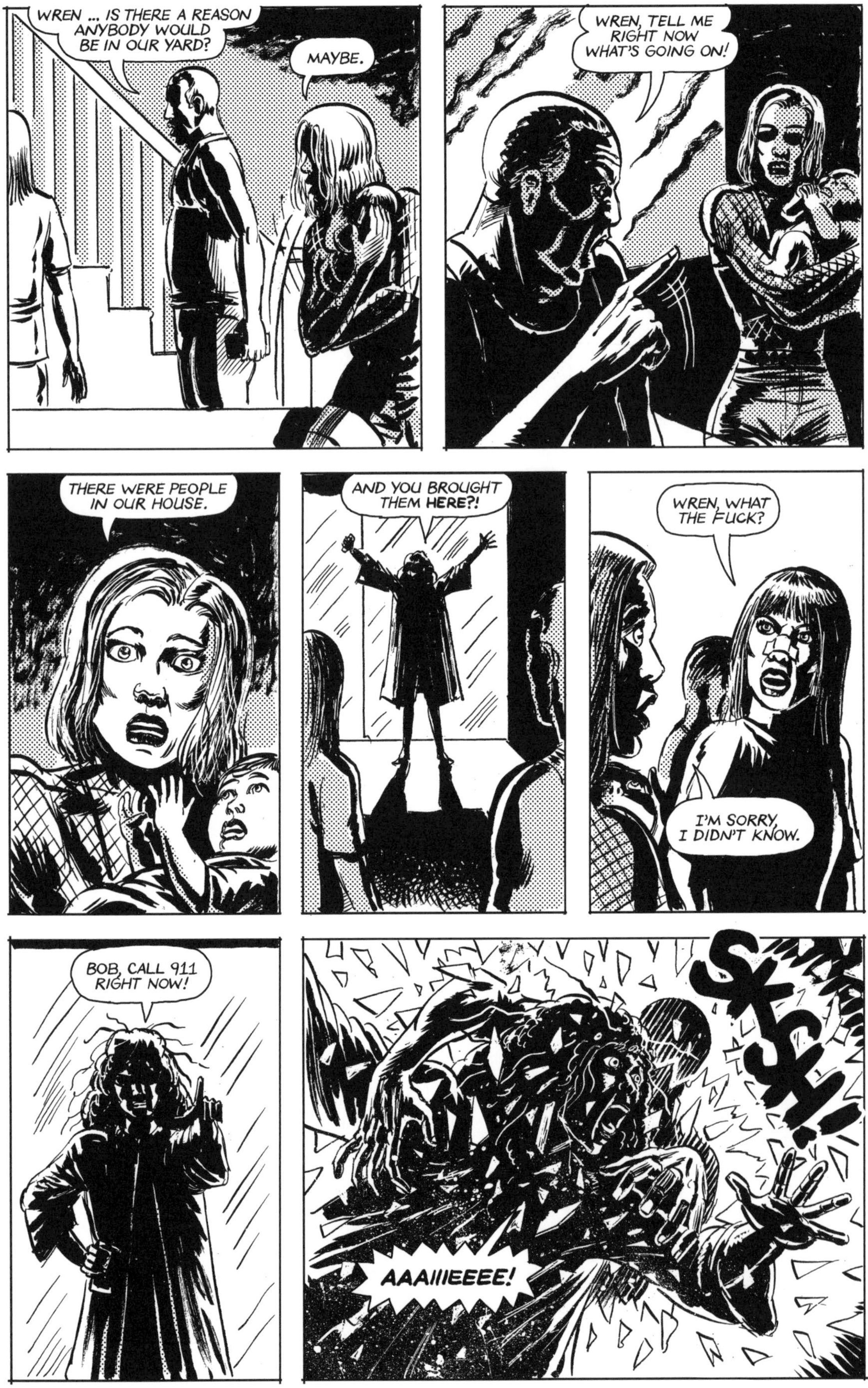
WREN ... IS THERE A REASON ANYBODY WOULD BE IN OUR YARD?
MAYBE.
WREN, TELL ME RIGHT NOW WHAT'S GOING ON!
THERE WERE PEOPLE IN OUR HOUSE.
AND YOU BROUGHT THEM **HERE?!**
WREN, WHAT THE FUCK?
I'M SORRY, I DIDN'T KNOW.
BOB, CALL 911 RIGHT NOW!
SKSH!
AAAIIIEEEE!

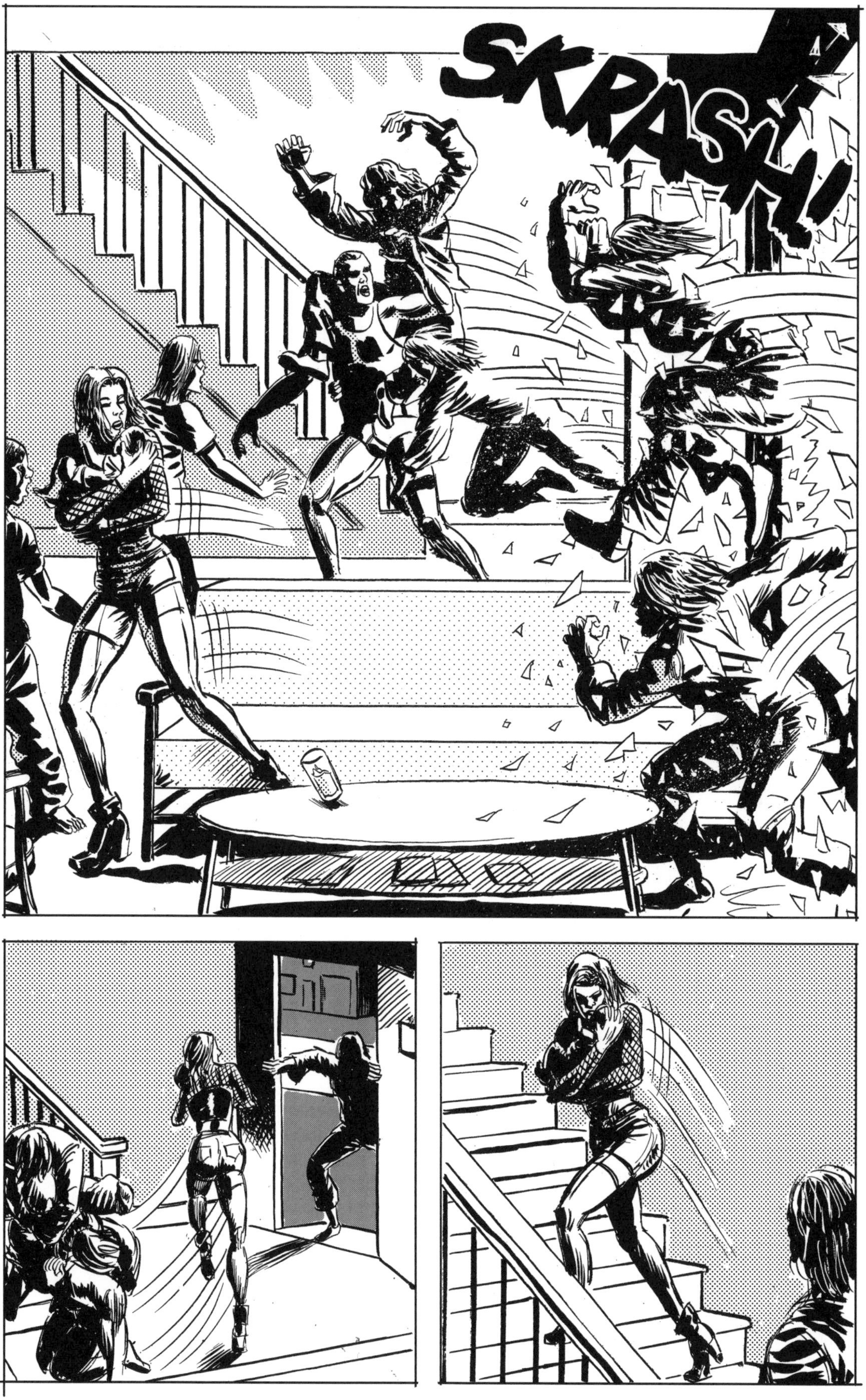
SKRASH!!

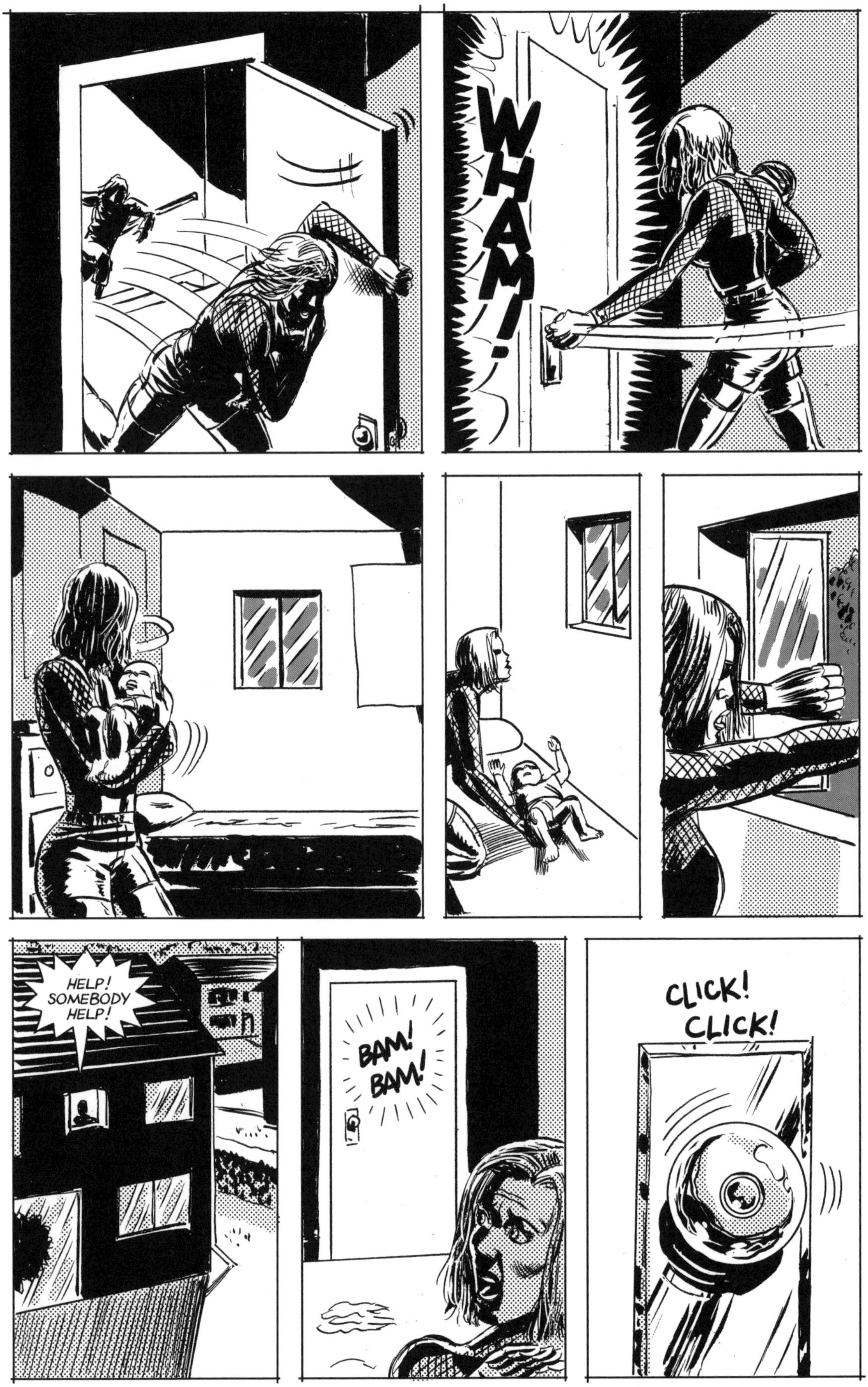
WHAM!
HELP! SOMEBODY HELP!
BAM! BAM!
CLICK! CLICK!

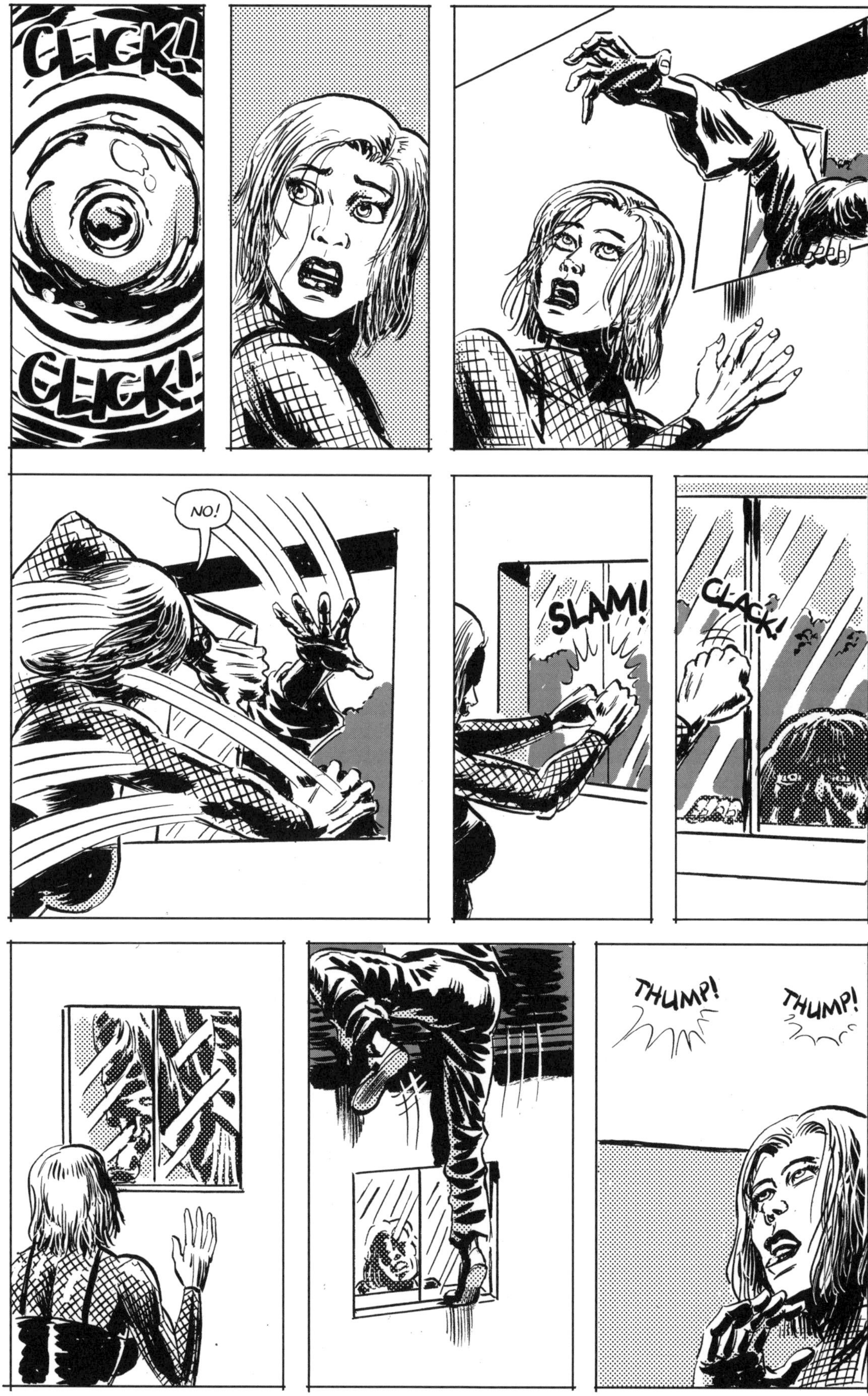
CLICK!
CLICK!
NO!
SLAM!
CLACK!
THUMP!
THUMP!

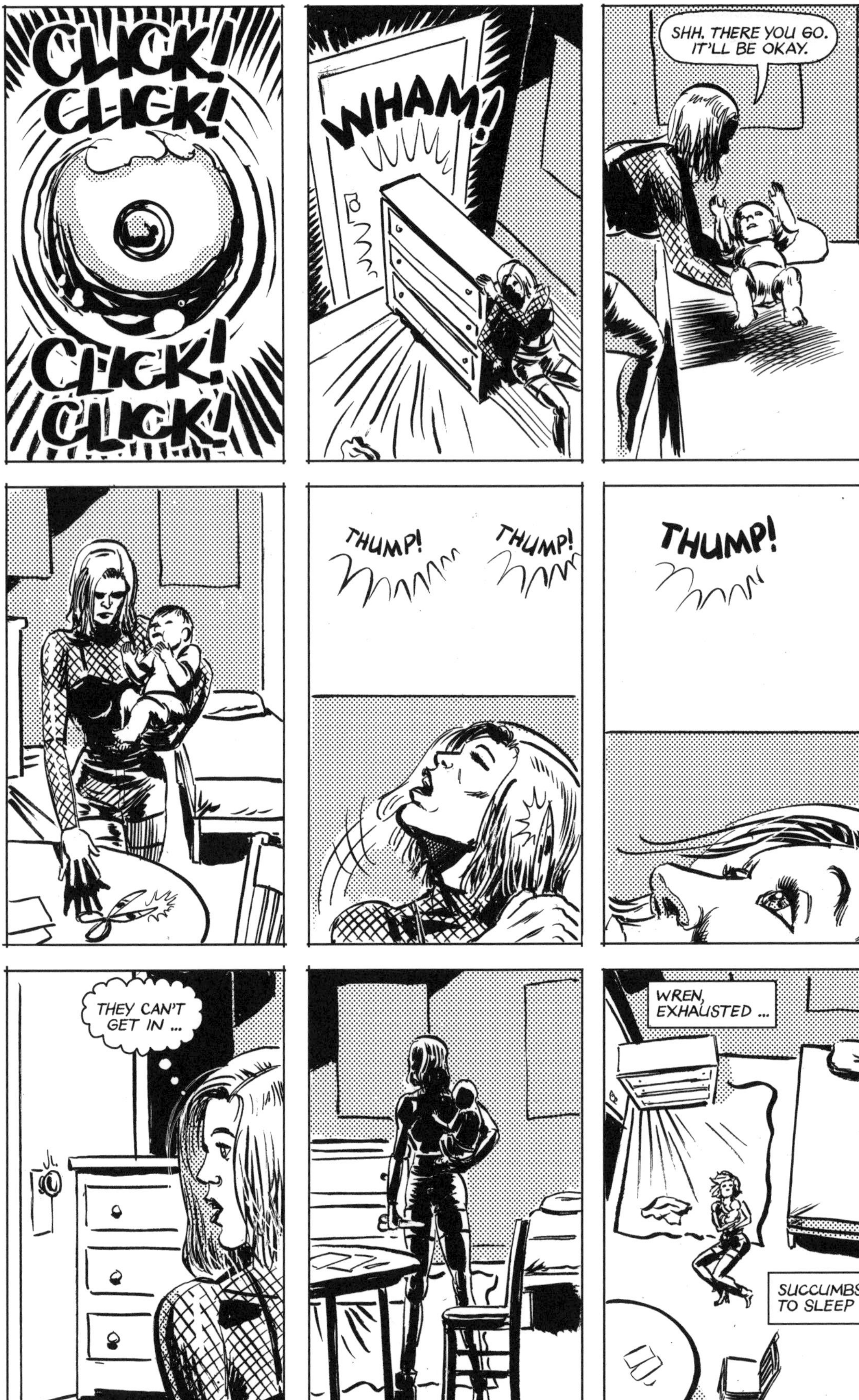
CLICK! CLICK!
CLICK! CLICK!
WHAM!
SHH, THERE YOU GO. IT'LL BE OKAY.
THUMP!
THUMP!
THUMP!
THUMP!
THEY CAN'T GET IN ...
WREN, EXHAUSTED ...
SUCCUMBS TO SLEEP ...

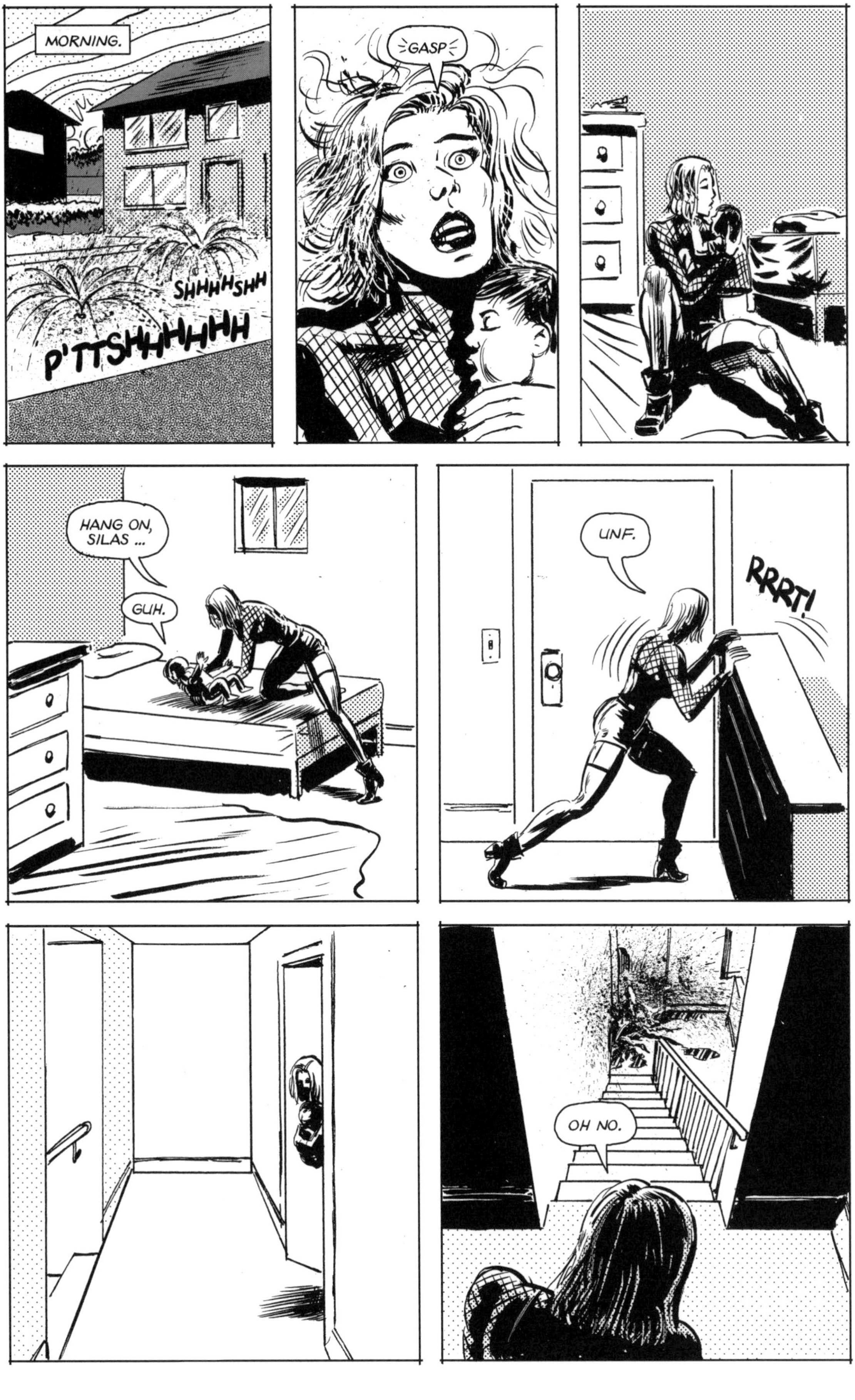
MORNING.
SHHHHSHH
P'TTSHHHHHH
GASP
HANG ON, SILAS ...
GUH.
UNF.
RRRT!
OH NO.

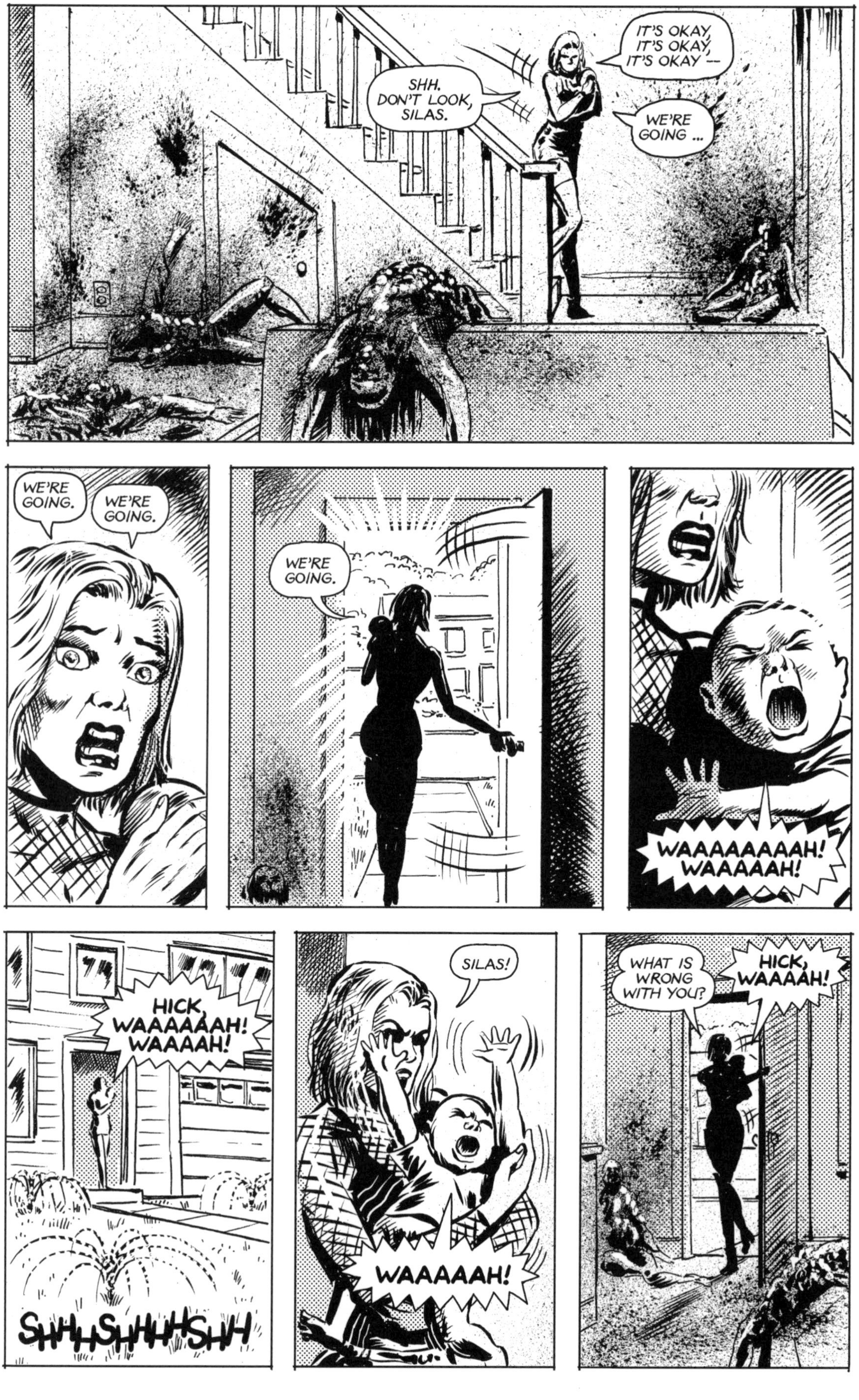

IT'S OKAY, IT'S OKAY, IT'S OKAY --
SHH. DON'T LOOK, SILAS.
WE'RE GOING ...
WE'RE GOING.
WE'RE GOING.
WE'RE GOING.
WAAAAAAAAH! WAAAAAH!
HICK, WAAAAAAH! WAAAAH!
SHHHSHHHHSHH
SILAS!
WAAAAAH!
WHAT IS WRONG WITH YOU?
HICK, WAAAAH!

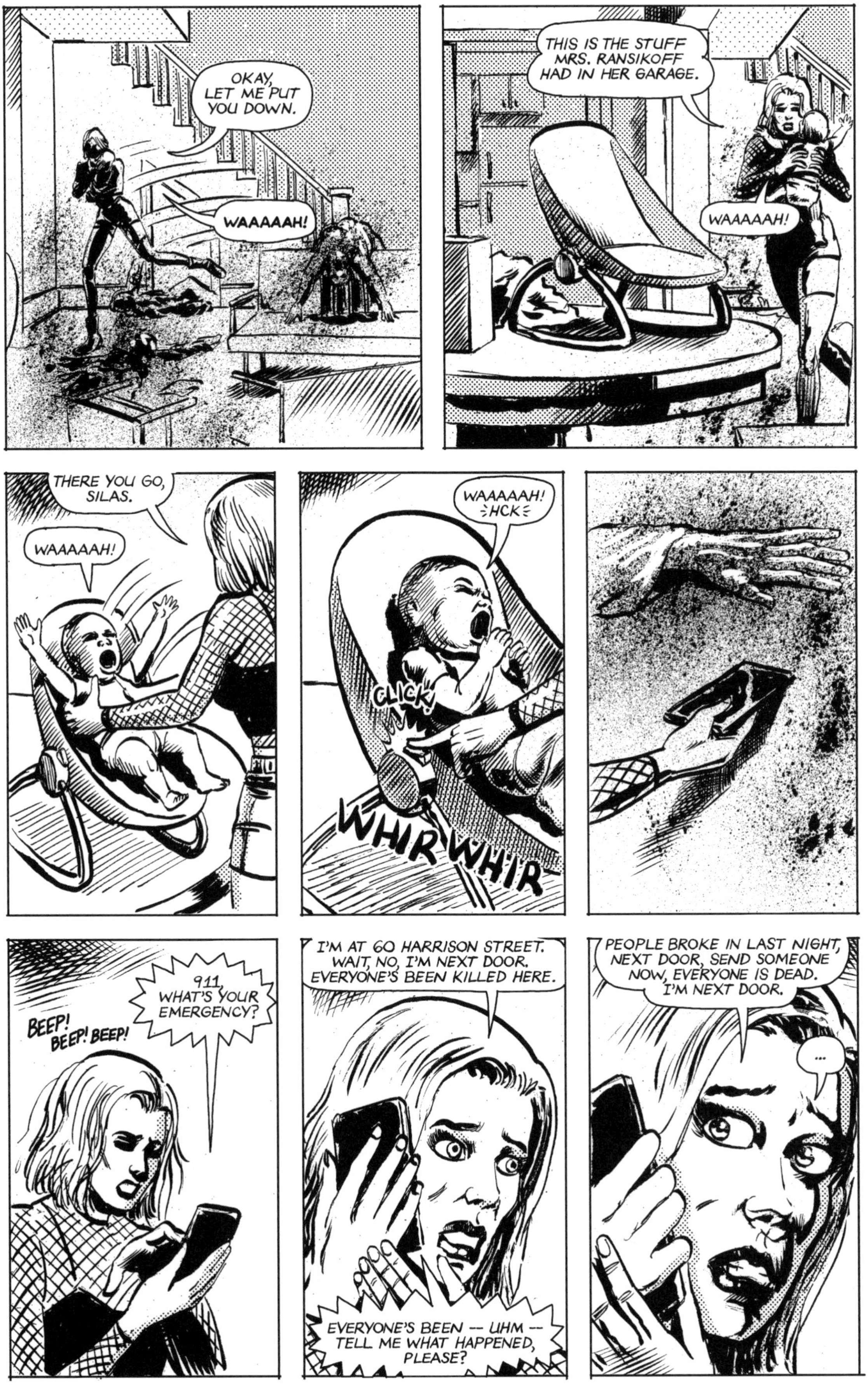
OKAY, LET ME PUT YOU DOWN.
WAAAAAH!
THIS IS THE STUFF MRS. RANSIKOFF HAD IN HER GARAGE.
WAAAAAH!
THERE YOU GO, SILAS.
WAAAAAH!
WAAAAAH! HCK
CLICK!
WHIR WHIR
BEEP! BEEP! BEEP!
911, WHAT'S YOUR EMERGENCY?
I'M AT 60 HARRISON STREET. WAIT, NO, I'M NEXT DOOR. EVERYONE'S BEEN KILLED HERE.
EVERYONE'S BEEN -- UHM -- TELL ME WHAT HAPPENED, PLEASE?
PEOPLE BROKE IN LAST NIGHT, NEXT DOOR, SEND SOMEONE NOW, EVERYONE IS DEAD. I'M NEXT DOOR.
...

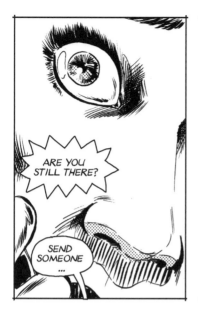

ARE YOU STILL THERE?

SEND SOMEONE ...

THE MIRROR.

WHIR WHIR WHIR-

NO REFLECTION ...

WHIR WHIR WHIR WHIR WHIR WHIR

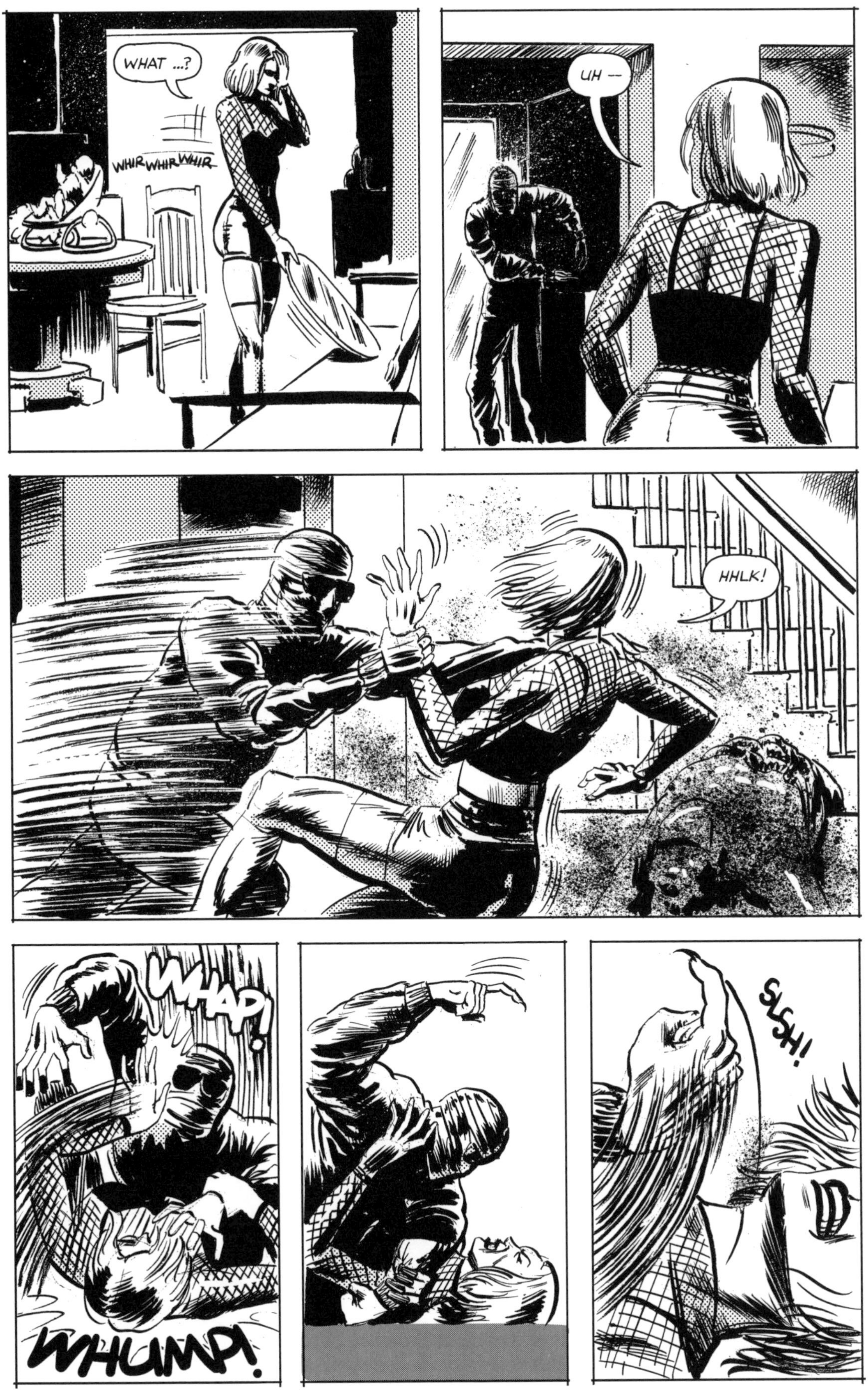
WHAT ...?
WHIR WHIR WHIR
UH --
HHLK!
WHAP!
WHUMP!
SLSH!

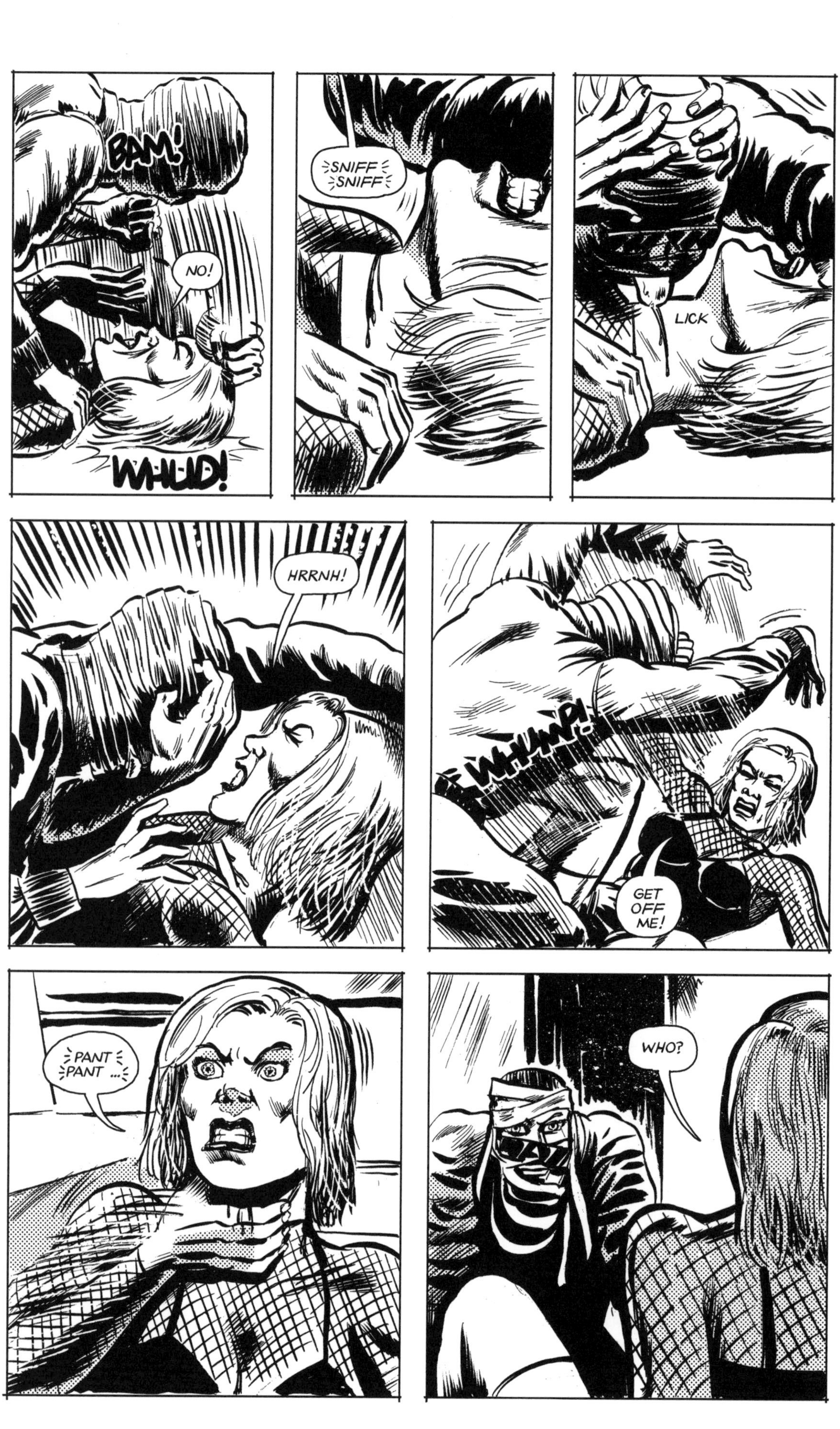
BAM!
NO!
WHUD!
SNIFF SNIFF
LICK
HRRNH!
WHUMP!
GET OFF ME!
PANT PANT ...
WHO?

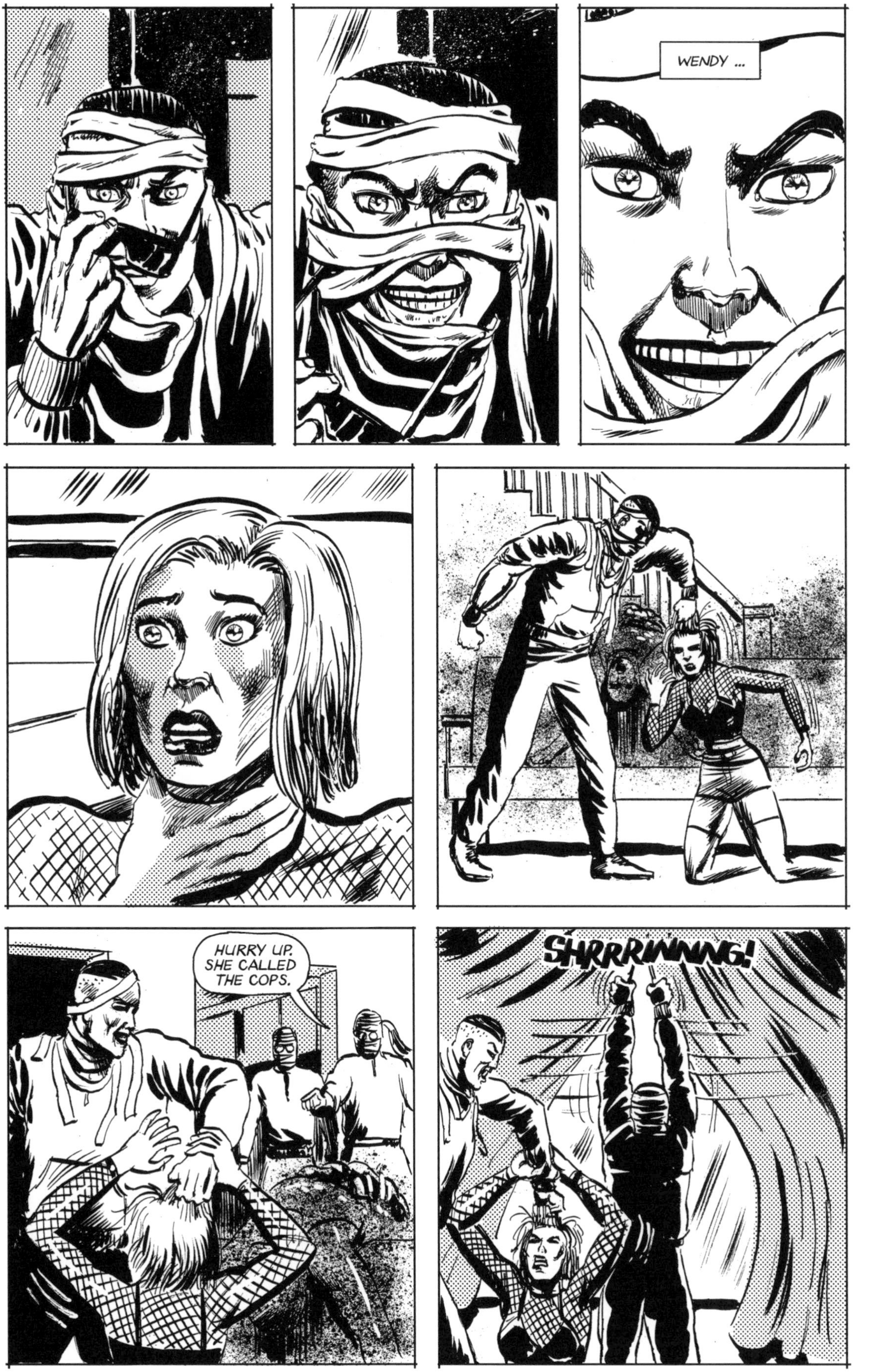
WENDY ...
HURRY UP. SHE CALLED THE COPS.
SHRRRINNNG!

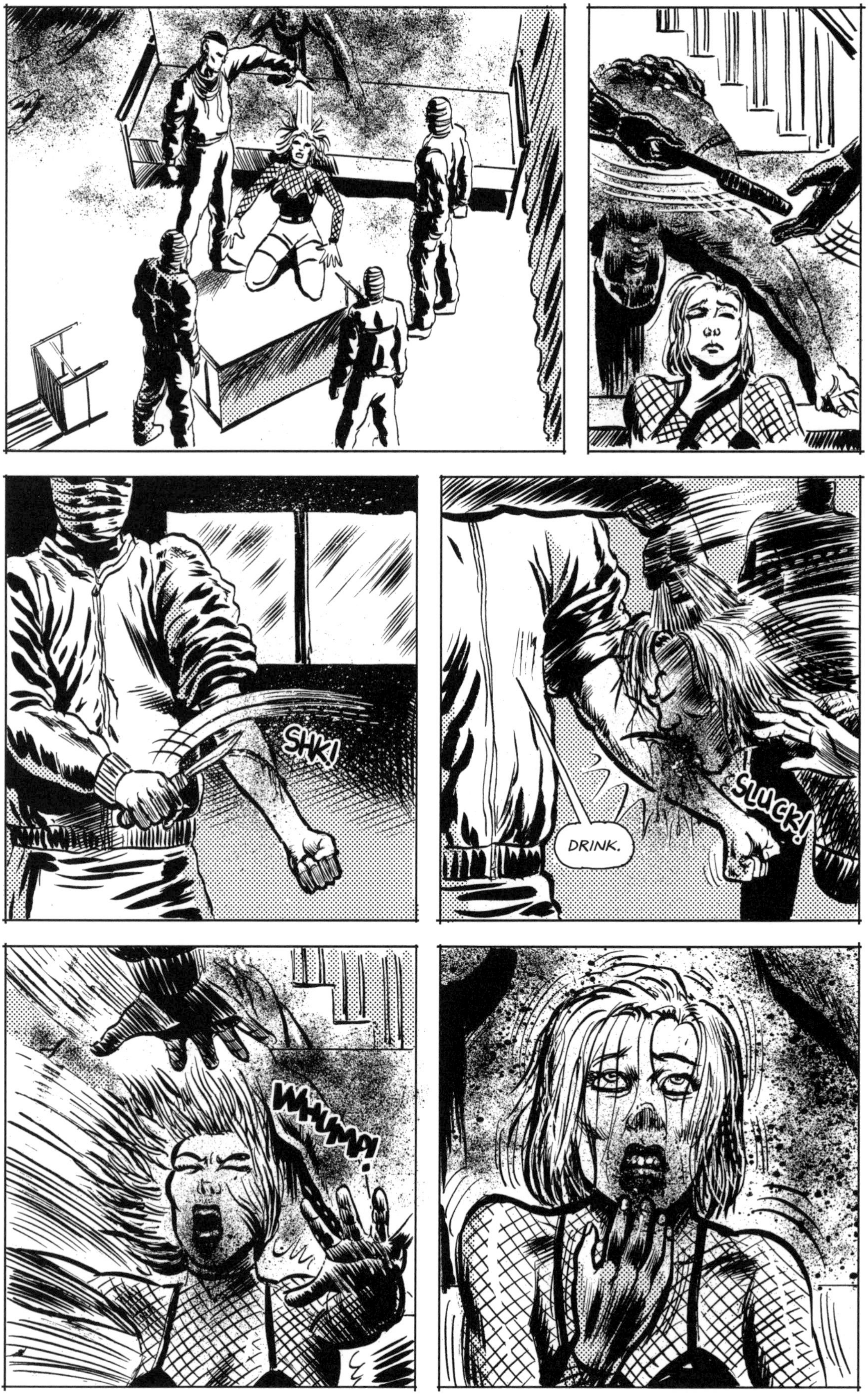
SHK!
DRINK.
SLUCK!
WHUMP!

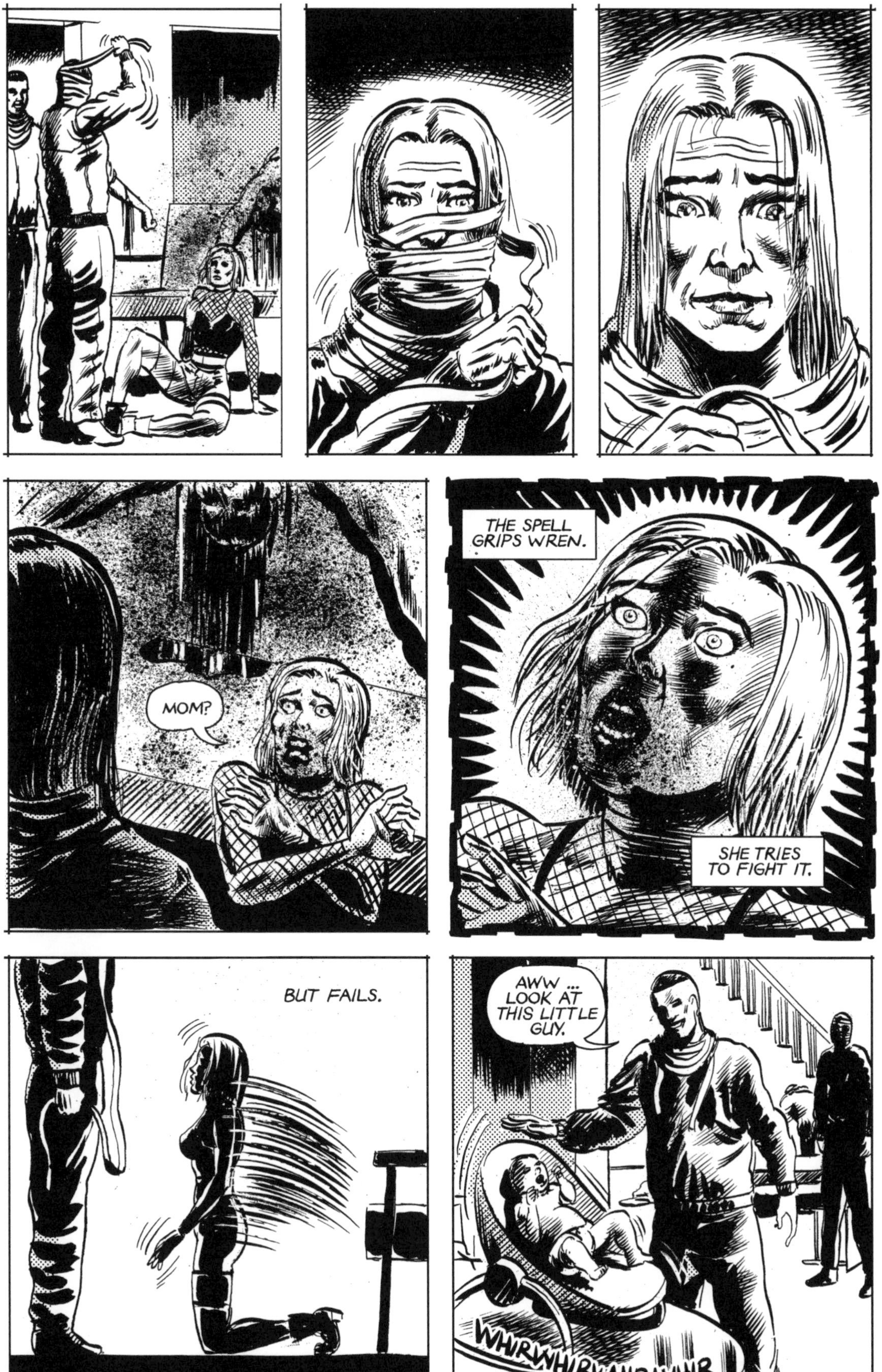

MOM?
THE SPELL GRIPS WREN.
SHE TRIES TO FIGHT IT.
BUT FAILS.
AWW ... LOOK AT THIS LITTLE GUY.
WHIRWHIRWHIRWHIR

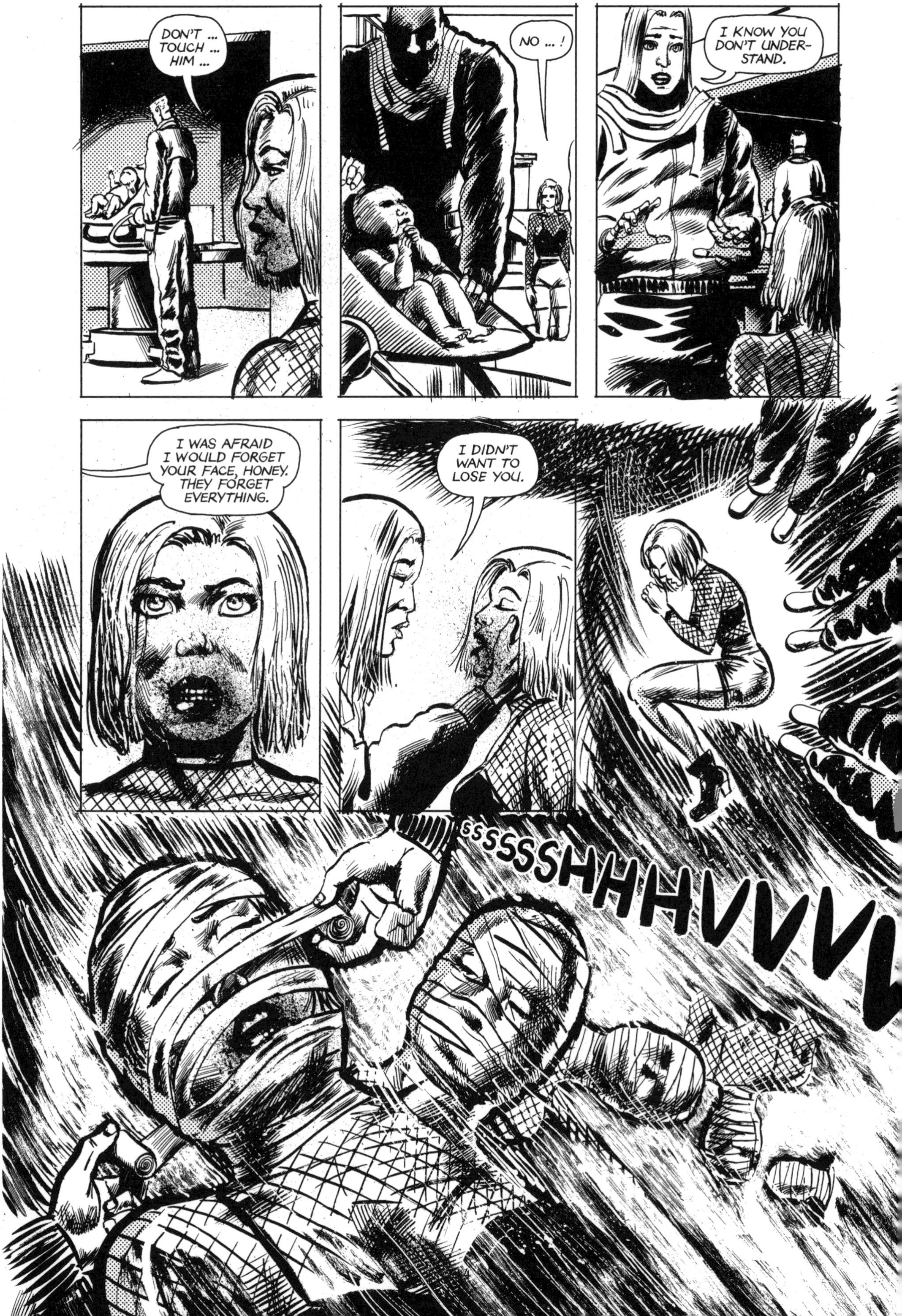
DON'T ... TOUCH ... HIM ...
NO ... !
I KNOW YOU DON'T UNDER-STAND.
I WAS AFRAID I WOULD FORGET YOUR FACE, HONEY. THEY FORGET EVERYTHING.
I DIDN'T WANT TO LOSE YOU.
SSSSSSSHHHHVVVVV

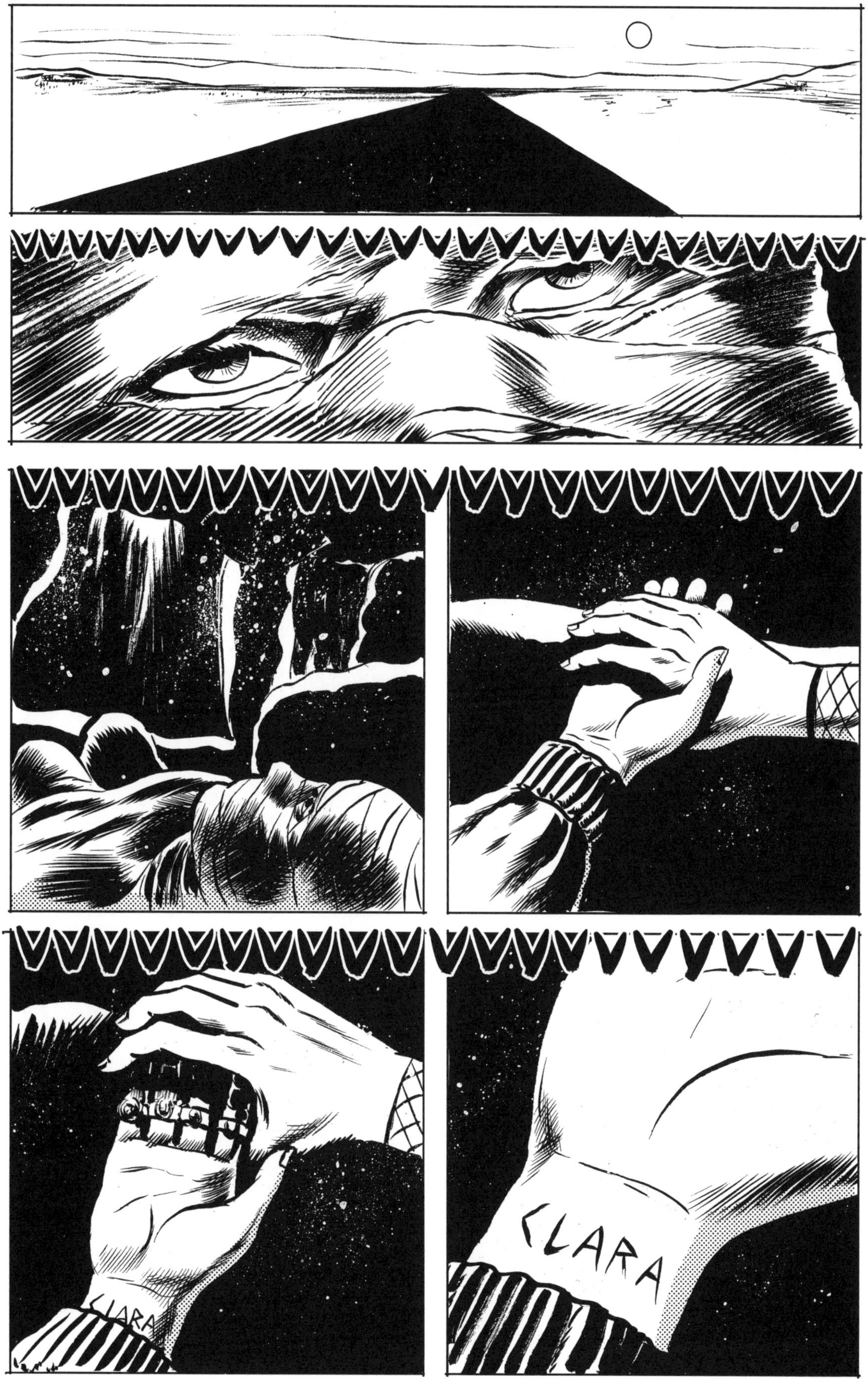
CLARA
CLARA

WE'RE GOING TO TAKE YOU WHERE YOU CAN FIND WHO YOU REALLY ARE.

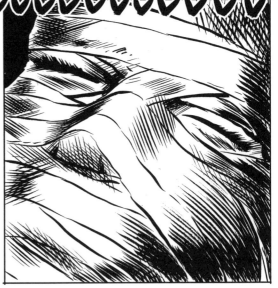

MUCH LATER ...

HUH?

NO NO NO NO ...

SHHHRK!
CHK!
THE FUCK ...?
PRIK
OH GOD.
NO!
WHAM!
BAM!
NO!
PLEASE NO. OH, GOD, PLEASE.
SCRTCH! SCRTCH!
SCRTCH! SCRTCH!
SCRTCH! SCRTCH!

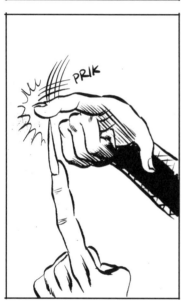

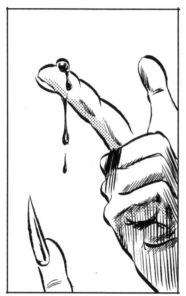

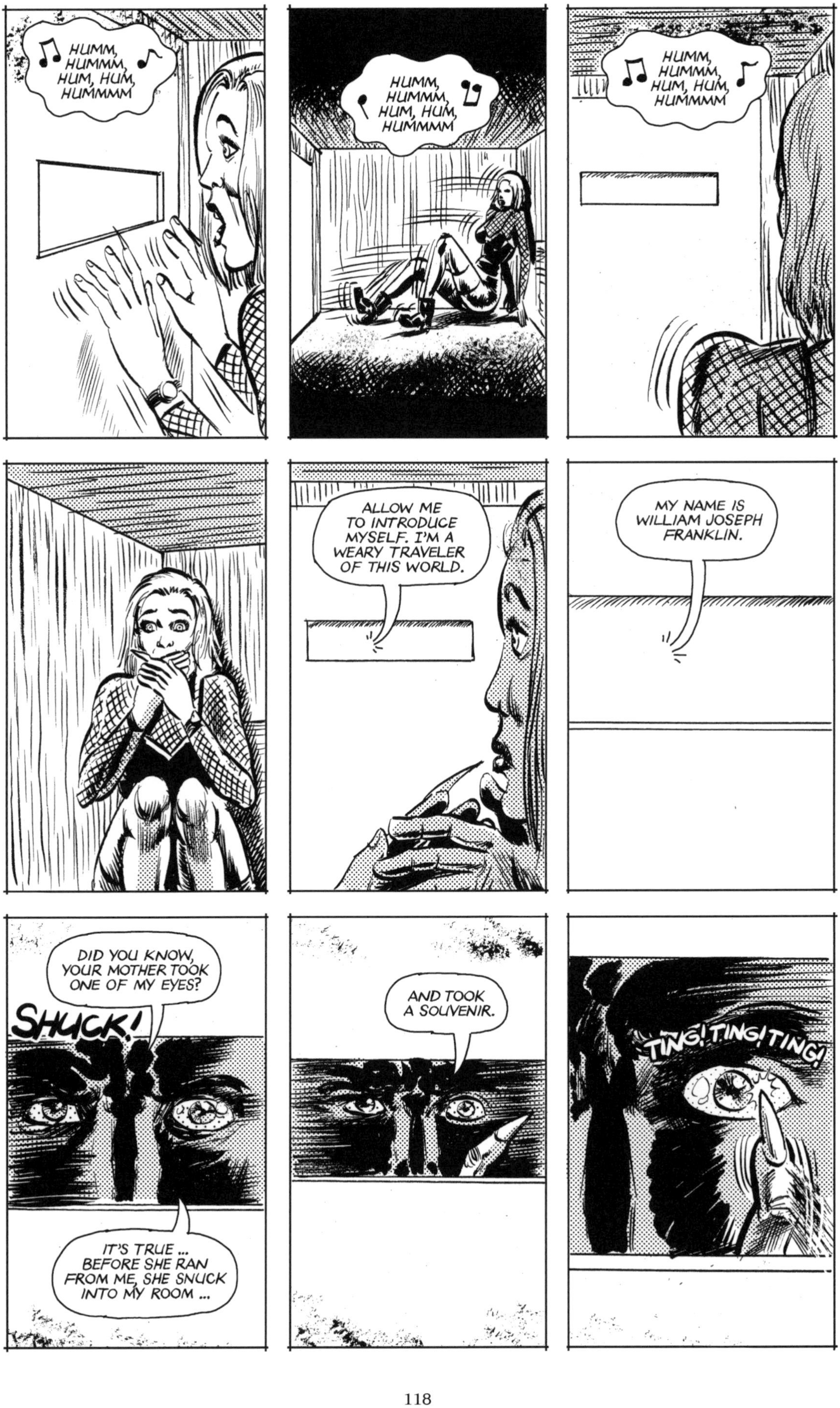

HUMM, HUMMM, HUM, HUM, HUMMMM
HUMM, HUMMM, HUM, HUM, HUMMMM
HUMM, HUMMM, HUM, HUM, HUMMMM
ALLOW ME TO INTRODUCE MYSELF. I'M A WEARY TRAVELER OF THIS WORLD.
MY NAME IS WILLIAM JOSEPH FRANKLIN.
DID YOU KNOW, YOUR MOTHER TOOK ONE OF MY EYES?
SHUCK!
IT'S TRUE ... BEFORE SHE RAN FROM ME, SHE SNUCK INTO MY ROOM ...
AND TOOK A SOUVENIR.
TING! TING! TING!

NOOOO!

BAM!

AAAAIIIEEE!

≩ PANT, PANT, PANT ≩

DO YOU KNOW WHY BABIES SCREAM?

BECAUSE BIRTH IS ALWAYS PAINFUL. EVERYTHING THAT HAPPENED BEFORE ...

IS DISAPPEARING, BLUEBIRD.

YOUR BIG ADVENTURE BEGINS TODAY. YOU'LL BE ABLE TO WRITE THE STORY OF YOUR LIFE FROM THE VERY FIRST WORDS.

IN MY LIFE, I SLEEP I WAKE ... I'VE SEEN IT ALL. THE EARTH FUCKS THE SKY, THE SKY FUCKS THE RAIN ... THE RAIN FUCKS THE WORMS IN THE DIRT ...

THE WORMS FUCK THE DEAD IN THE GROUND, THE DEAD FUCK FLOWERS TO LIFE ... IT'S ALL A GAS.

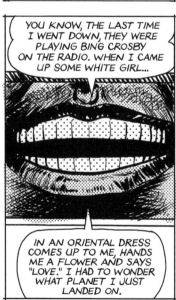

YOU KNOW, THE LAST TIME I WENT DOWN, THEY WERE PLAYING BING CROSBY ON THE RADIO. WHEN I CAME UP SOME WHITE GIRL...

IN AN ORIENTAL DRESS COMES UP TO ME, HANDS ME A FLOWER AND SAYS "LOVE." I HAD TO WONDER WHAT PLANET I JUST LANDED ON.

AFTER YOUR MOTHER LEFT, I HAD TO CHANGE SOME RULES. NO MORE CREEPY-CRAWLS INTO HOMES, ONLY SNACKING ON SPOOK BAIT. KEEPING QUIET FOR A WHILE. I ALWAYS KNEW YOUR MOTHER WOULD COME BACK. THEY ALWAYS DO. BUT I NEVER COULD'VE KNOWN WHAT A BEAUTIFUL PRIZE SHE WOULD BRING.

I NEVER KNEW YOU, BUT THE MOMENT I SAW YOU, I KNEW I LOVED YOU.

WHAT HAVE YOU DONE WITH HIM?

WHO?

THE BABY. WHERE IS HE?

AH. YOU REMEMBER THE BABY. ONE OF WEIRD WENDY'S LITTLE PROJECTS ... YOU HAVE TO LET THAT GO.

NO!

WHAT'S THE BABY'S NAME?

I ... CAN'T ....

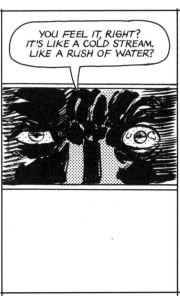

YOU FEEL IT, RIGHT? IT'S LIKE A COLD STREAM. LIKE A RUSH OF WATER?

THAT'S ME. RUSHING OVER YOU.

THE GIRLS COME UP WITH DIFFERENT WAYS TO REMEMBER THINGS.

WRITING ON THE INSIDE OF THEIR THIGHS THE NAME OF SOME OLD FLAME ...

OR A GRANDMA WHO USED TO MAKE THEM MAPLE STEW. FOR WEIRD WENDY, THAT BABY IS A MEMORY OF A MEMORY, A LIFE THAT SHE MIGHT'VE READ IN A BOOK SOMEWHERE...

THE BEAUTY IS: THE PAST DOESN'T MATTER. YOU'LL SOON FORGET THE WORLD.

AND LOVE WHAT YOU REALLY ARE ... JUST LIKE YOUR MOTHER LOVES IT.

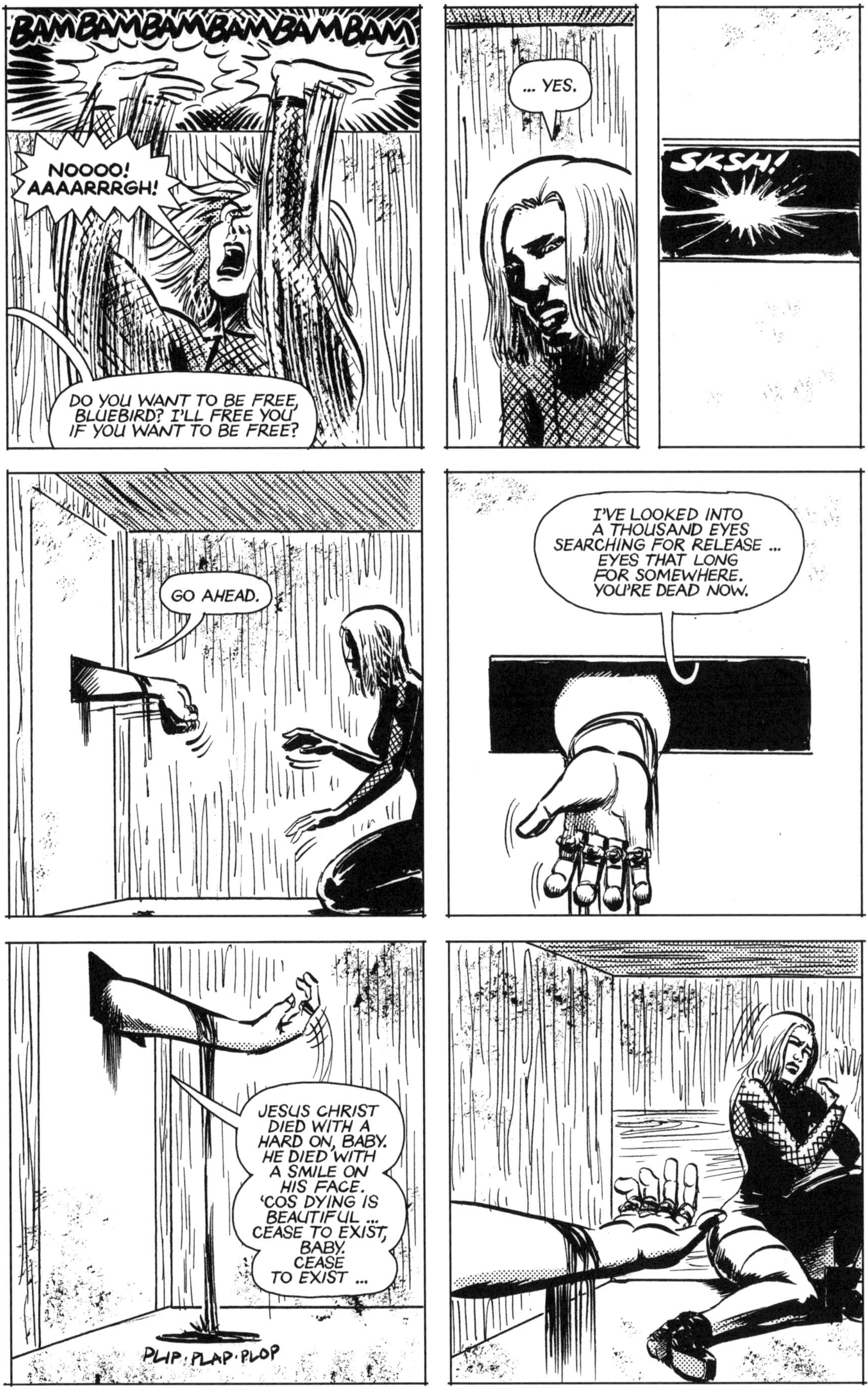
BAMBAMBAMBAMBAMBAM
NOOOO! AAAARRRGH!
DO YOU WANT TO BE FREE, BLUEBIRD? I'LL FREE YOU IF YOU WANT TO BE FREE?
... YES.
SKSH!
GO AHEAD.
I'VE LOOKED INTO A THOUSAND EYES SEARCHING FOR RELEASE ... EYES THAT LONG FOR SOMEWHERE. YOU'RE DEAD NOW.
JESUS CHRIST DIED WITH A HARD ON, BABY. HE DIED WITH A SMILE ON HIS FACE. 'COS DYING IS BEAUTIFUL ... CEASE TO EXIST, BABY. CEASE TO EXIST ...
PLIP · PLAP · PLOP

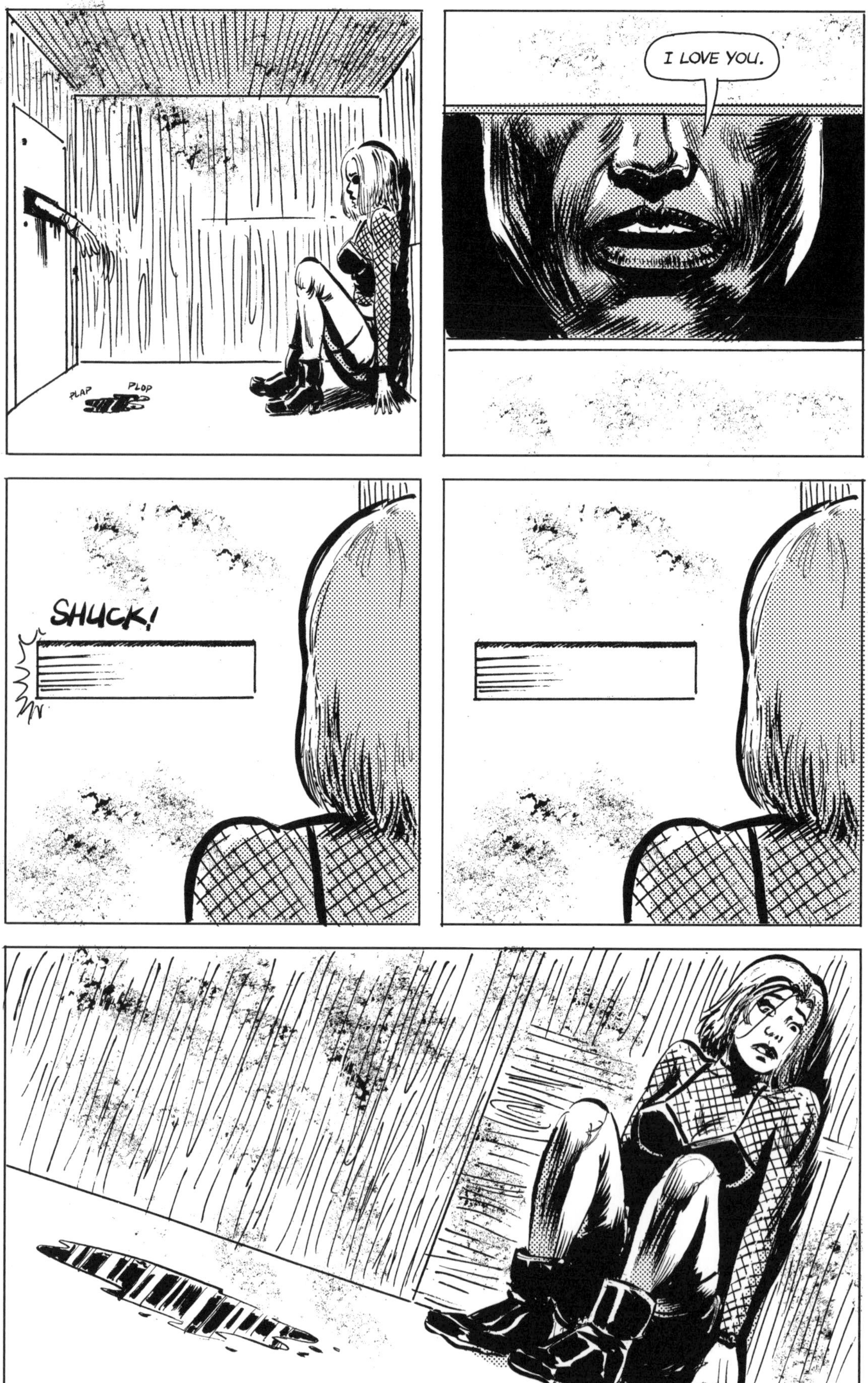
PLAP
PLOP
I LOVE YOU.
SHUCK!

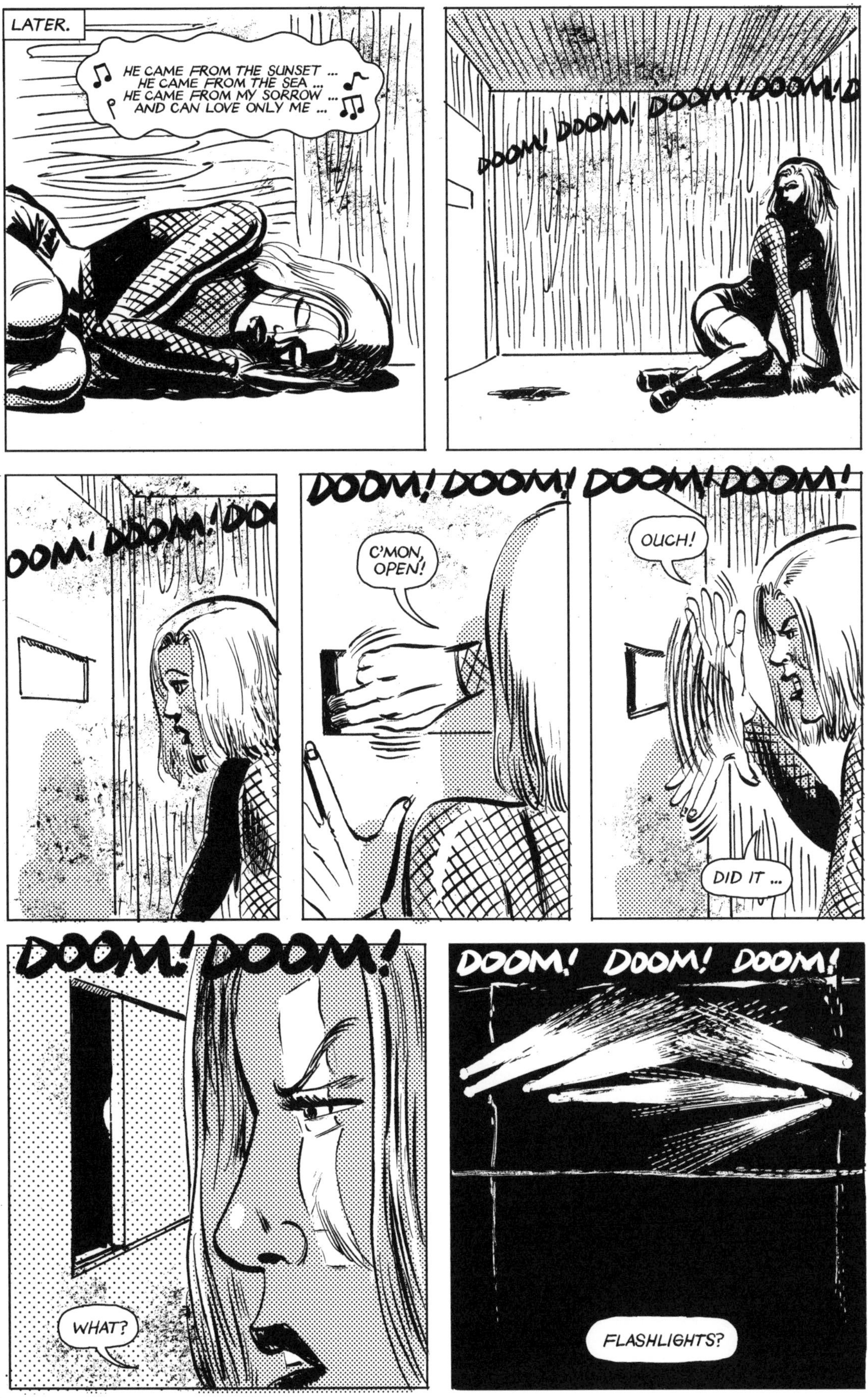
LATER.
HE CAME FROM THE SUNSET ... HE CAME FROM THE SEA ... HE CAME FROM MY SORROW ... AND CAN LOVE ONLY ME ...
DOOM! DOOM! DOOM! DOOM! D
OOM! DOOM! DO
DOOM! DOOM! DOOM! DOOM!
C'MON, OPEN!
OUCH!
DID IT ...
DOOM! DOOM!
WHAT?
DOOM! DOOM! DOOM!
FLASHLIGHTS?

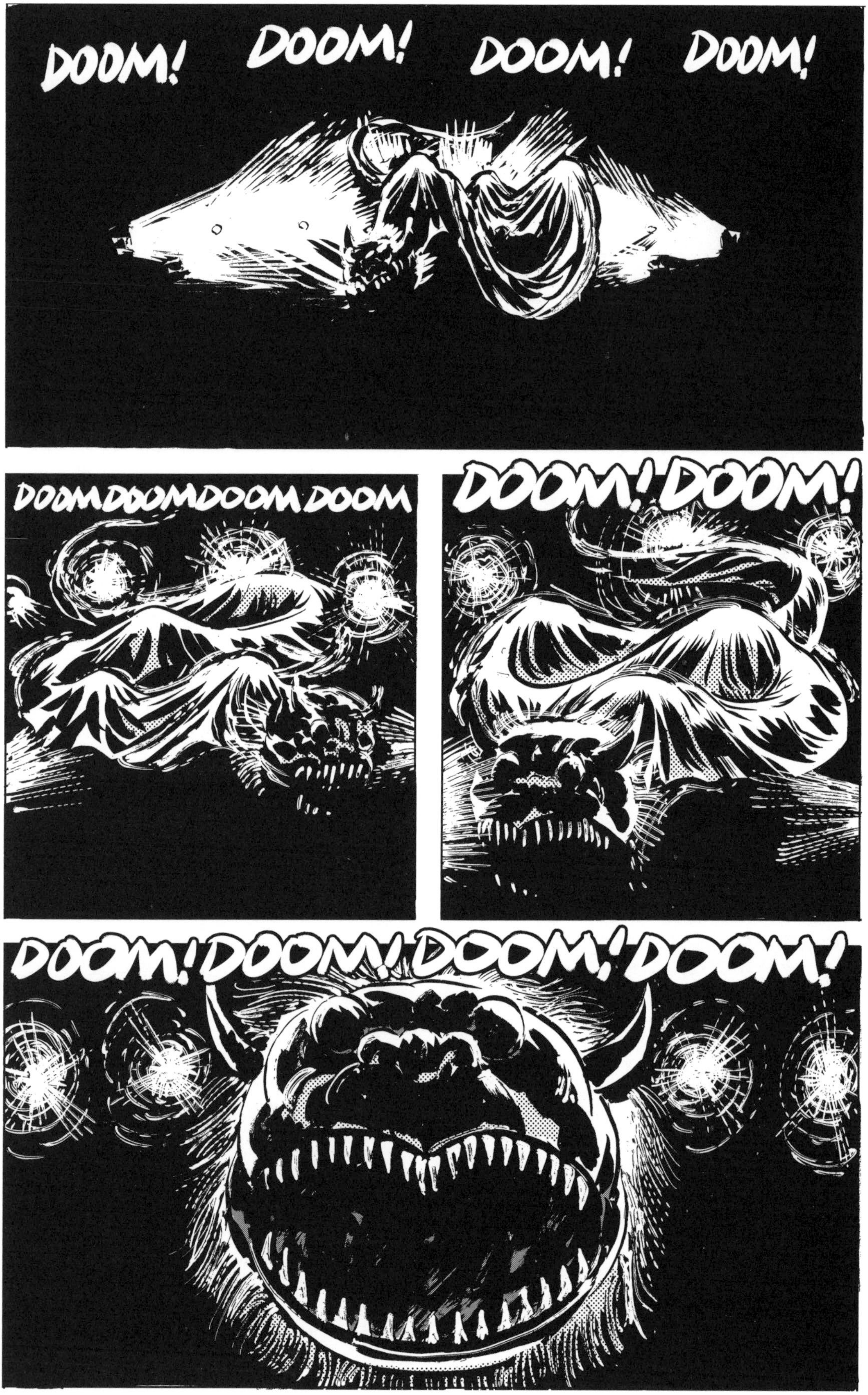
DOOM! DOOM! DOOM! DOOM!
DOOMDOOMDOOMDOOM
DOOM! DOOM!
DOOM! DOOM! DOOM! DOOM!

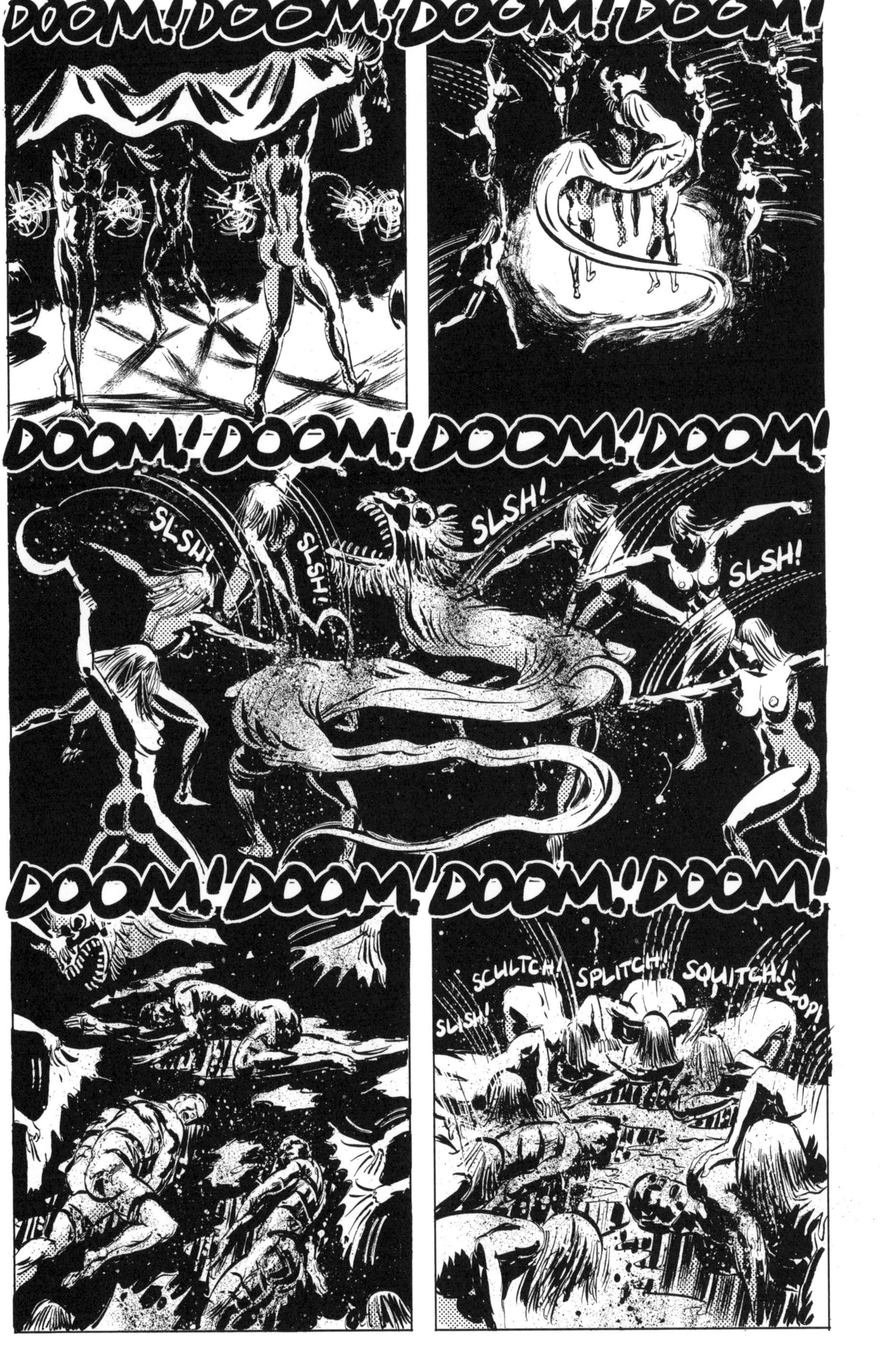
DOOM! DOOM! DOOM! DOOM!
DOOM! DOOM! DOOM! DOOM!
SLSH!
SLSH!
SLSH!
SLSH!
DOOM! DOOM! DOOM! DOOM!
SLSH!
SCULTCH!
SPLITCH!
SQUITCH!
SLOP!

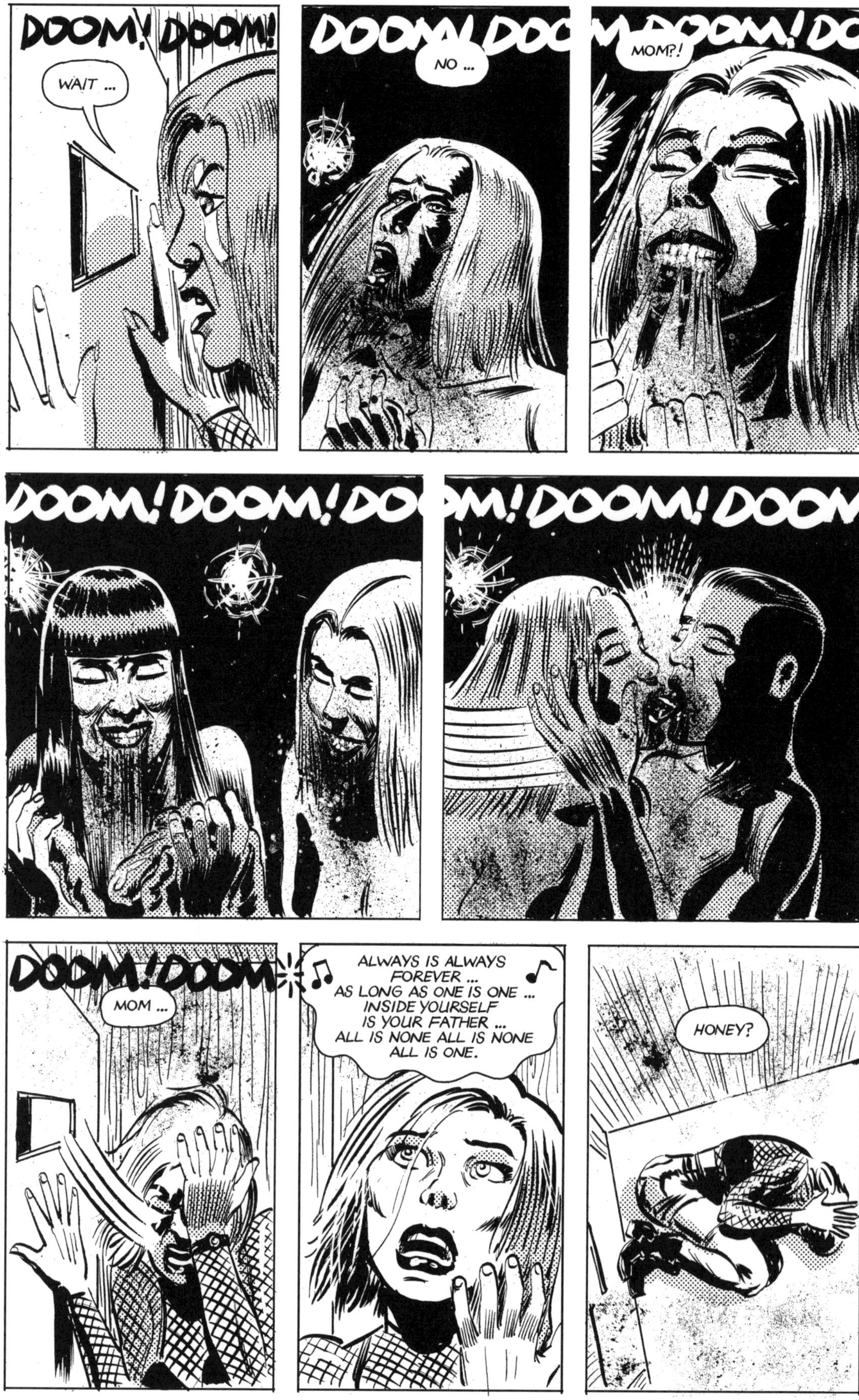
DOOM! DOOM!
WAIT ...
DOOM! DOOM! DOOM! DO
NO ...
MOM?!
DOOM! DOOM! DOOM! DOOM! DOOM
DOOM! DOOM
MOM ...
ALWAYS IS ALWAYS
FOREVER ...
AS LONG AS ONE IS ONE ...
INSIDE YOURSELF
IS YOUR FATHER ...
ALL IS NONE ALL IS NONE
ALL IS ONE.
HONEY?

DO YOU WANT TO COME OUT NOW?

DO YOU WANT TO COME OUT AND JOIN US?

WHAT HAVE YOU DONE, MOM?

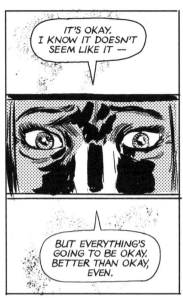

IT'S OKAY. I KNOW IT DOESN'T SEEM LIKE IT —

BUT EVERYTHING'S GOING TO BE OKAY. BETTER THAN OKAY, EVEN.

HOW CAN IT BE?

HOW CAN ANYTHING EVER BE OKAY AGAIN?

YOU JUST ... YOU JUST HAVE TO LET GO OF THE WAY YOU USED TO SEE THINGS.

AND DO WHAT HE WANTS YOU TO?

IT'S NOT LIKE THAT. IT DOESN'T HAVE TO BE LIKE THAT. IT'S NOT ABOUT SURRENDERING ... OR IF IT IS, IT'S ABOUT SURRENDERING TO YOURSELF ...

BABY, I DON'T HAVE THE WORDS BUT I JUST WANT YOU TO KNOW EVERYTHING'S GOING TO BE OKAY.

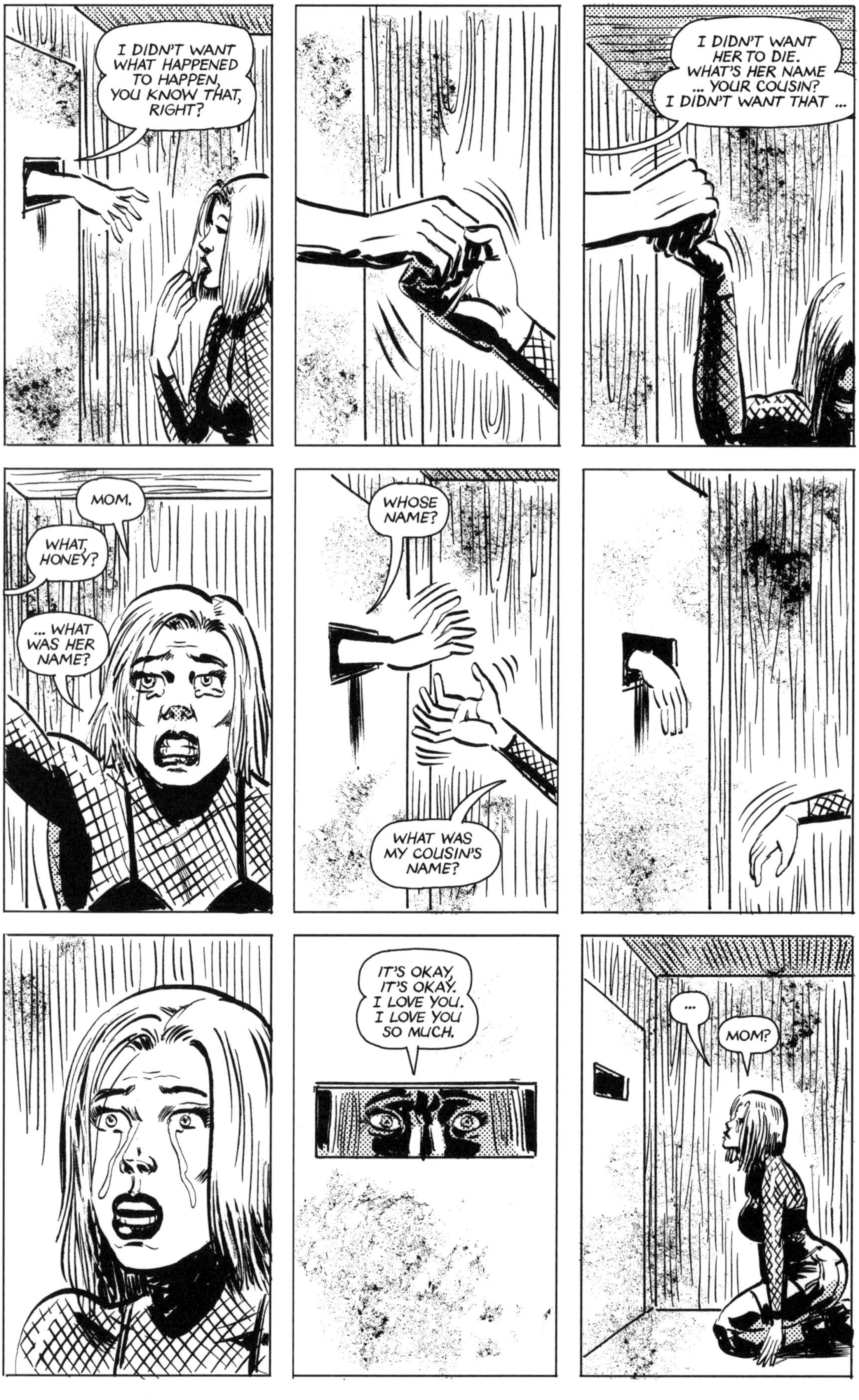
I DIDN'T WANT WHAT HAPPENED TO HAPPEN, YOU KNOW THAT, RIGHT?
I DIDN'T WANT HER TO DIE. WHAT'S HER NAME ... YOUR COUSIN? I DIDN'T WANT THAT ...
MOM.
WHAT, HONEY?
... WHAT WAS HER NAME?
WHOSE NAME?
WHAT WAS MY COUSIN'S NAME?
IT'S OKAY, IT'S OKAY. I LOVE YOU. I LOVE YOU SO MUCH.
...
MOM?

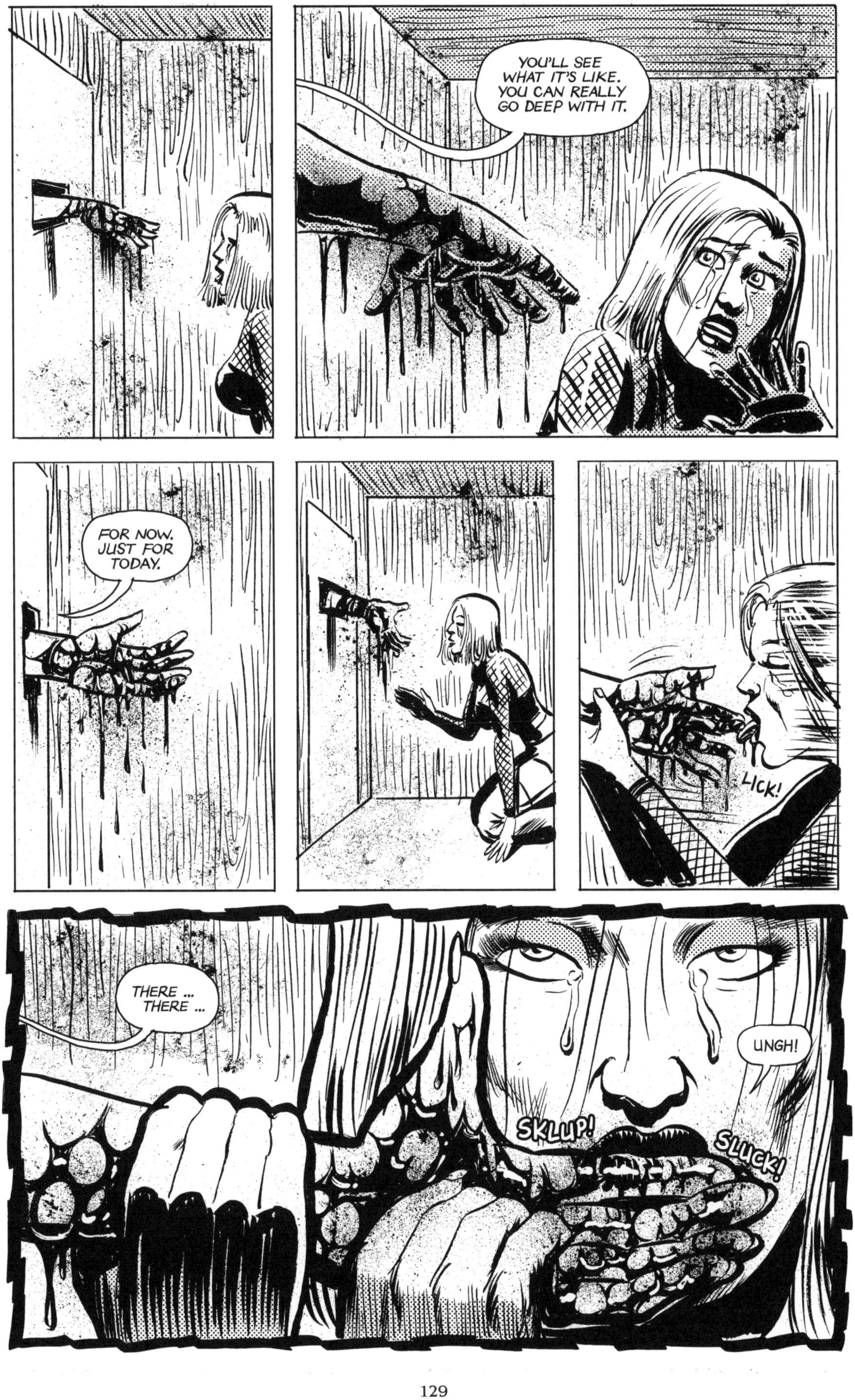
YOU'LL SEE WHAT IT'S LIKE. YOU CAN REALLY GO DEEP WITH IT.
FOR NOW. JUST FOR TODAY.
LICK!
THERE ... THERE ...
UNGH!
SKLUP!
SLUCK!

AAAH ...

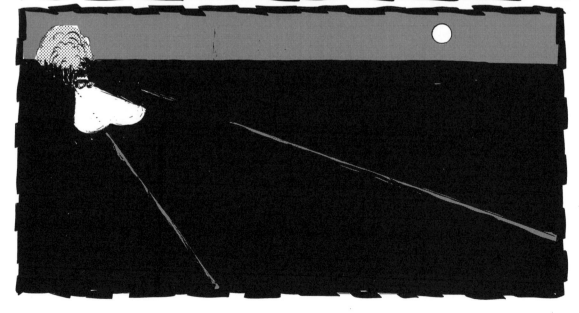

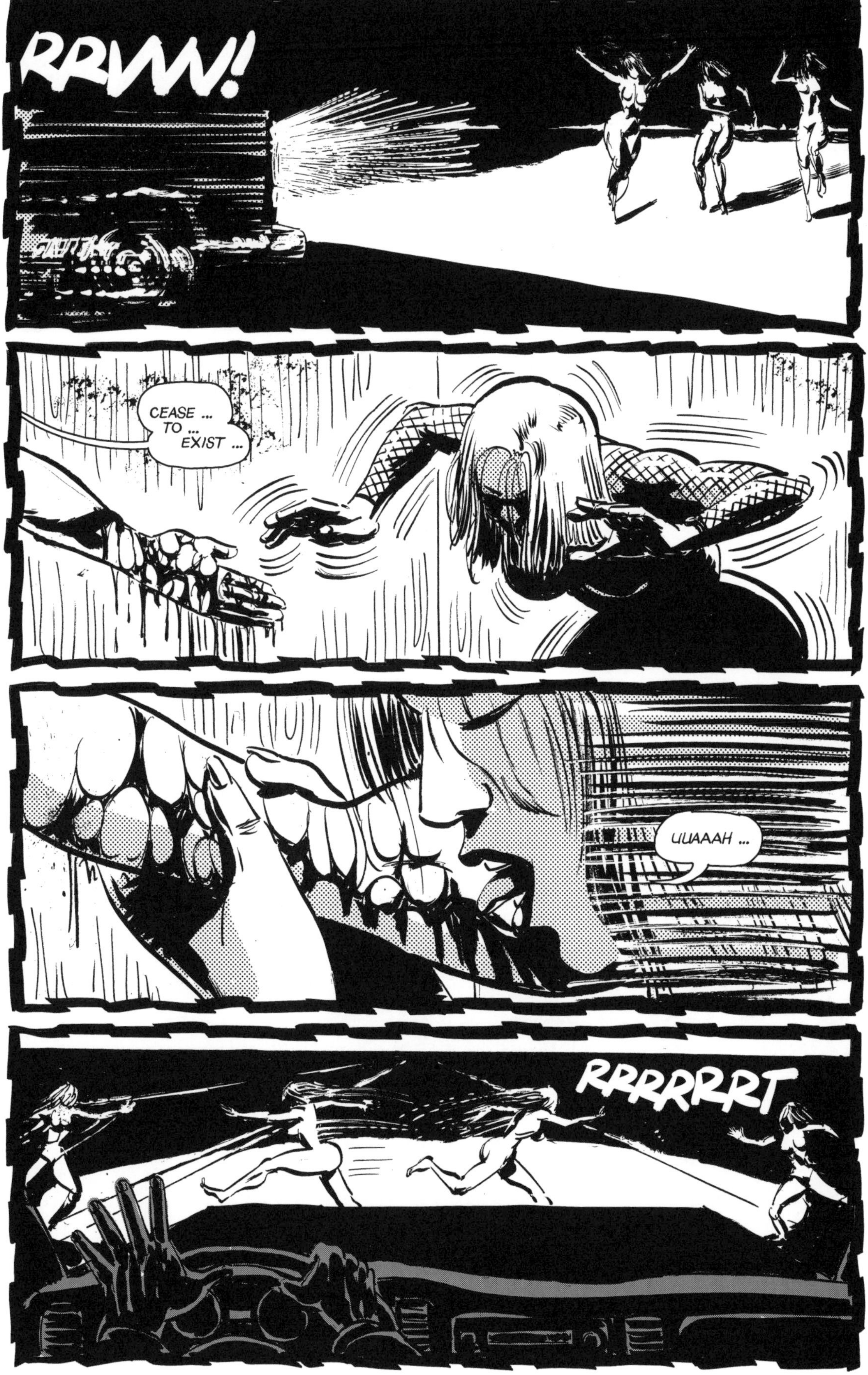
RRVVN!
CEASE ... TO ... EXIST ...
UUAAAH ...
RRRRRRT

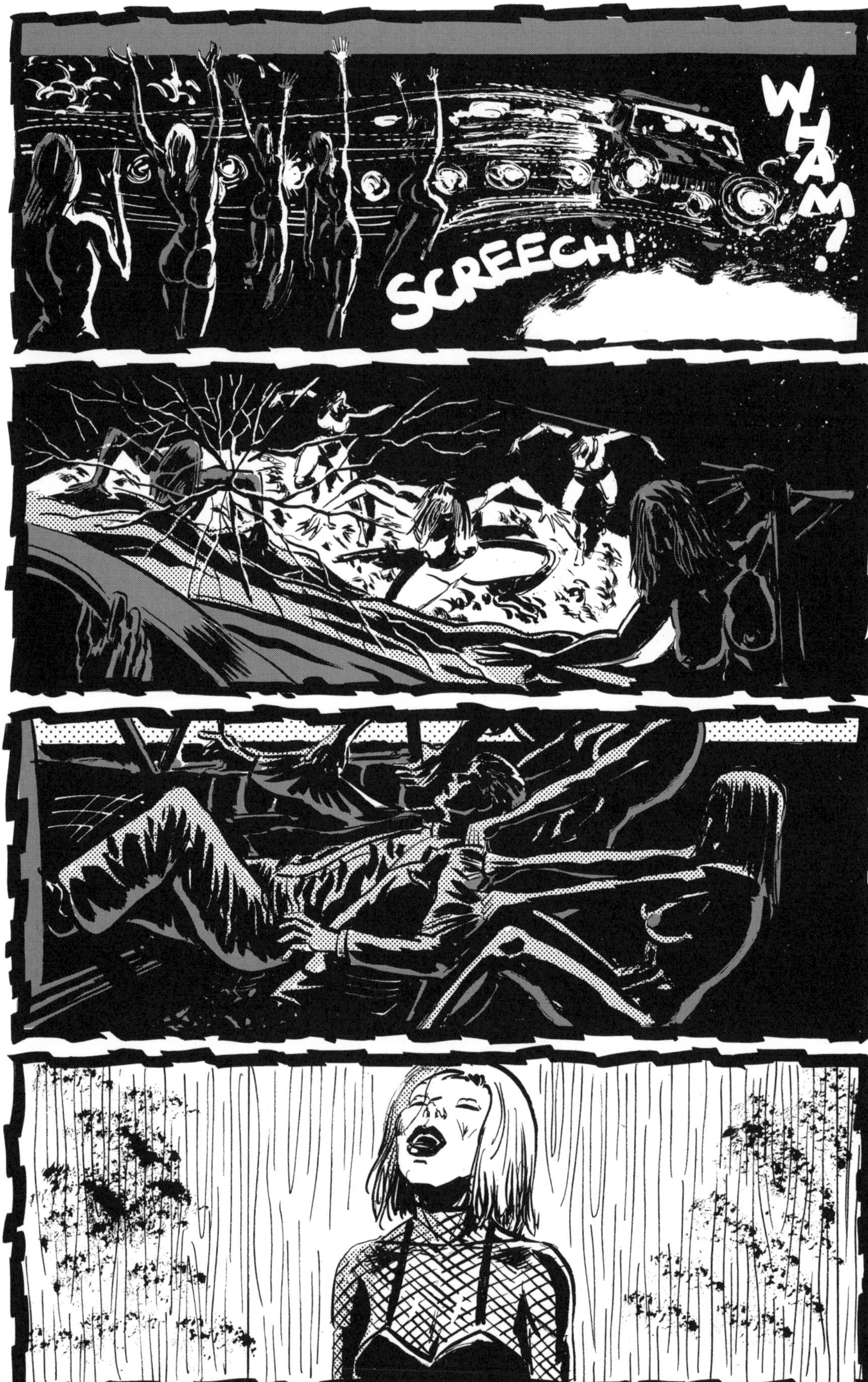
SCREECH!
WHAM!

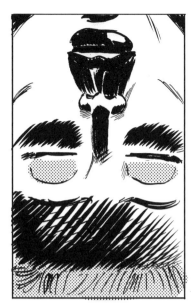

WHAT THE FUCK?

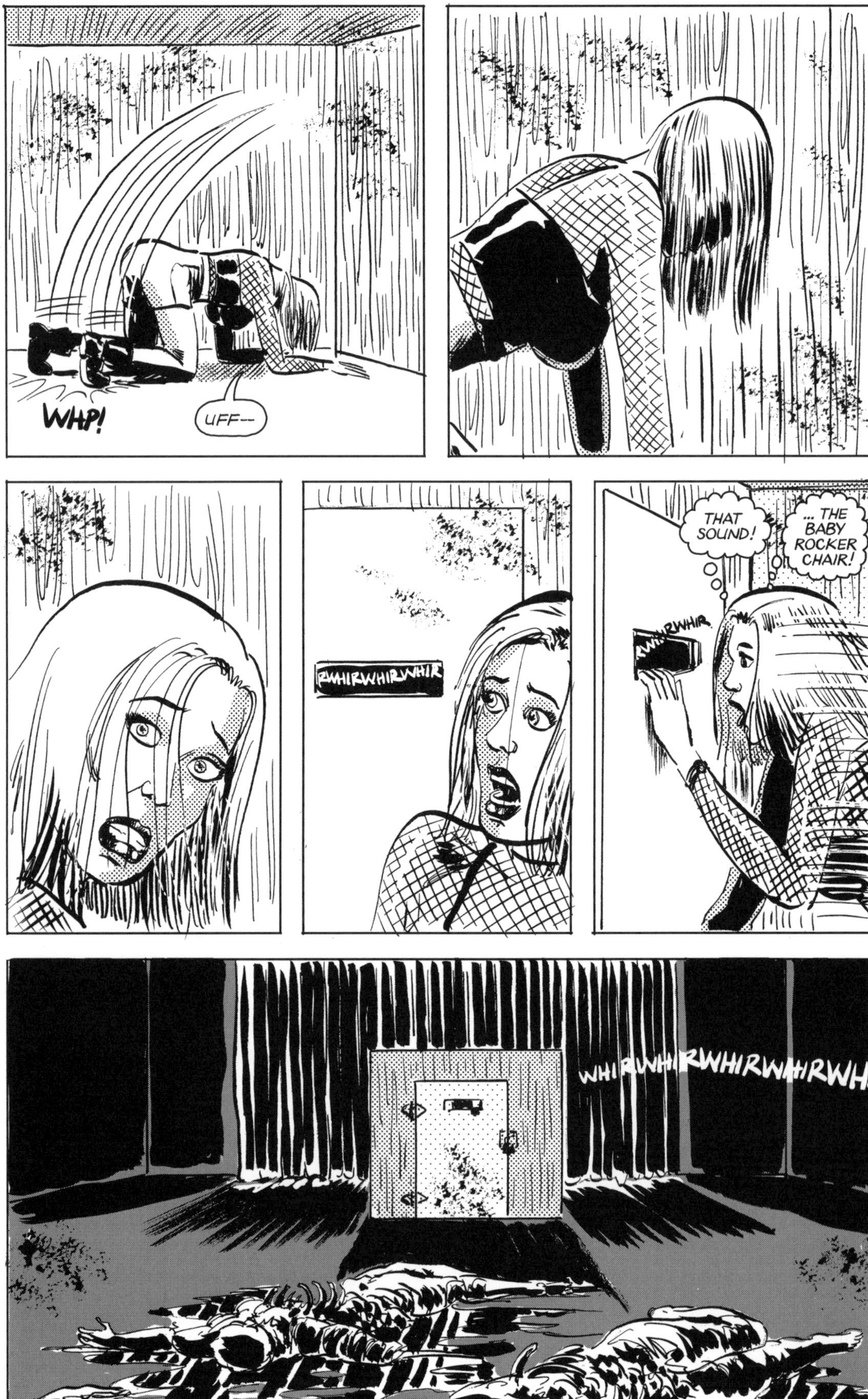
WHP!
UFF--
RWHIRWHIRWHIR
THAT SOUND!
... THE BABY ROCKER CHAIR!
RWHIR
WHIRWHIRWHIRWHIRWHIRWH

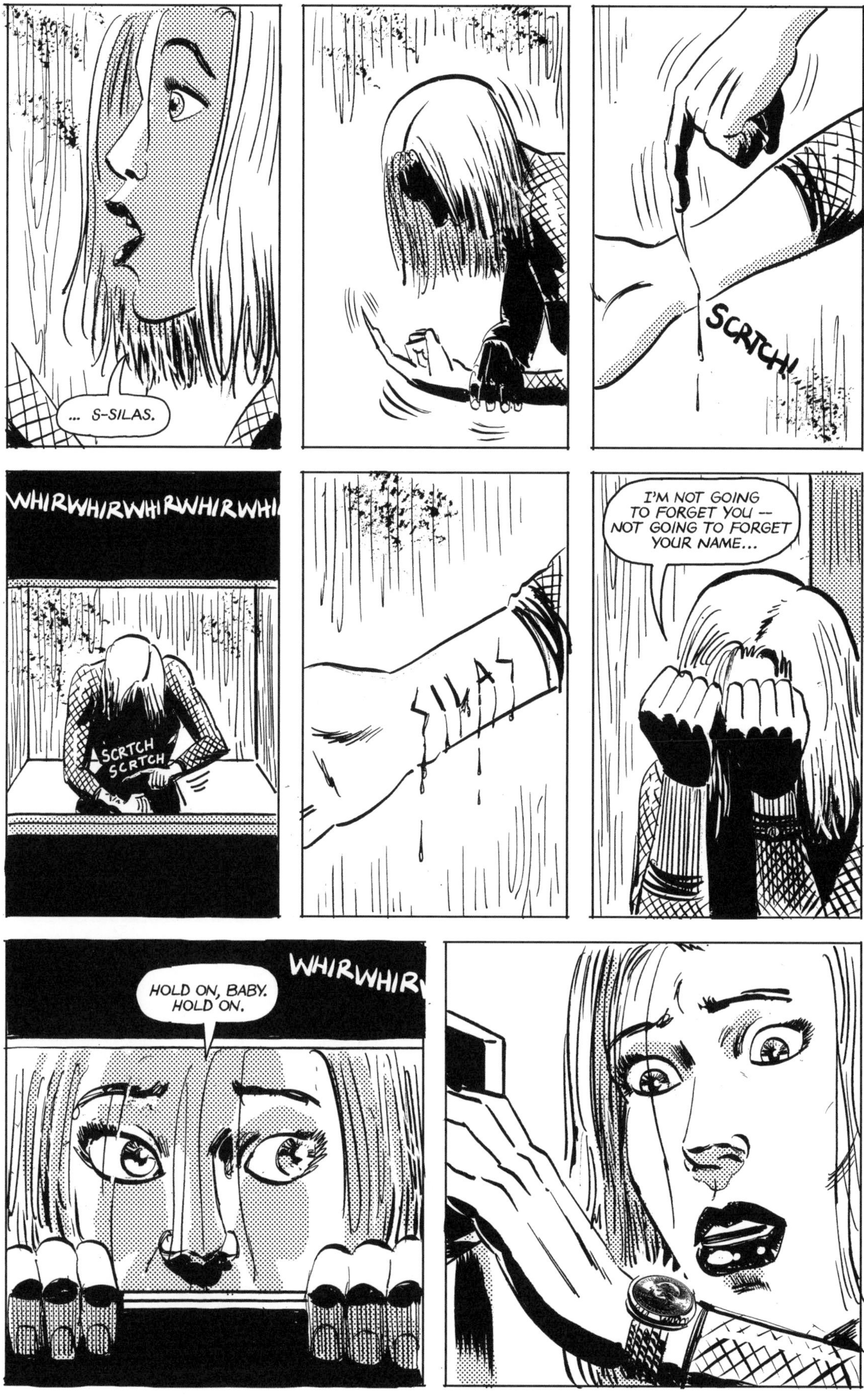
... S-SILAS.
SCRTCH!
WHIRWHIRWHIRWHIRWHI
SCRTCH
SCRTCH
SILAS
I'M NOT GOING TO FORGET YOU -- NOT GOING TO FORGET YOUR NAME...
HOLD ON, BABY. HOLD ON.
WHIRWHIR

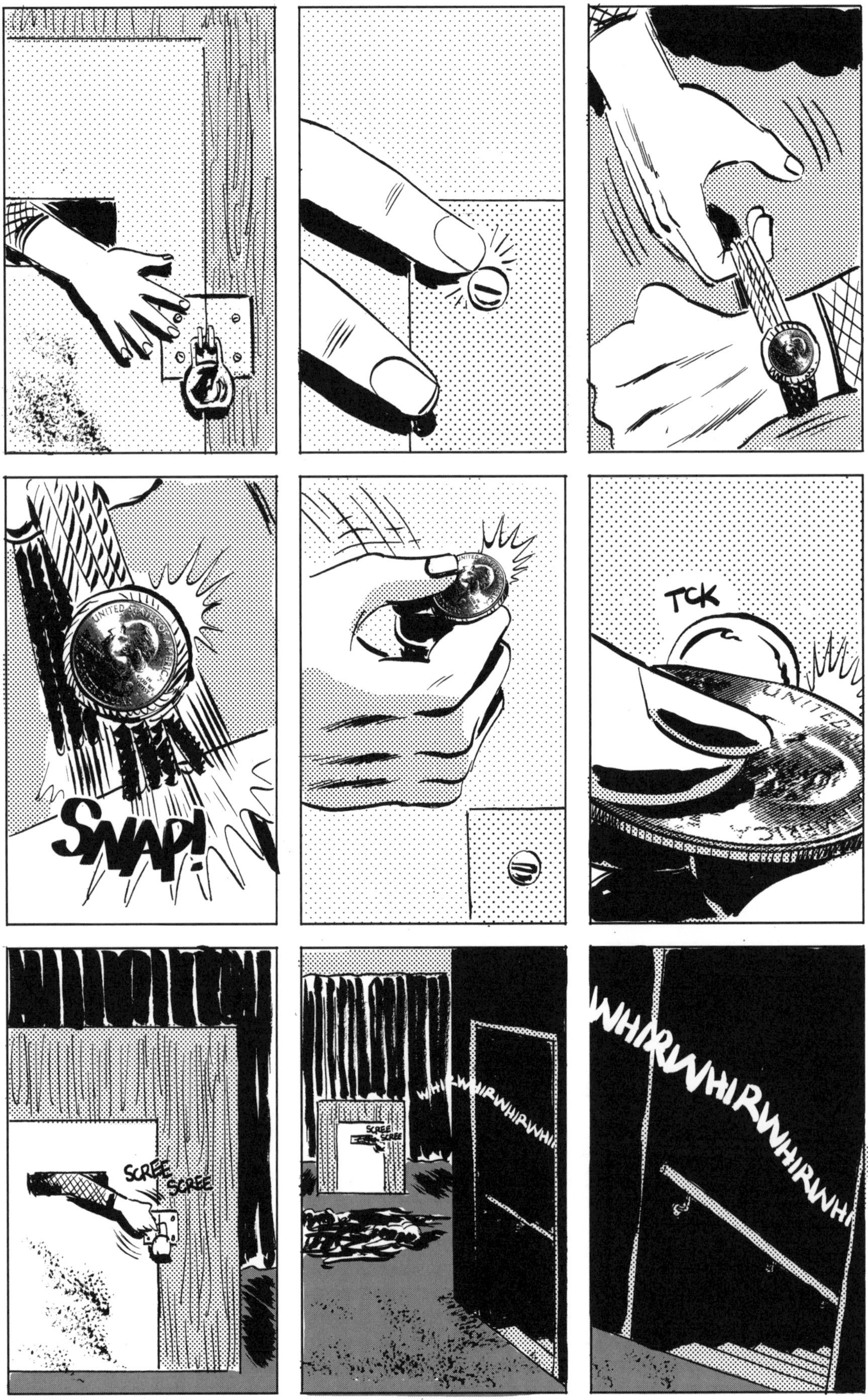
SNAP!
TCK
SCREE SCREE
SCREE SCREE
WHIRWHIRWHI
WHIRWHIRWHIRWHI

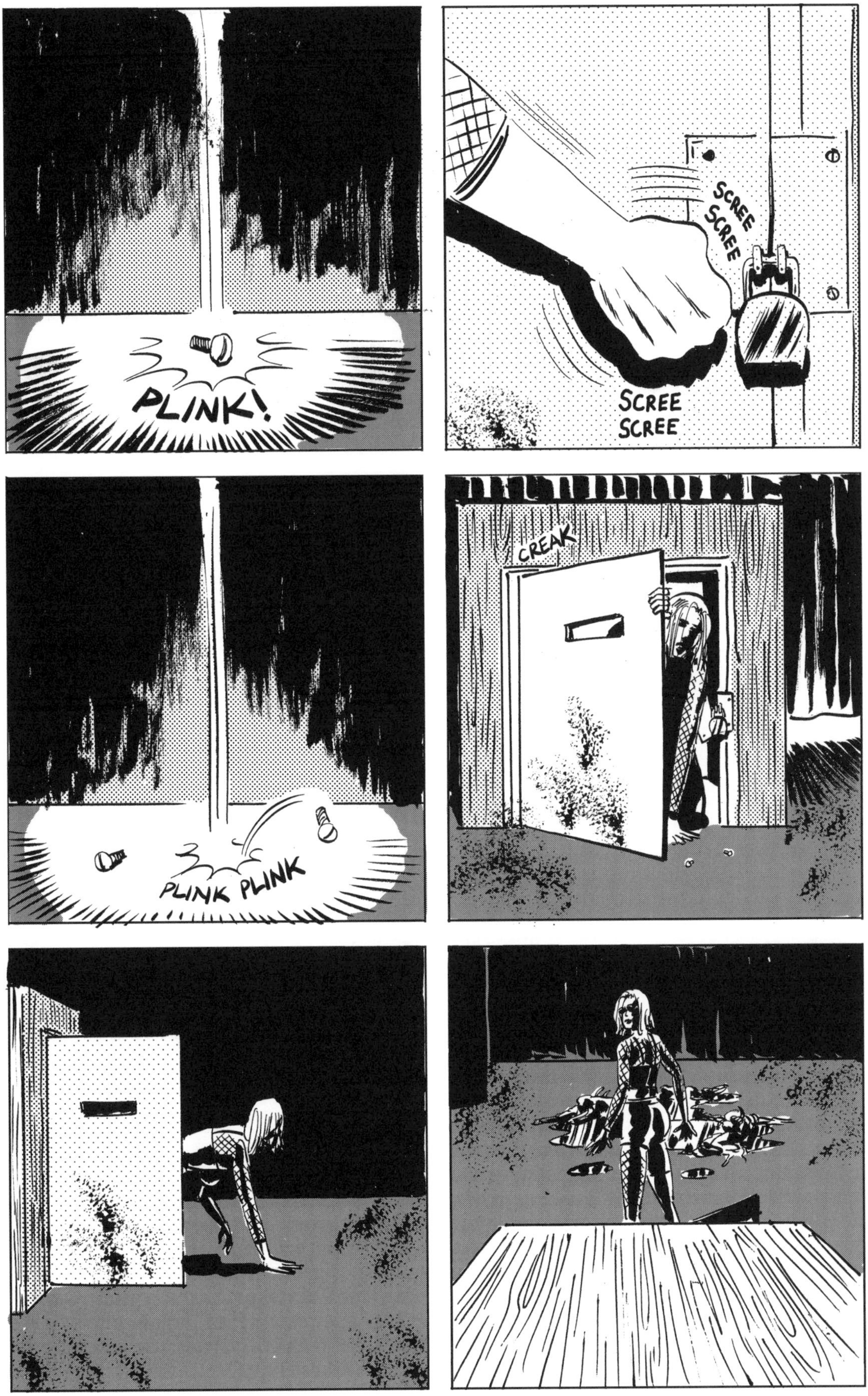
PLINK!
SCREE
SCREE
SCREE
SCREE
PLINK PLINK
CREAK

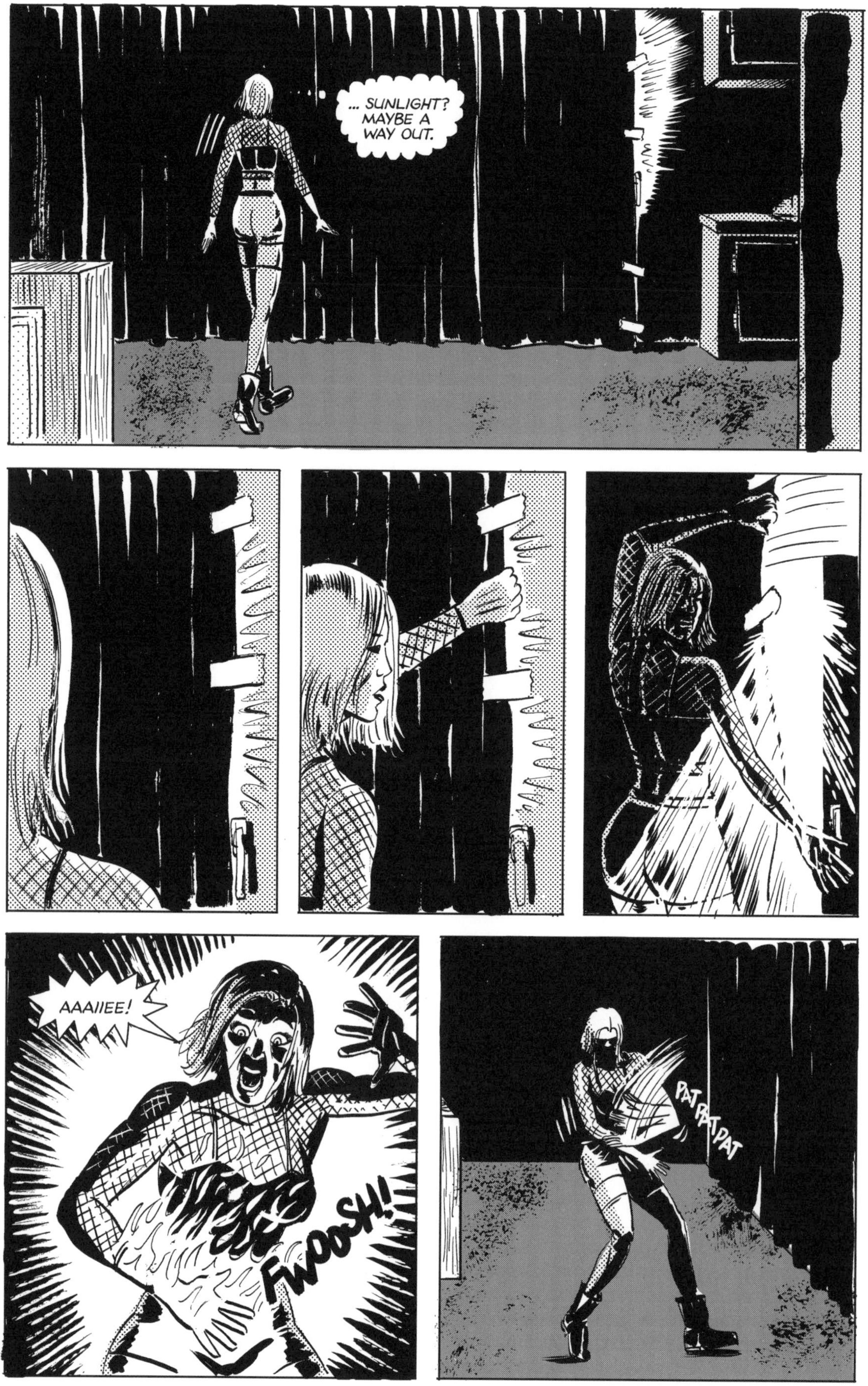

... SUNLIGHT? MAYBE A WAY OUT.
AAAIIEE!
FWOOSH!
PAT PAT PAT

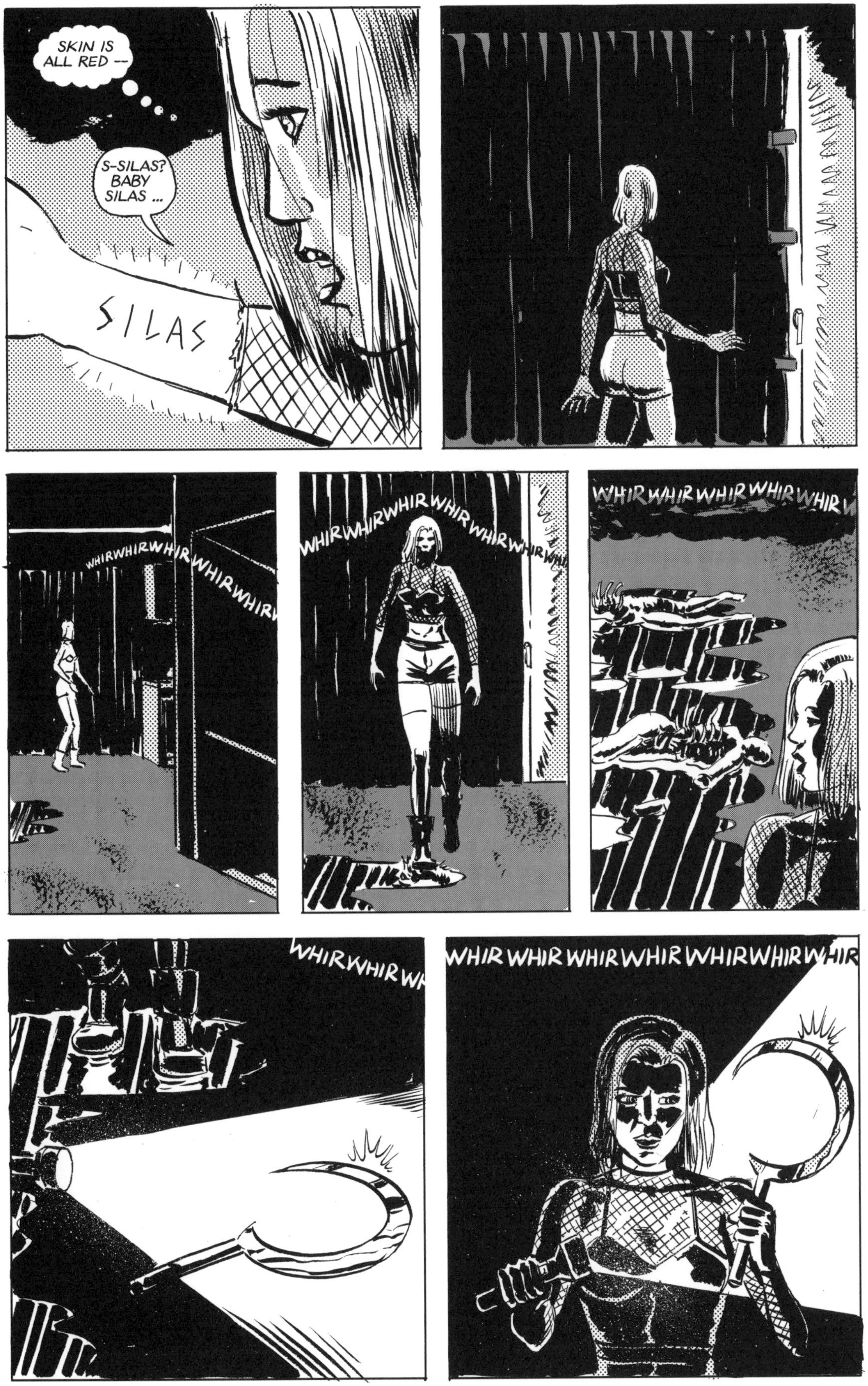
SKIN IS ALL RED --
S-SILAS? BABY SILAS ...
SILAS
WHIRWHIRWHIRWHIRWHIRW
WHIRWHIRWHIRWHIRWHIRWHIR
WHIRWHIRWHIRWHIRWHIR
WHIRWHIRWH
WHIR WHIR WHIR WHIR WHIR WHIR WHIR

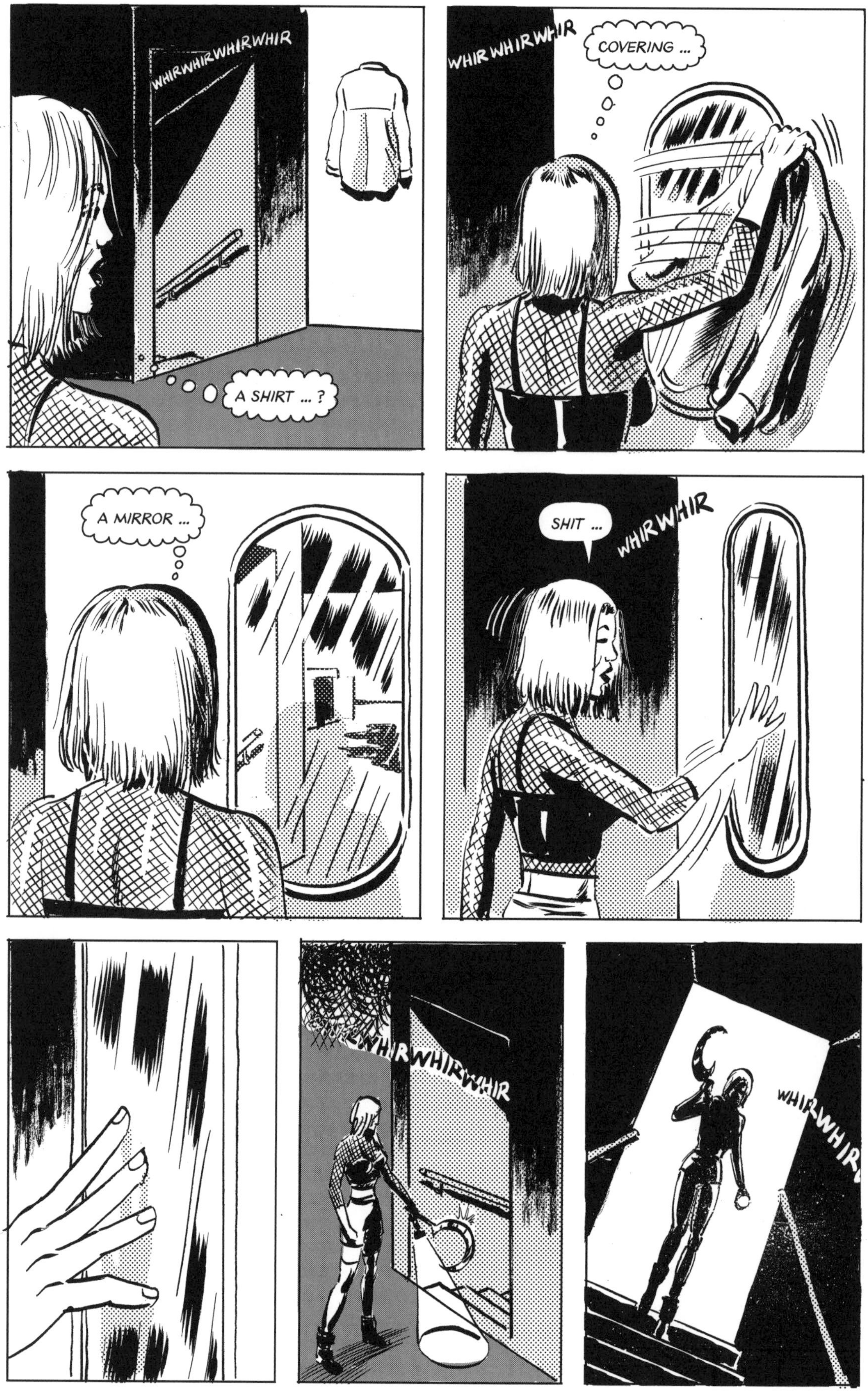
WHIRWHIRWHIRWHIR
A SHIRT ... ?
WHIRWHIRWHIR
COVERING ...
A MIRROR ...
SHIT ...
WHIRWHIR
WHIRWHIRWHIR
WHIRWHIR

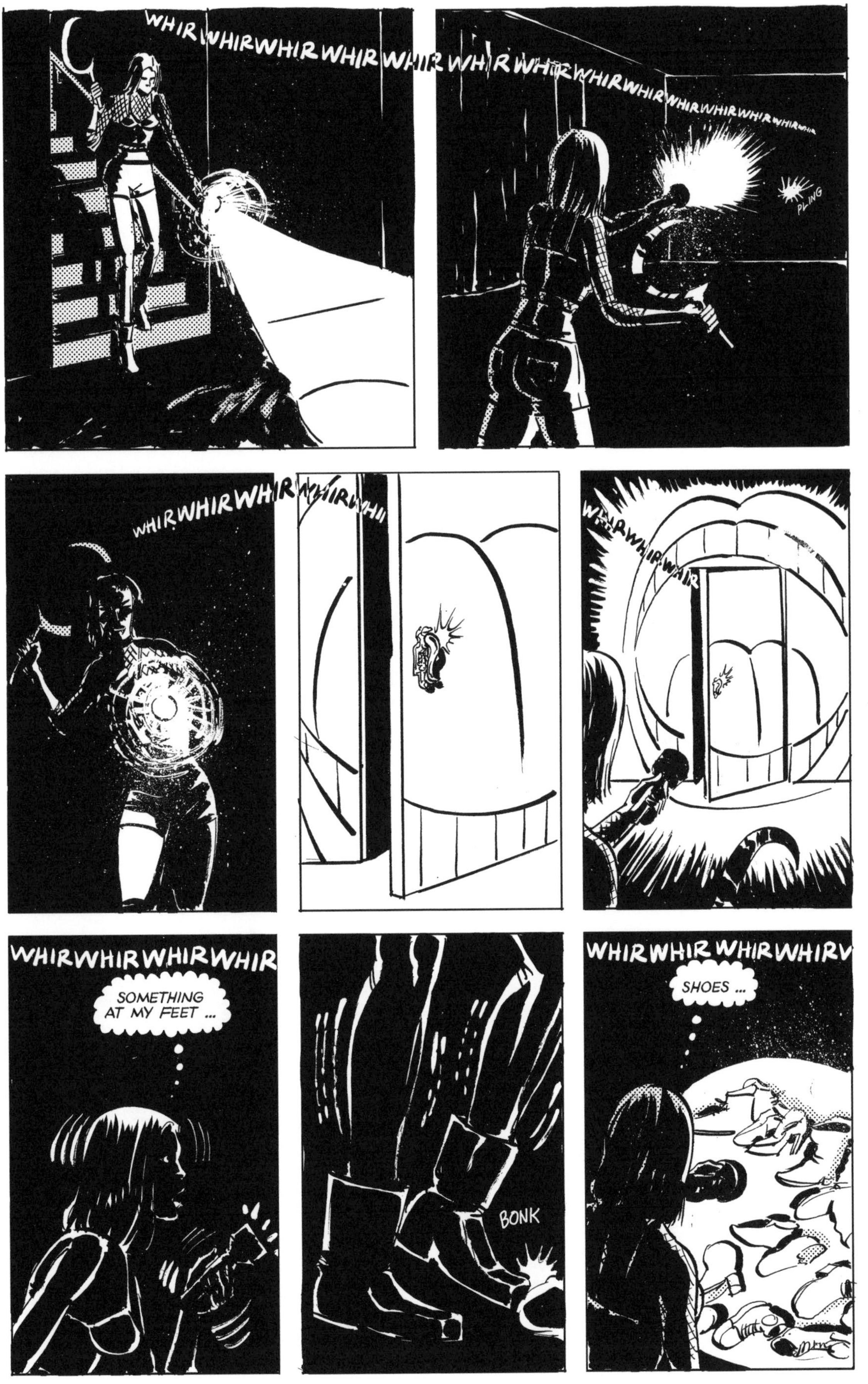
WHIRWHIRWHIRWHIRWHIRWHIRWHIRWHIRWHIRWHIRWHIRWHIR
PLING
WHIRWHIRWHIRWHIR
WHIRWHIRWHIR
WHIRWHIRWHIRWHIR
SOMETHING AT MY FEET ...
BONK
WHIRWHIR WHIRWHIR
SHOES ...

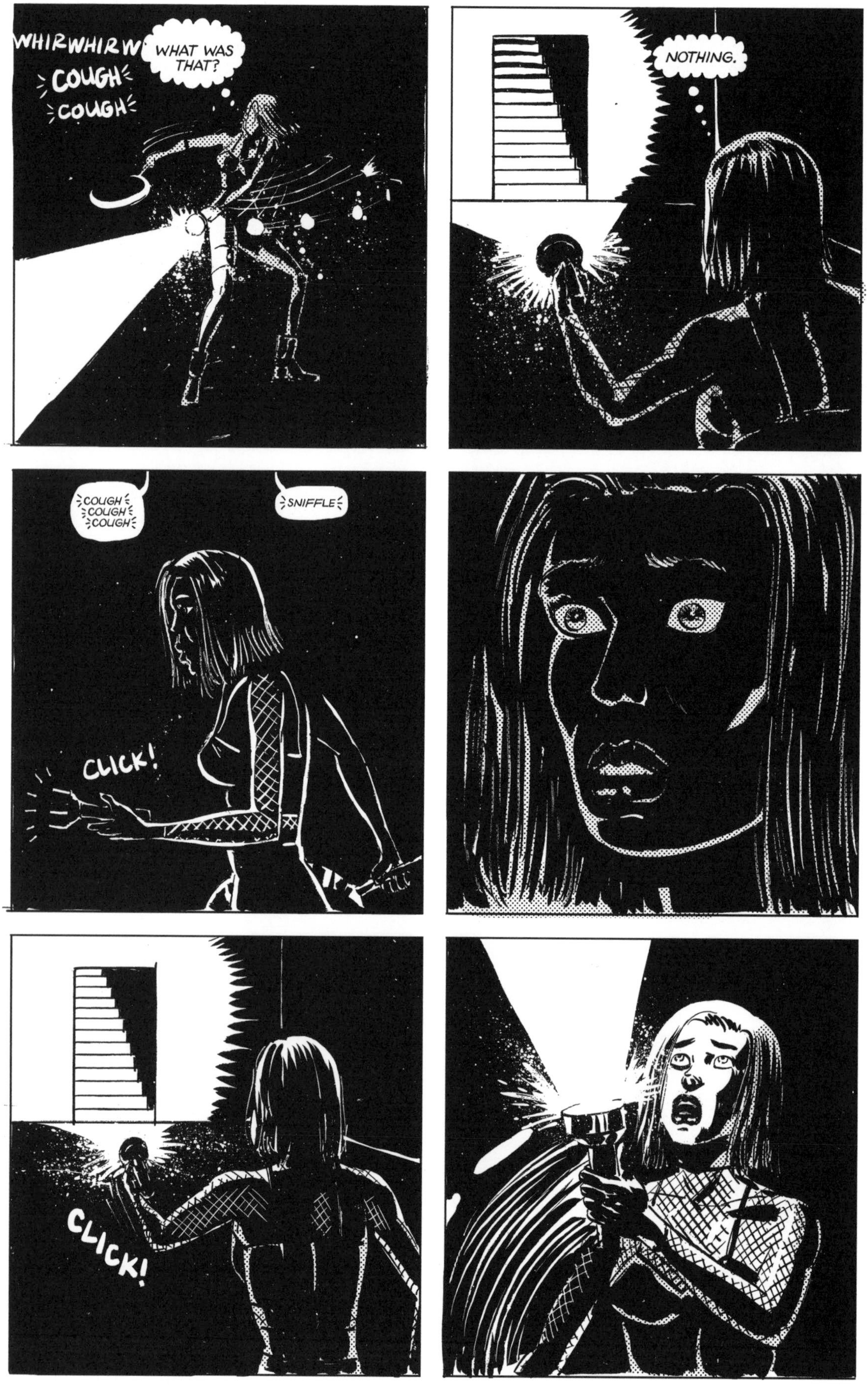

WHIRWHIRW
WHAT WAS THAT?
COUGH
COUGH
NOTHING.
COUGH COUGH COUGH
SNIFFLE
CLICK!
CLICK!

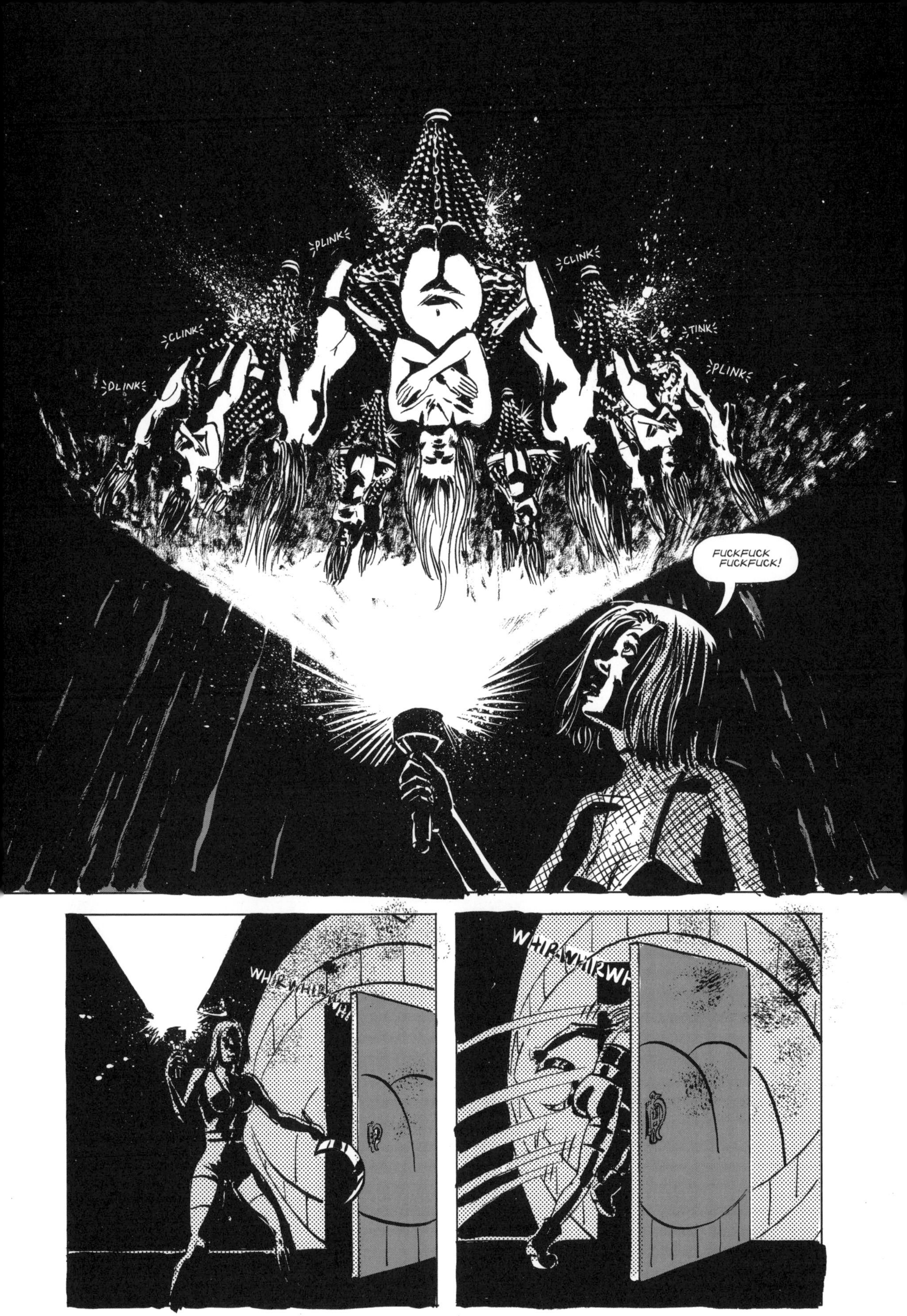
DLINK
CLINK
PLINK
CLINK
TINK
PLINK
FUCKFUCK FUCKFUCK!
WHIRWHIRWH
WHIRWHIRWH

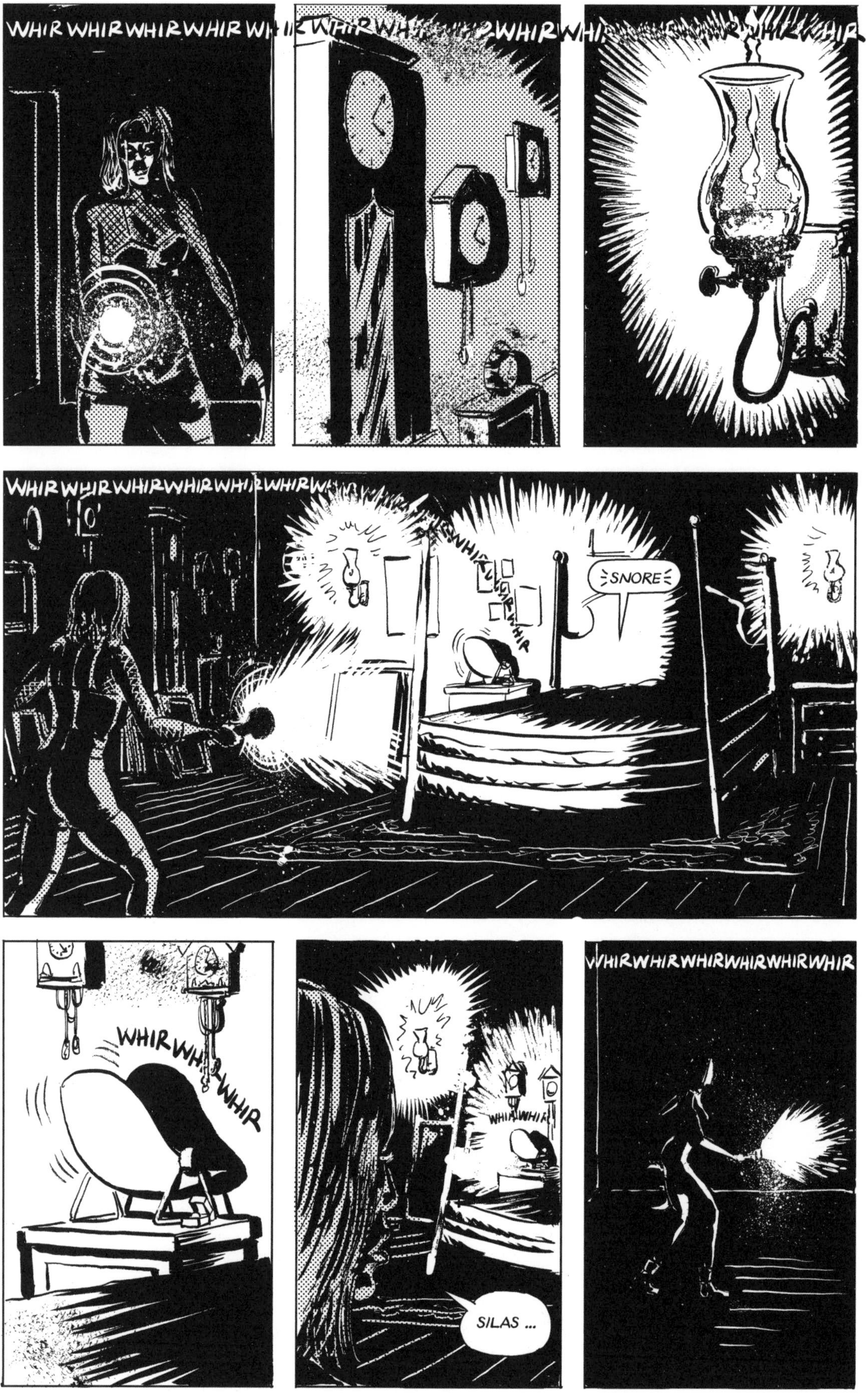
WHIR WHIR WHIR WHIR WHIR
WHIR WHIR WHIR
WHIR WHIR WHIR WHIR WHIR WHIR
SNORE
WHIR WHIR WHIR
WHIR WHIR
SILAS ...
WHIR WHIR WHIR WHIR WHIR

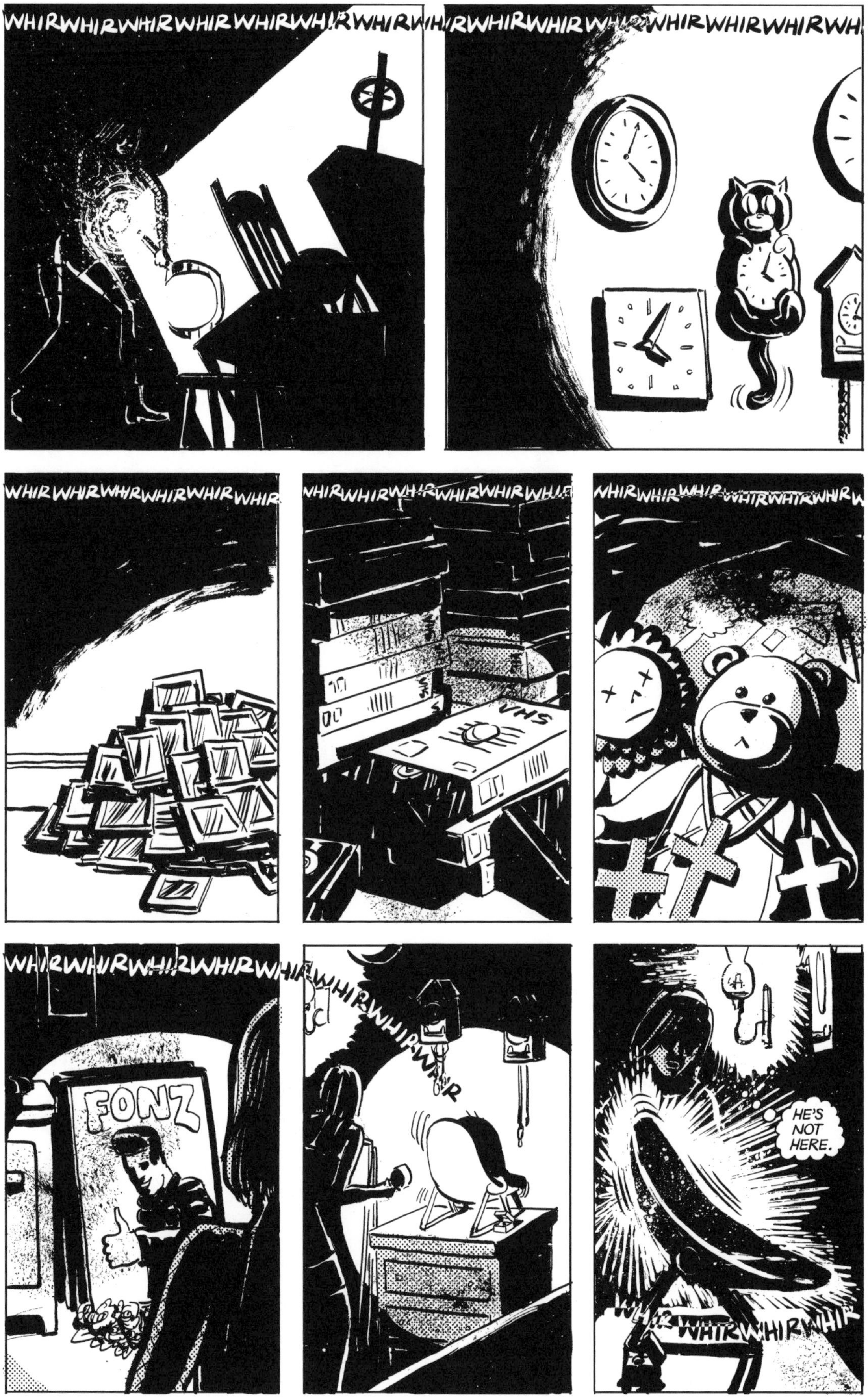
WHIRWHIRWHIRWHIRWHIRWHIRWHIR
WHIRWHIRWHIRWHIRWHIR
WHIRWHIRWHIRWHIRWHIRWHIR
WHIRWHIR
VHS
WHIRWHIRWHIRWHIR
WHIRWHIRWHIRWHIR
FONZ
WHIRWHIR
HE'S NOT HERE.
WHIRWHIRWHIR

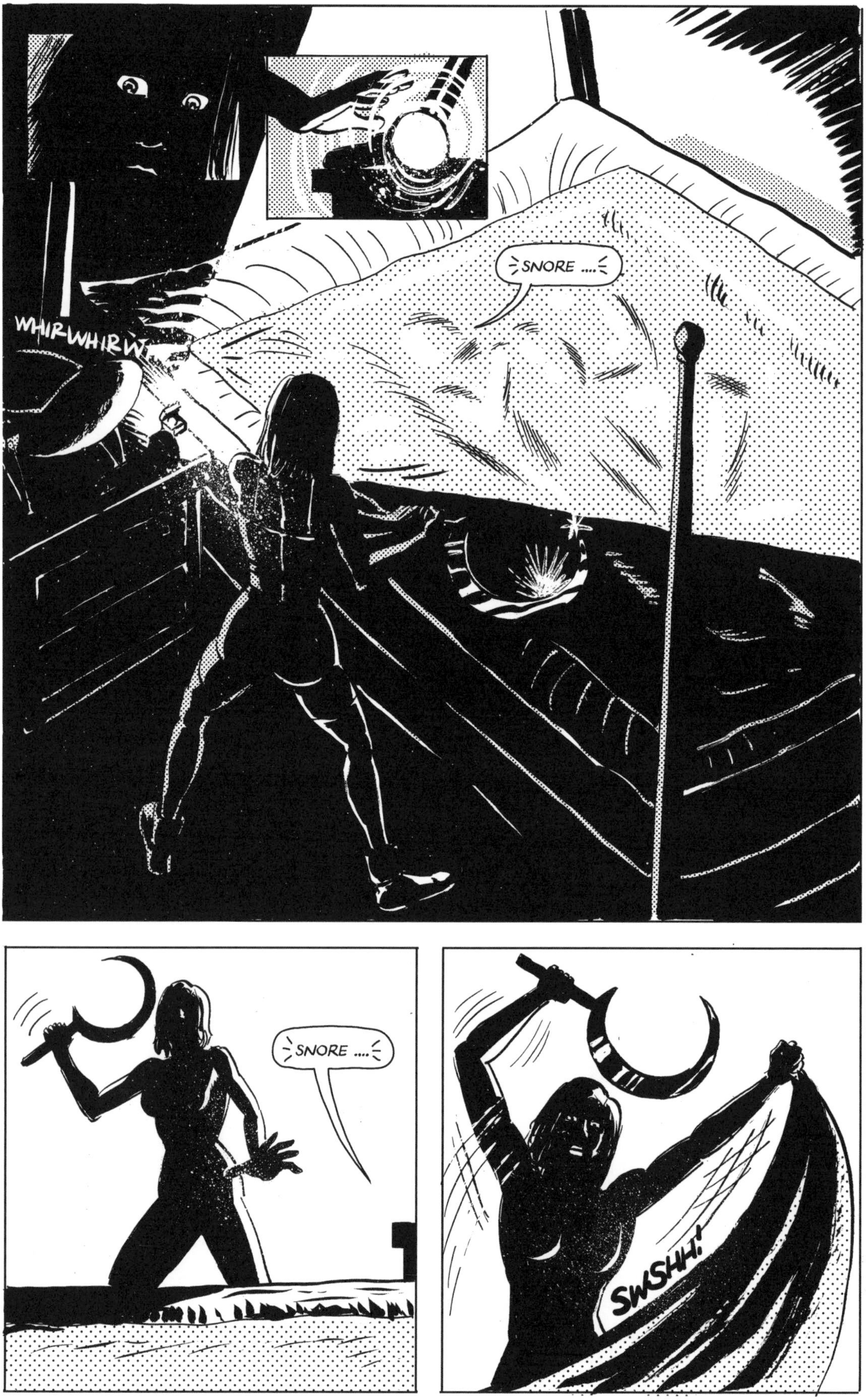
SNORE ....
WHIRWHIRW
SNORE ....
SWSHH!

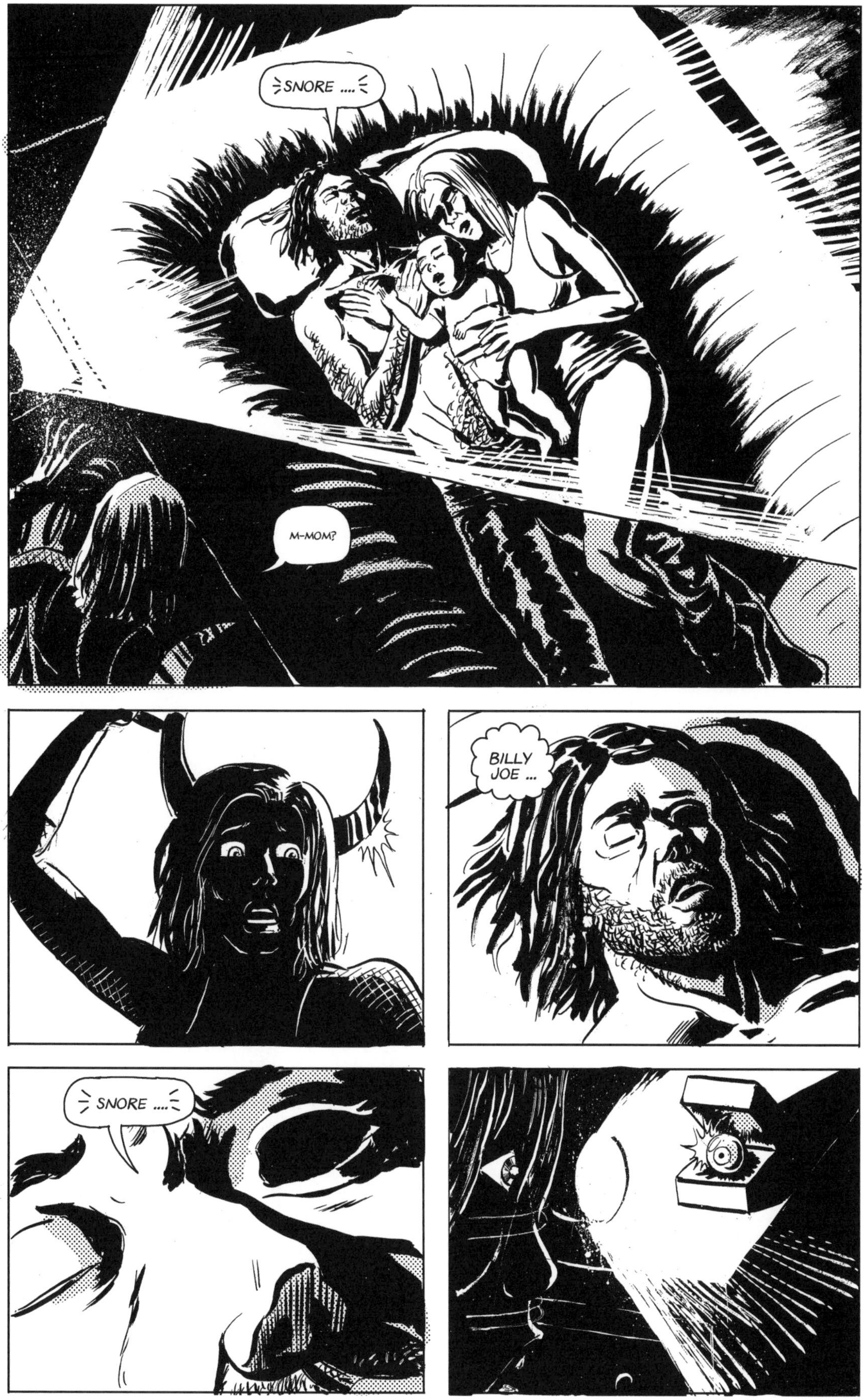
SNORE ....
M-MOM?
BILLY JOE ...
SNORE ....

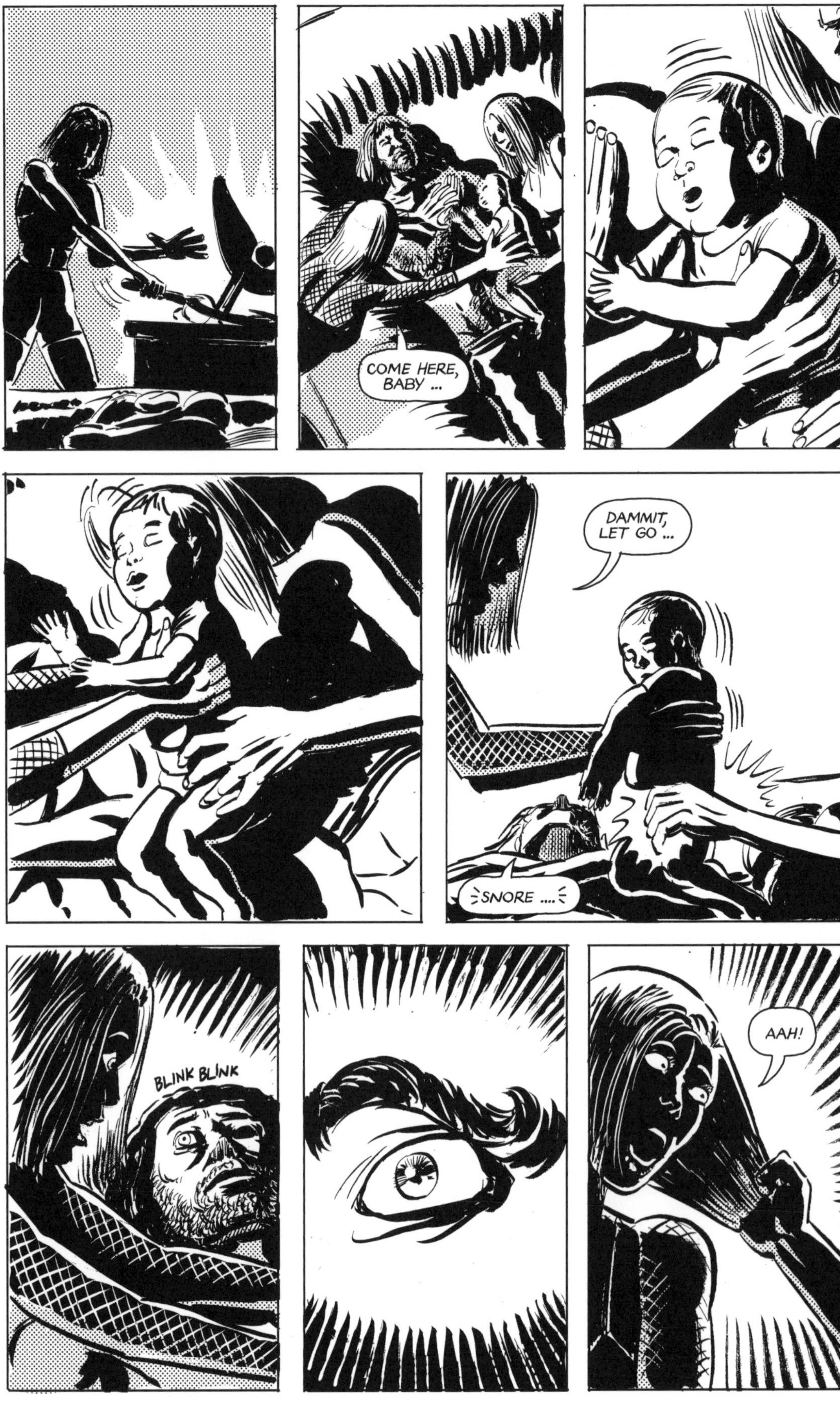
COME HERE, BABY ...
DAMMIT, LET GO ...
SNORE ....
BLINK BLINK
AAH!

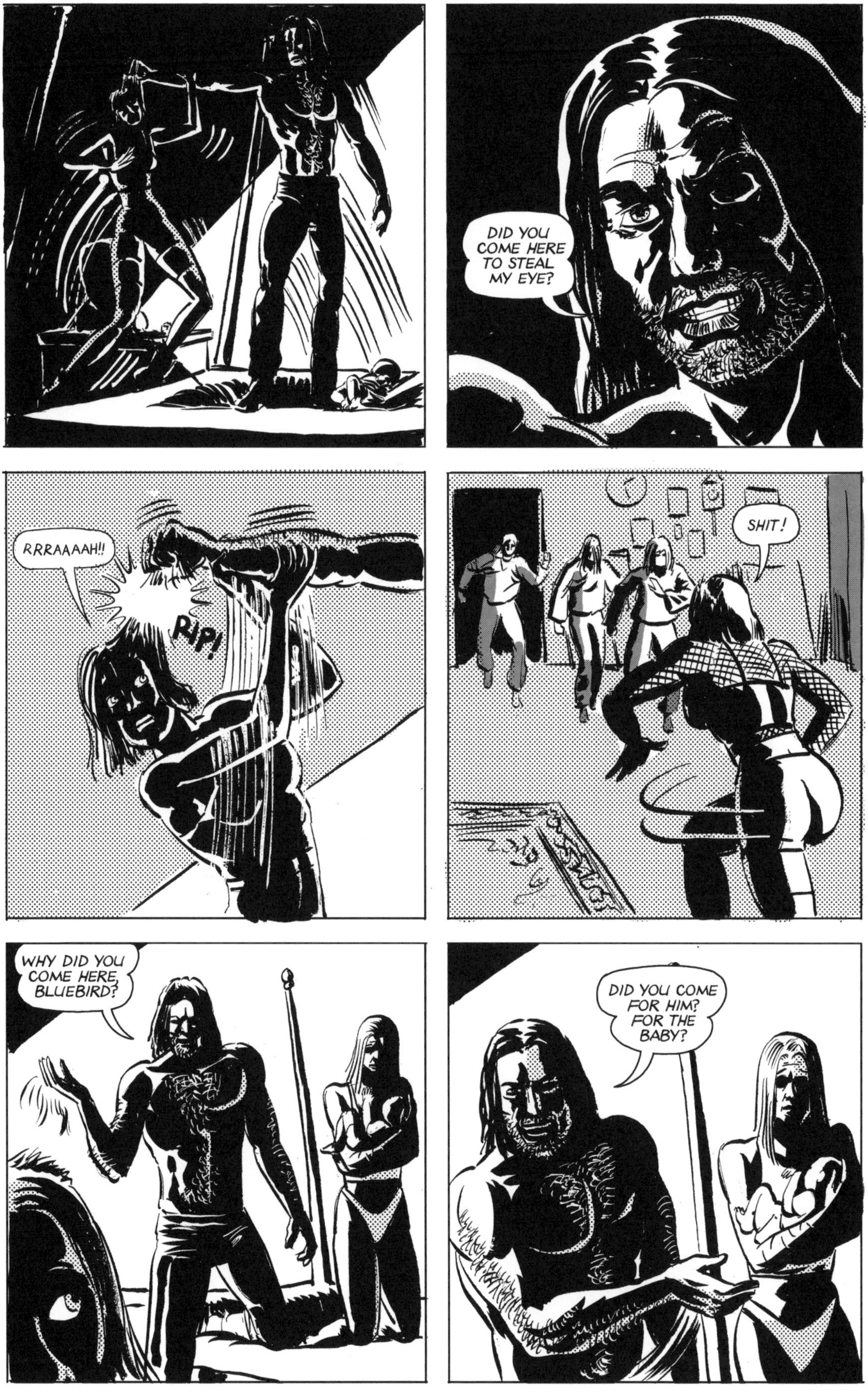
DID YOU COME HERE TO STEAL MY EYE?
RRRAAAAAH!!
RIP!
SHIT!
WHY DID YOU COME HERE, BLUEBIRD?
DID YOU COME FOR HIM? FOR THE BABY?

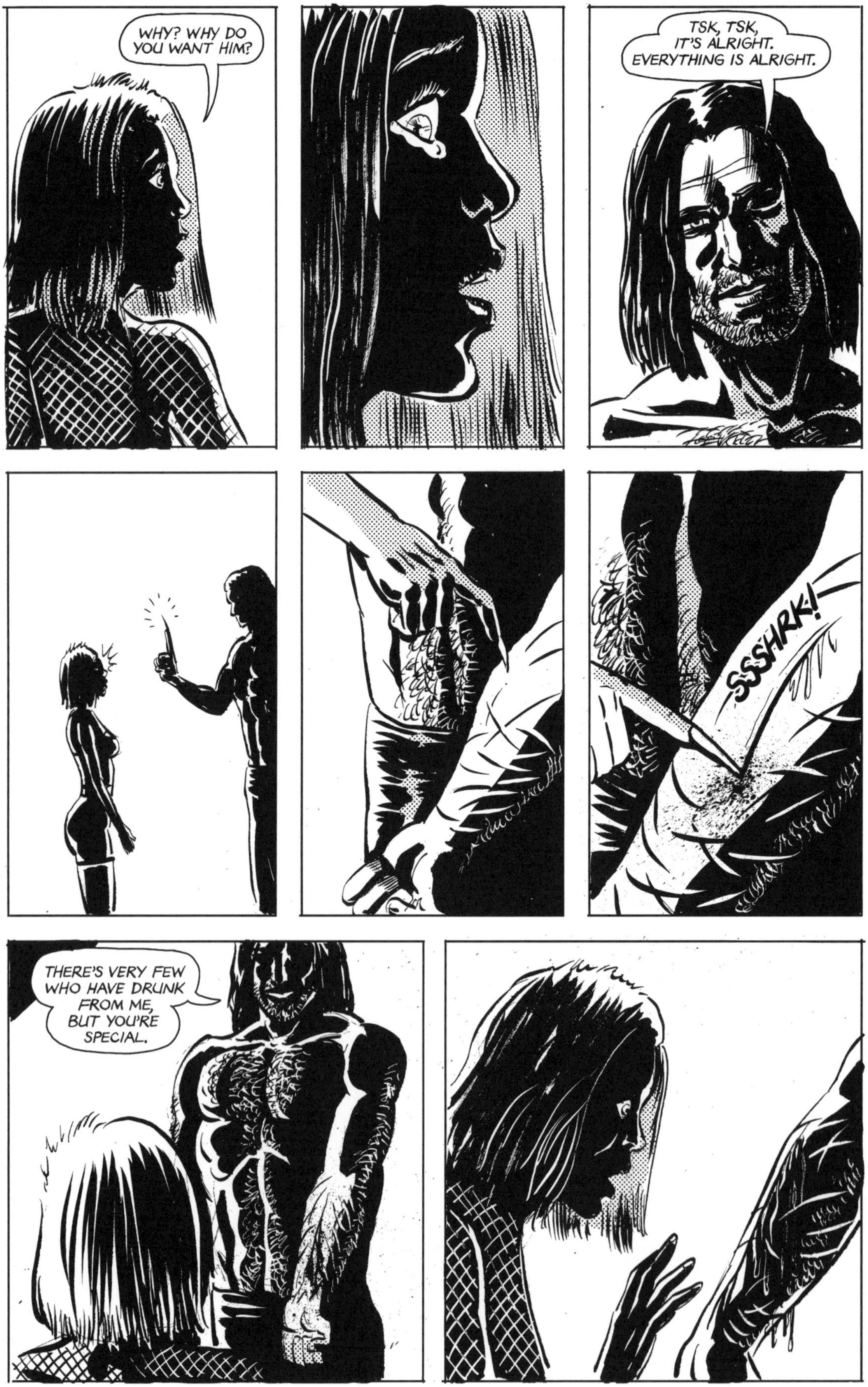
WHY? WHY DO YOU WANT HIM?
TSK, TSK, IT'S ALRIGHT. EVERYTHING IS ALRIGHT.
SSSHRK!
THERE'S VERY FEW WHO HAVE DRUNK FROM ME, BUT YOU'RE SPECIAL.

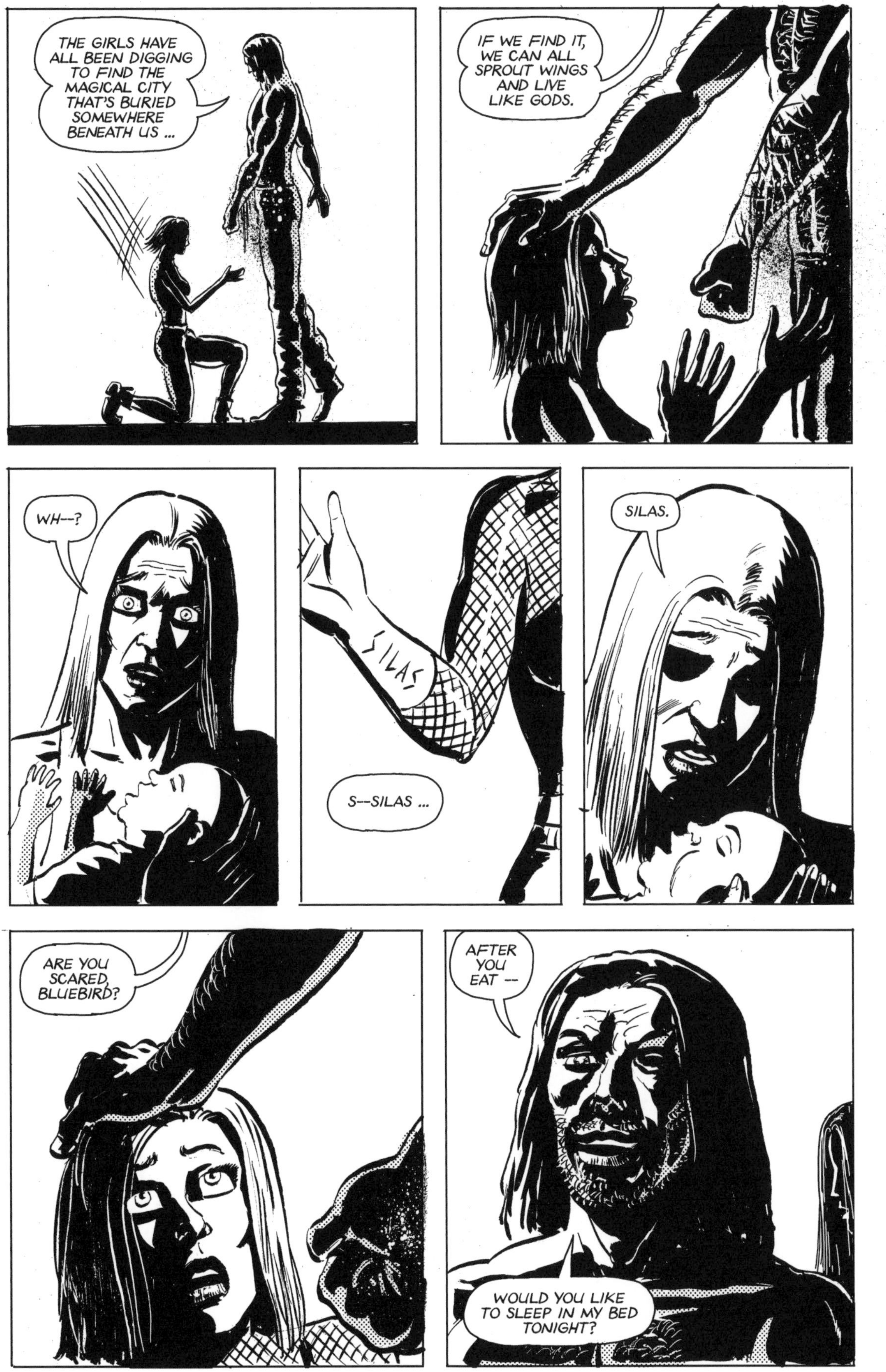
THE GIRLS HAVE ALL BEEN DIGGING TO FIND THE MAGICAL CITY THAT'S BURIED SOMEWHERE BENEATH US ...
IF WE FIND IT, WE CAN ALL SPROUT WINGS AND LIVE LIKE GODS.
WH--?
SILAS
S--SILAS ...
SILAS.
ARE YOU SCARED, BLUEBIRD?
AFTER YOU EAT --
WOULD YOU LIKE TO SLEEP IN MY BED TONIGHT?

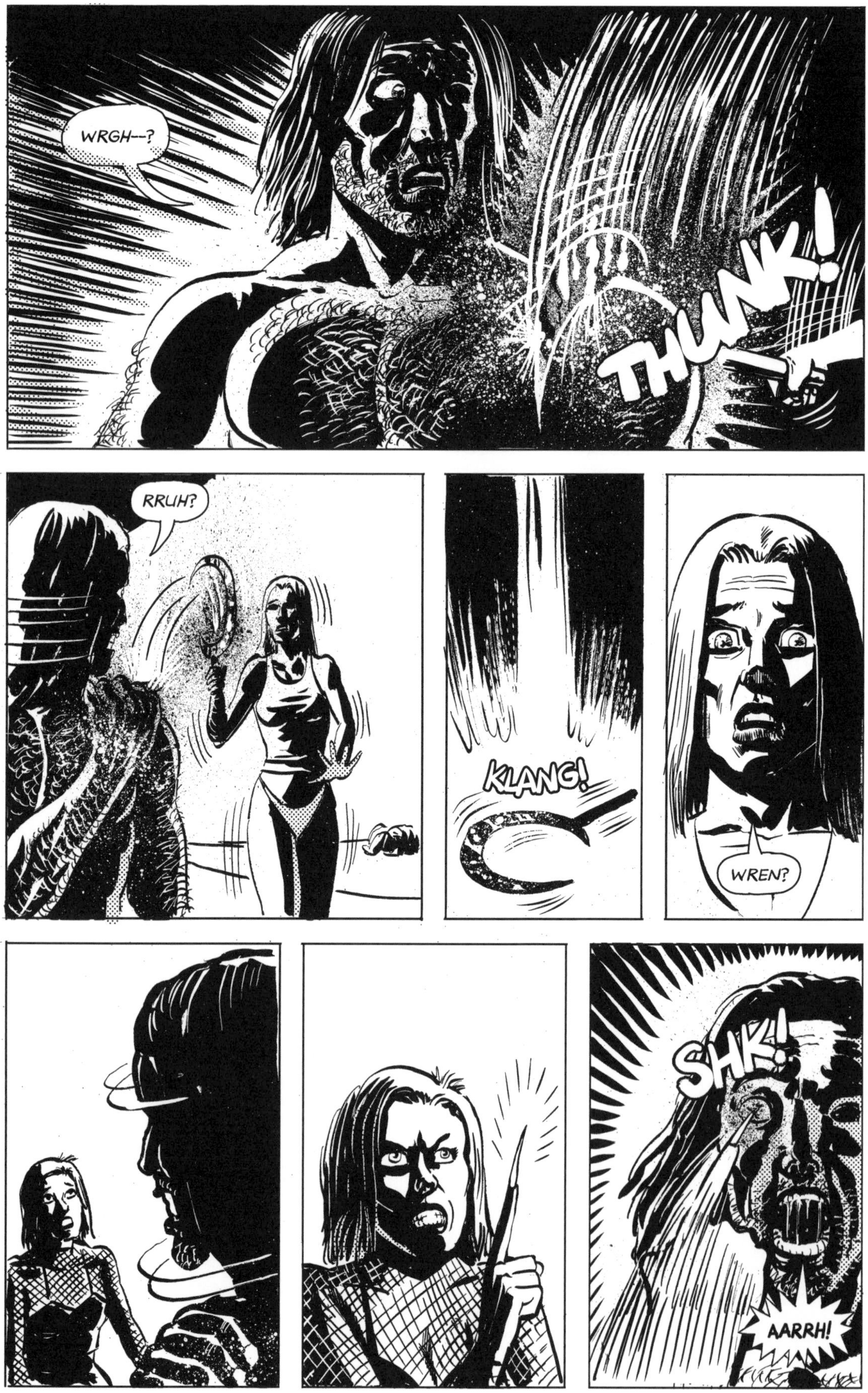
WRGH--?
THUNK!
RRUH?
KLANG!
WREN?
SHK!
AARRH!

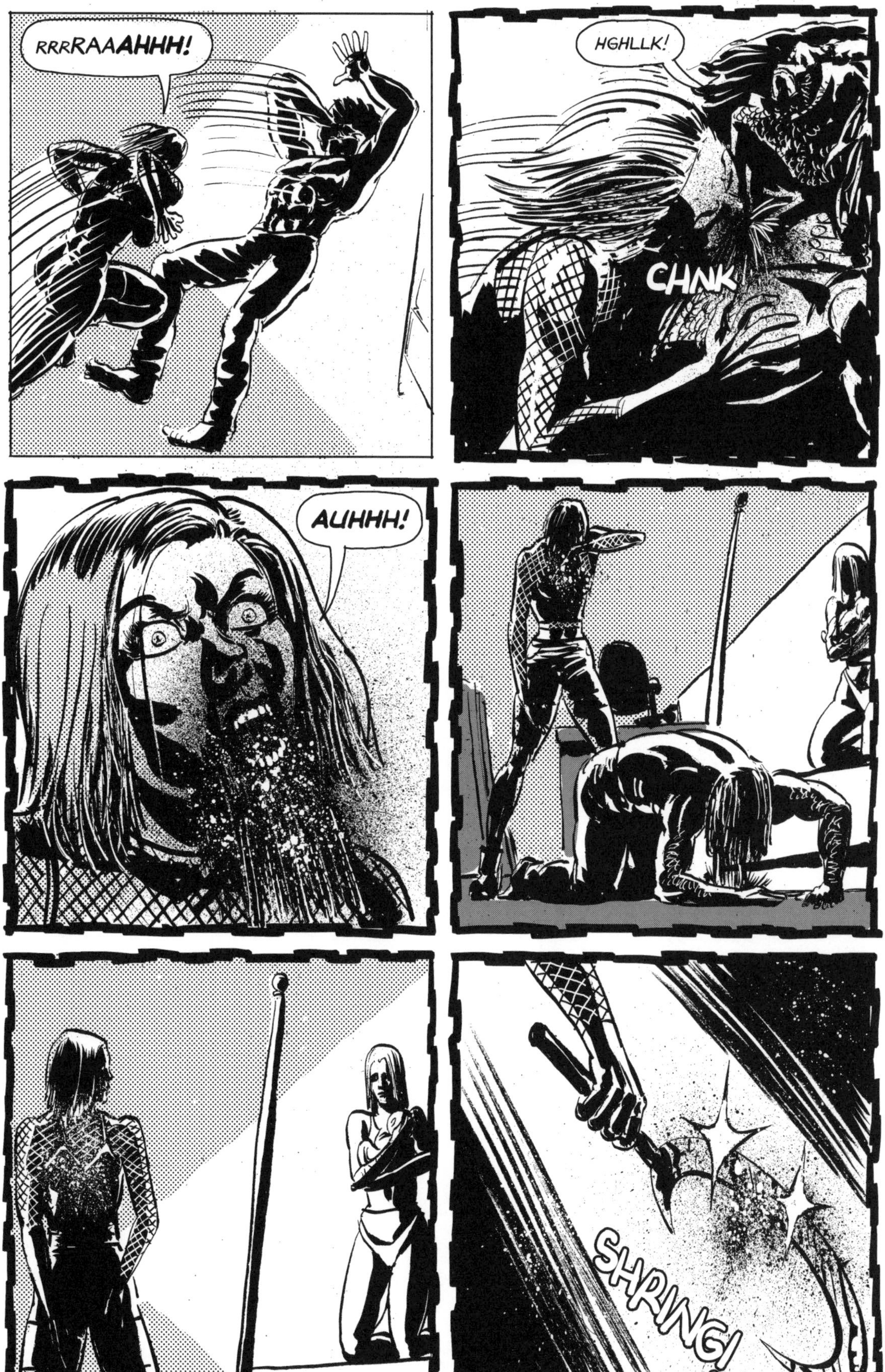
RRRRAAAHHH!
HGHLLK!
CHNK
AUHHH!
SHRING!

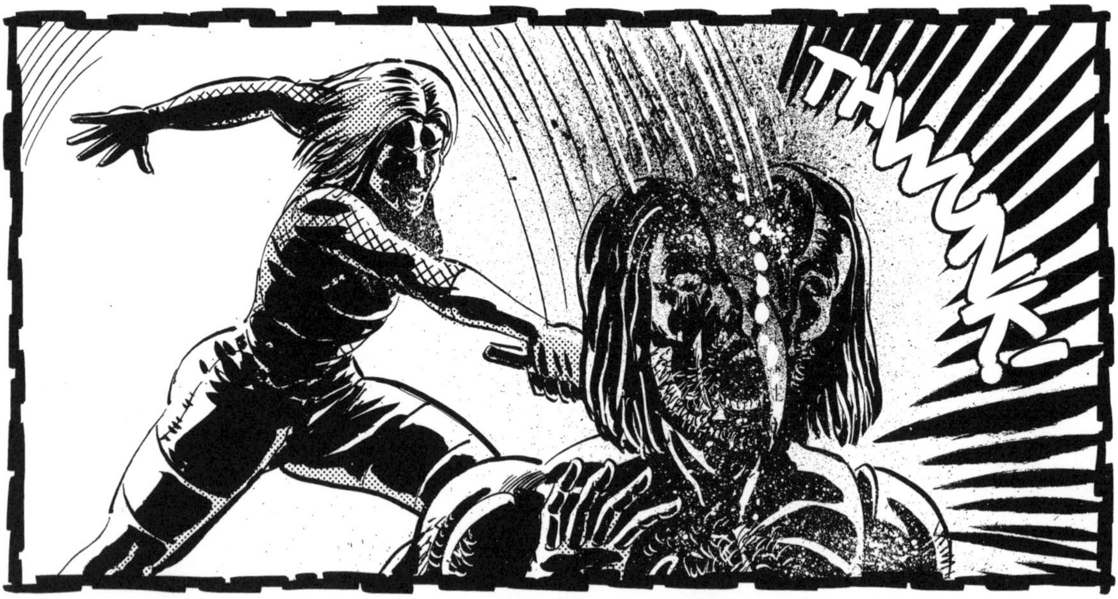
THWUNK!

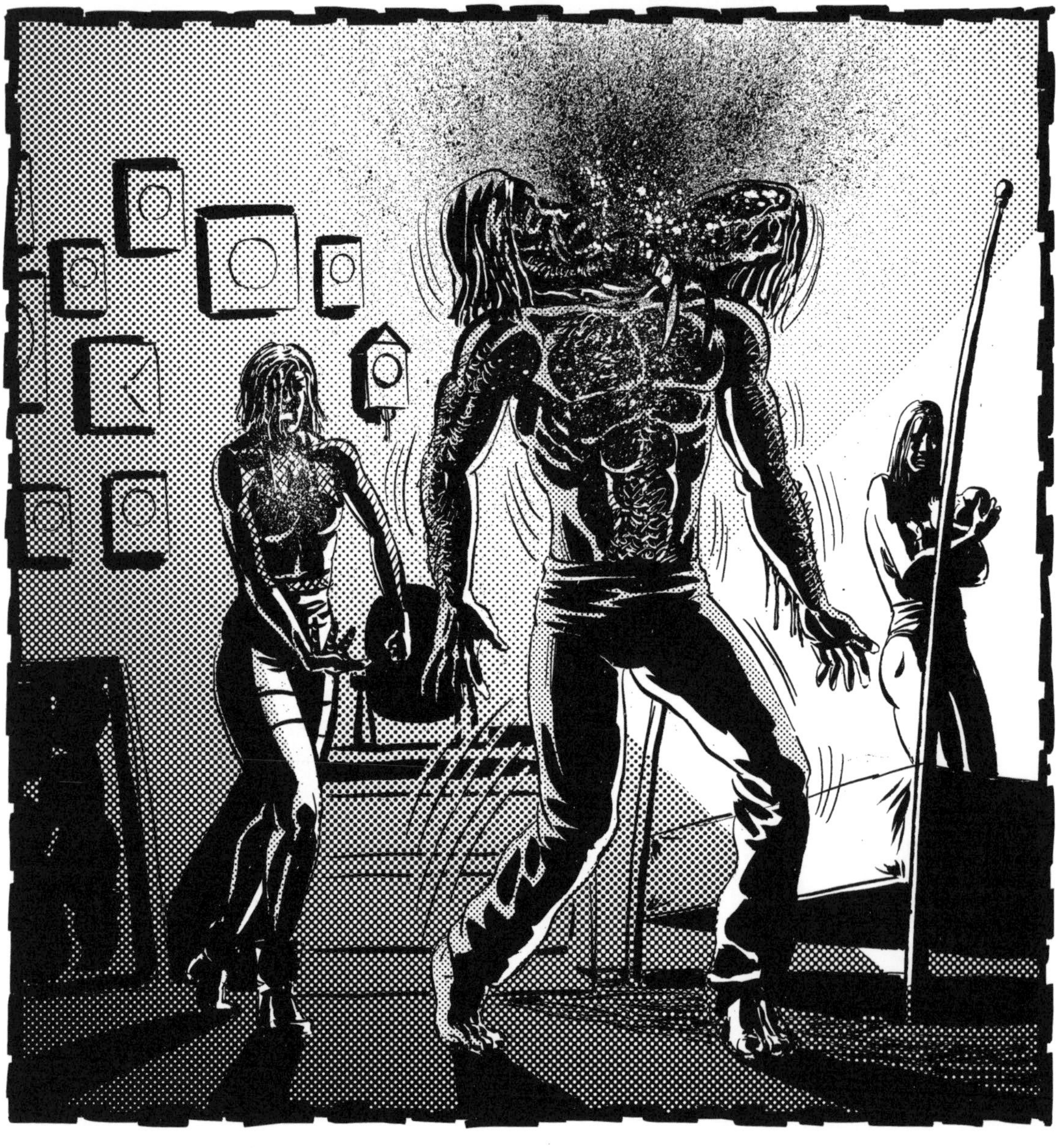

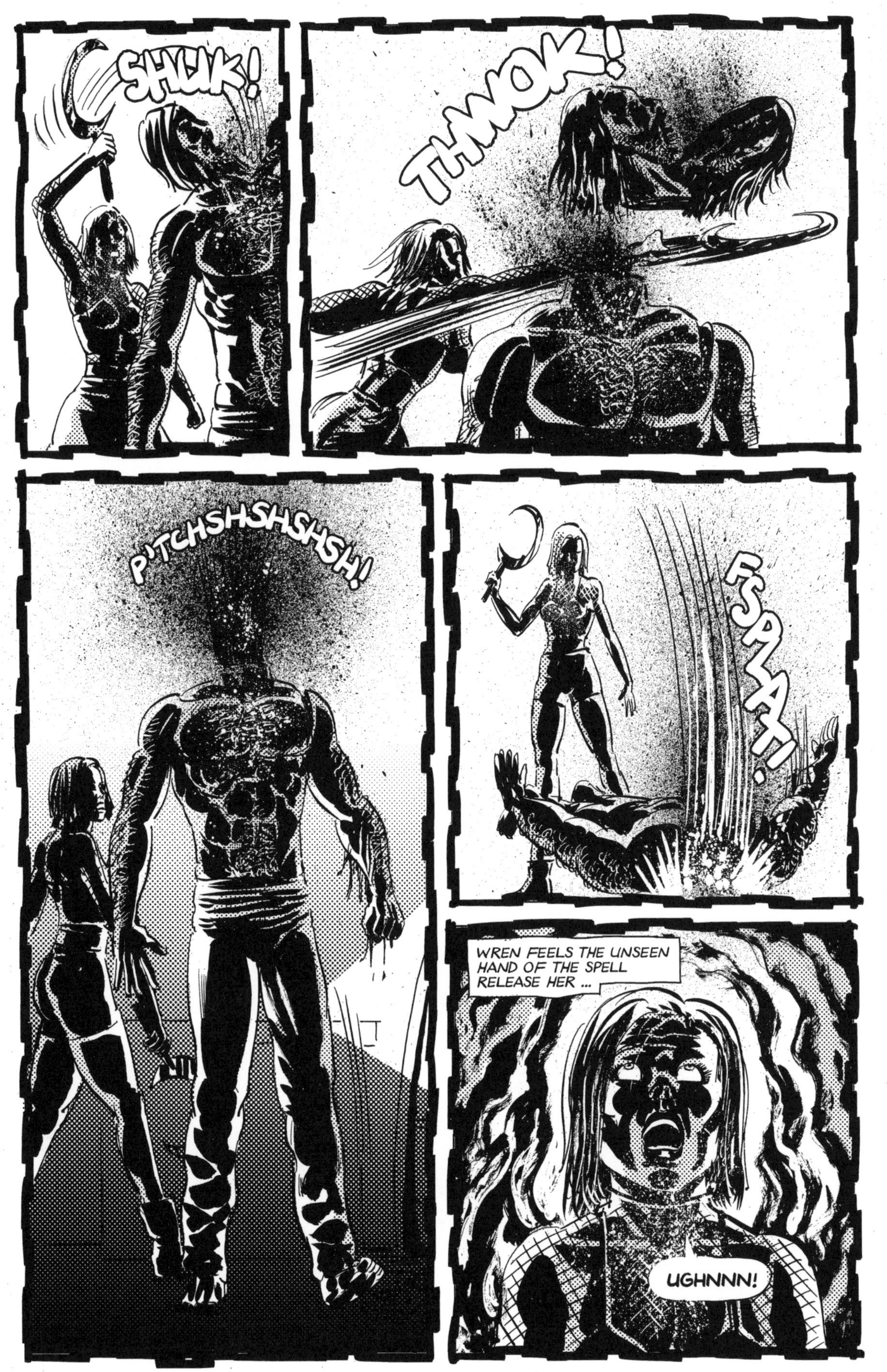
SHUK!
THWOK!
P'TCHSHSHSHSH!
FSPLAT!
WREN FEELS THE UNSEEN HAND OF THE SPELL RELEASE HER ...
UGHNNN!

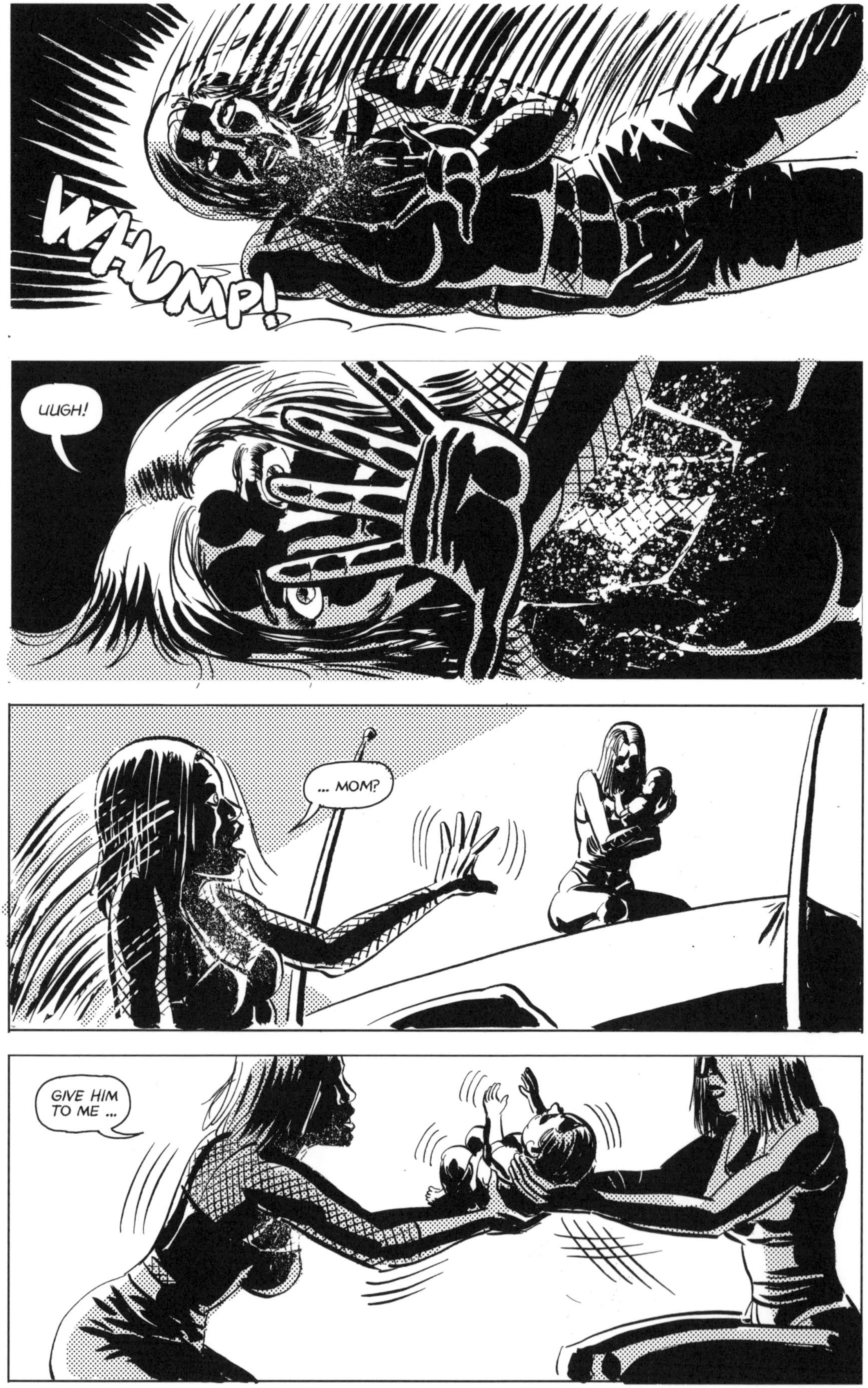
WHUMP!
UUGH!
... MOM?
GIVE HIM TO ME ...

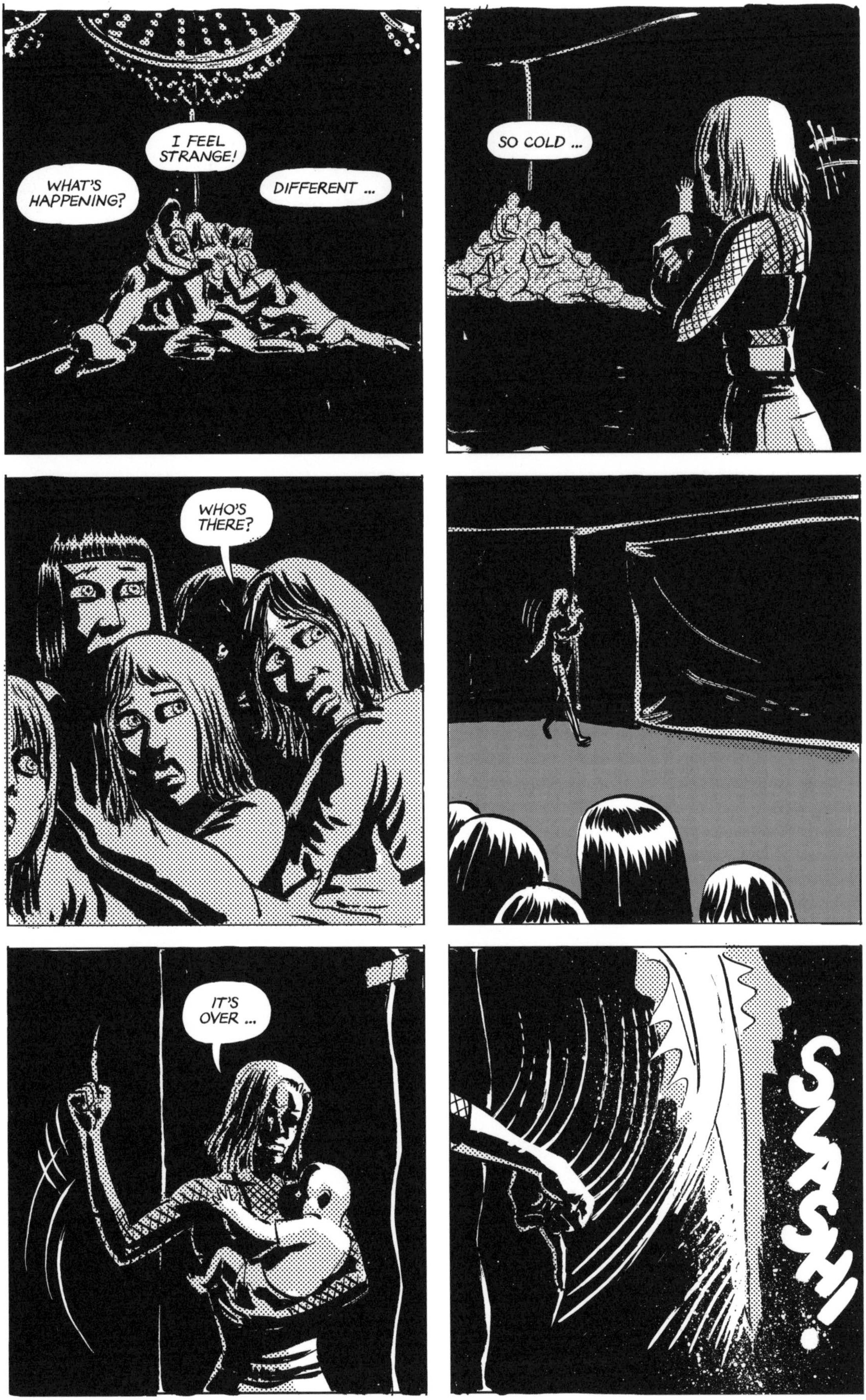
I FEEL STRANGE!
WHAT'S HAPPENING?
DIFFERENT ...
SO COLD ...
WHO'S THERE?
IT'S OVER ...
SHASHI!

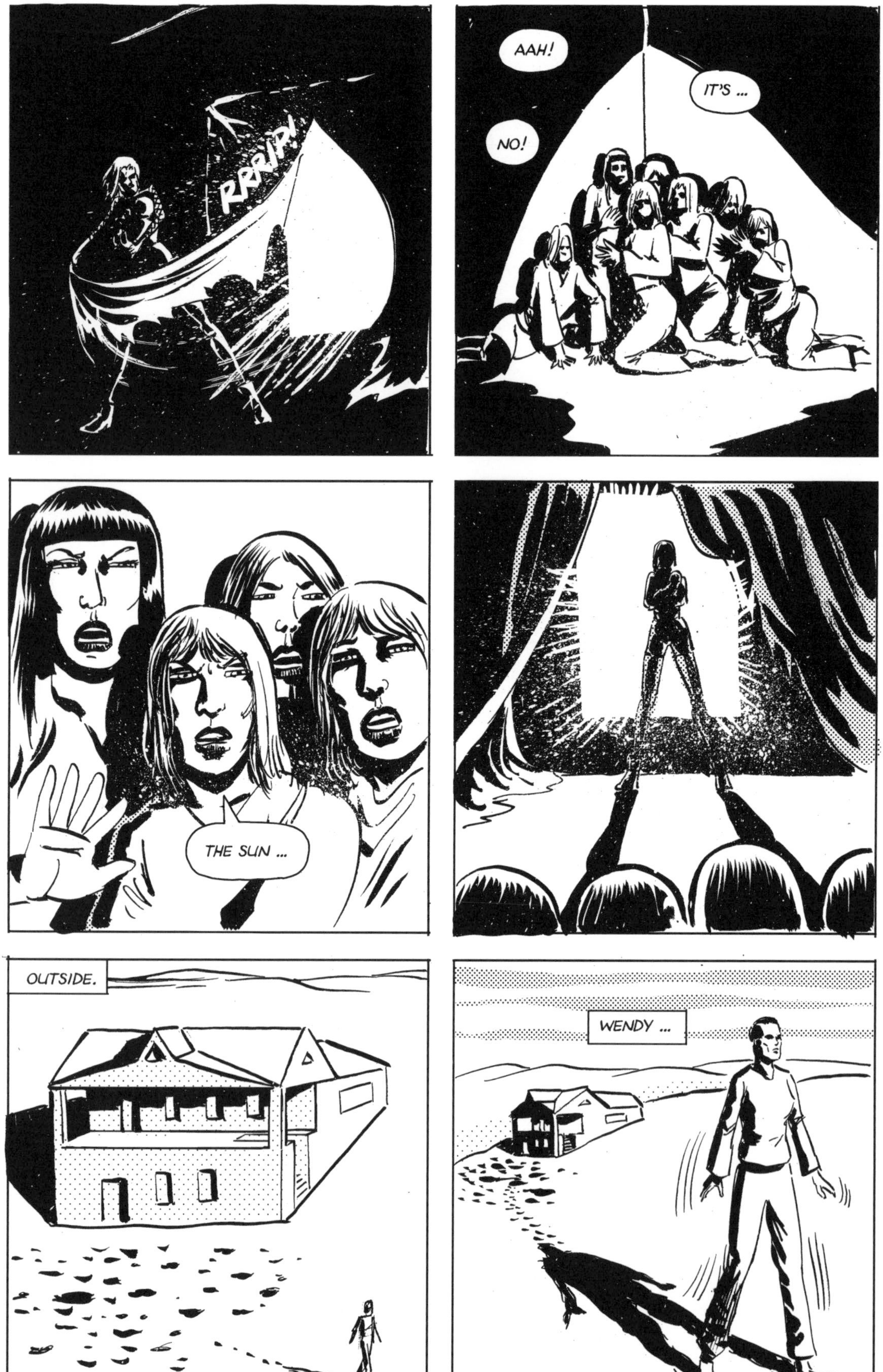
RRRIP!
AAH!
IT'S ...
NO!
THE SUN ...
OUTSIDE.
WENDY ...

HOME.

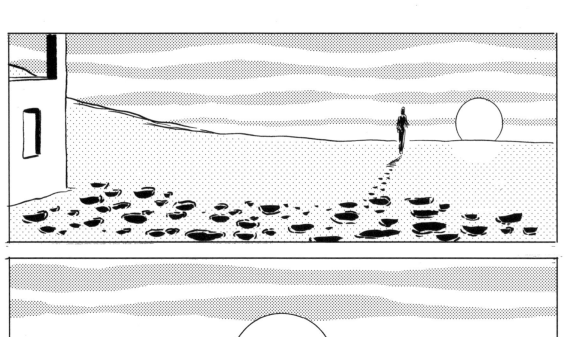

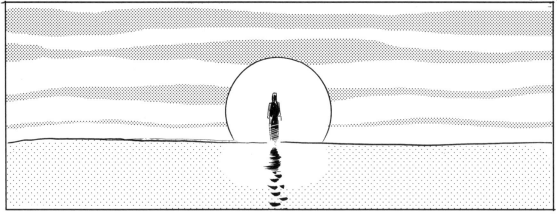

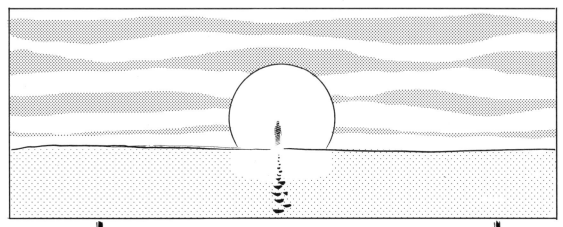

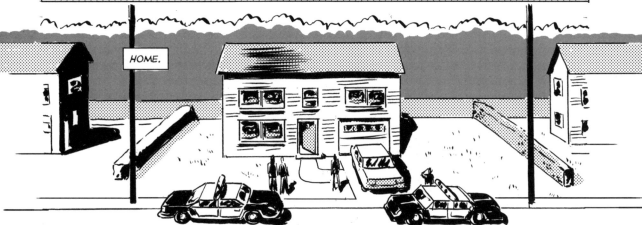

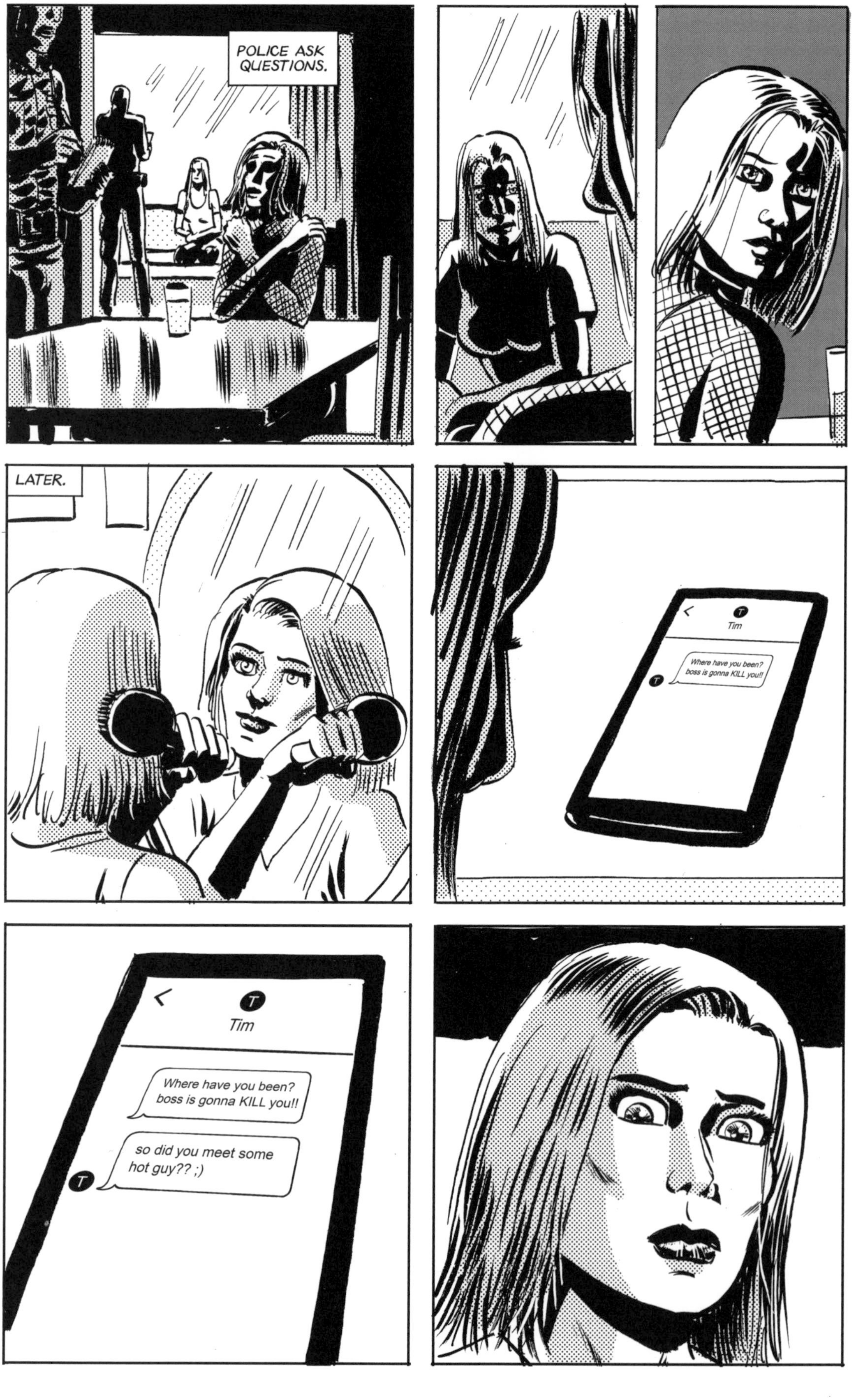
POLICE ASK QUESTIONS.
LATER.
Tim
Where have you been? boss is gonna KILL you!!
Tim
Where have you been? boss is gonna KILL you!!
so did you meet some hot guy?? ;)

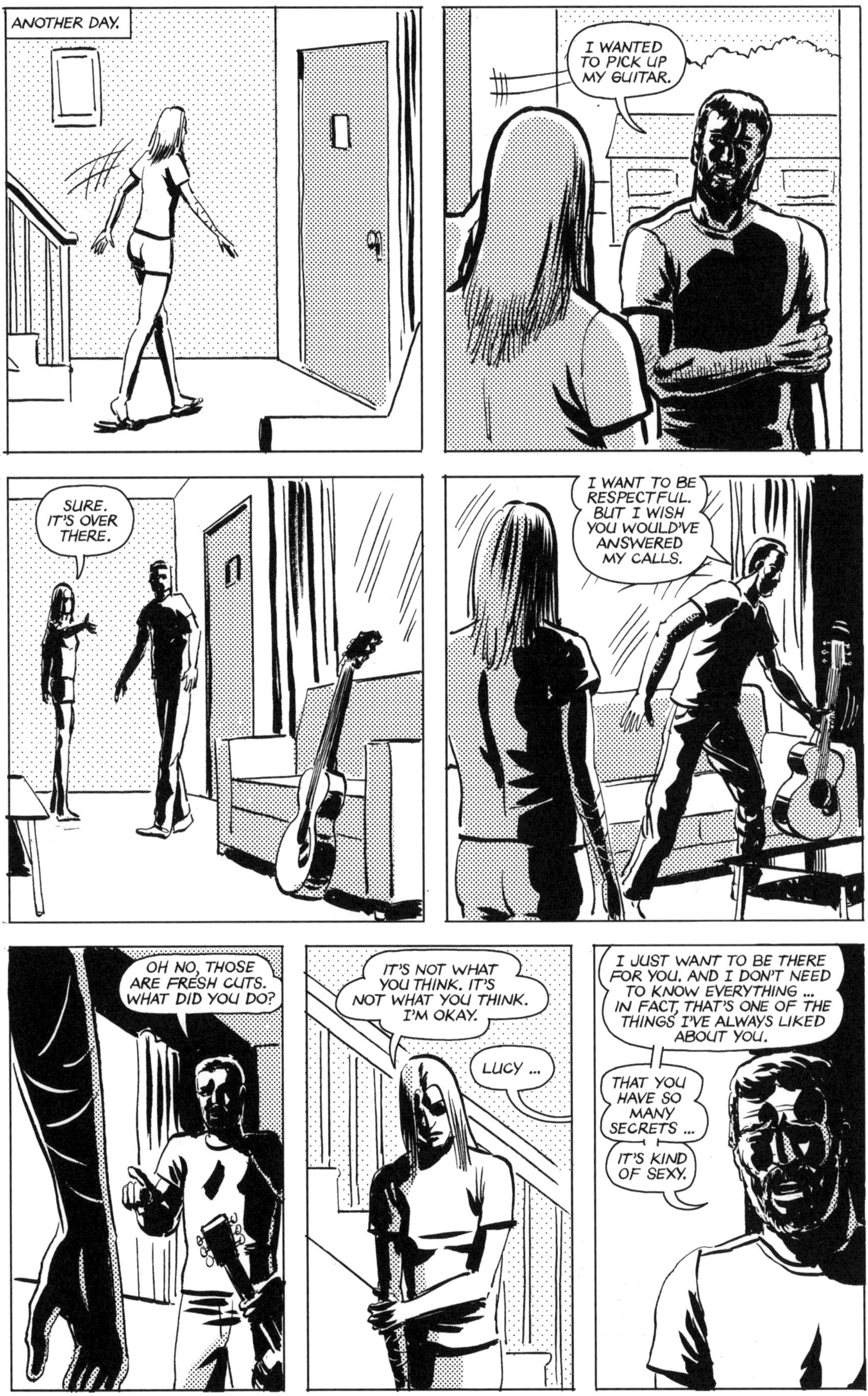
ANOTHER DAY.
I WANTED TO PICK UP MY GUITAR.
SURE. IT'S OVER THERE.
I WANT TO BE RESPECTFUL. BUT I WISH YOU WOULD'VE ANSWERED MY CALLS.
OH NO, THOSE ARE FRESH CUTS. WHAT DID YOU DO?
IT'S NOT WHAT YOU THINK. IT'S NOT WHAT YOU THINK. I'M OKAY.
LUCY ...
I JUST WANT TO BE THERE FOR YOU. AND I DON'T NEED TO KNOW EVERYTHING ... IN FACT, THAT'S ONE OF THE THINGS I'VE ALWAYS LIKED ABOUT YOU.
THAT YOU HAVE SO MANY SECRETS ...
IT'S KIND OF SEXY.

HAHAHA ...

LET'S FUCK ...

ANOTHER DAY.

BOUNCE, BOUNCE, BOUNCE --

IN A MOMENT, WREN IMAGINES HERSELF ELSEWHERE ...

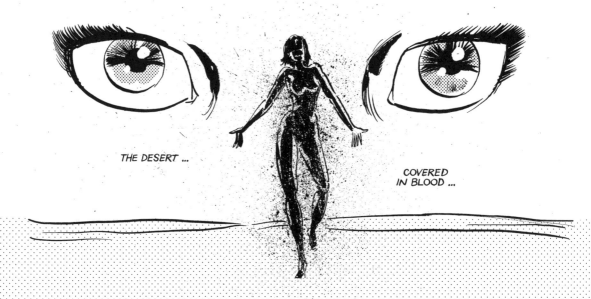

THE DESERT ...

COVERED IN BLOOD ...

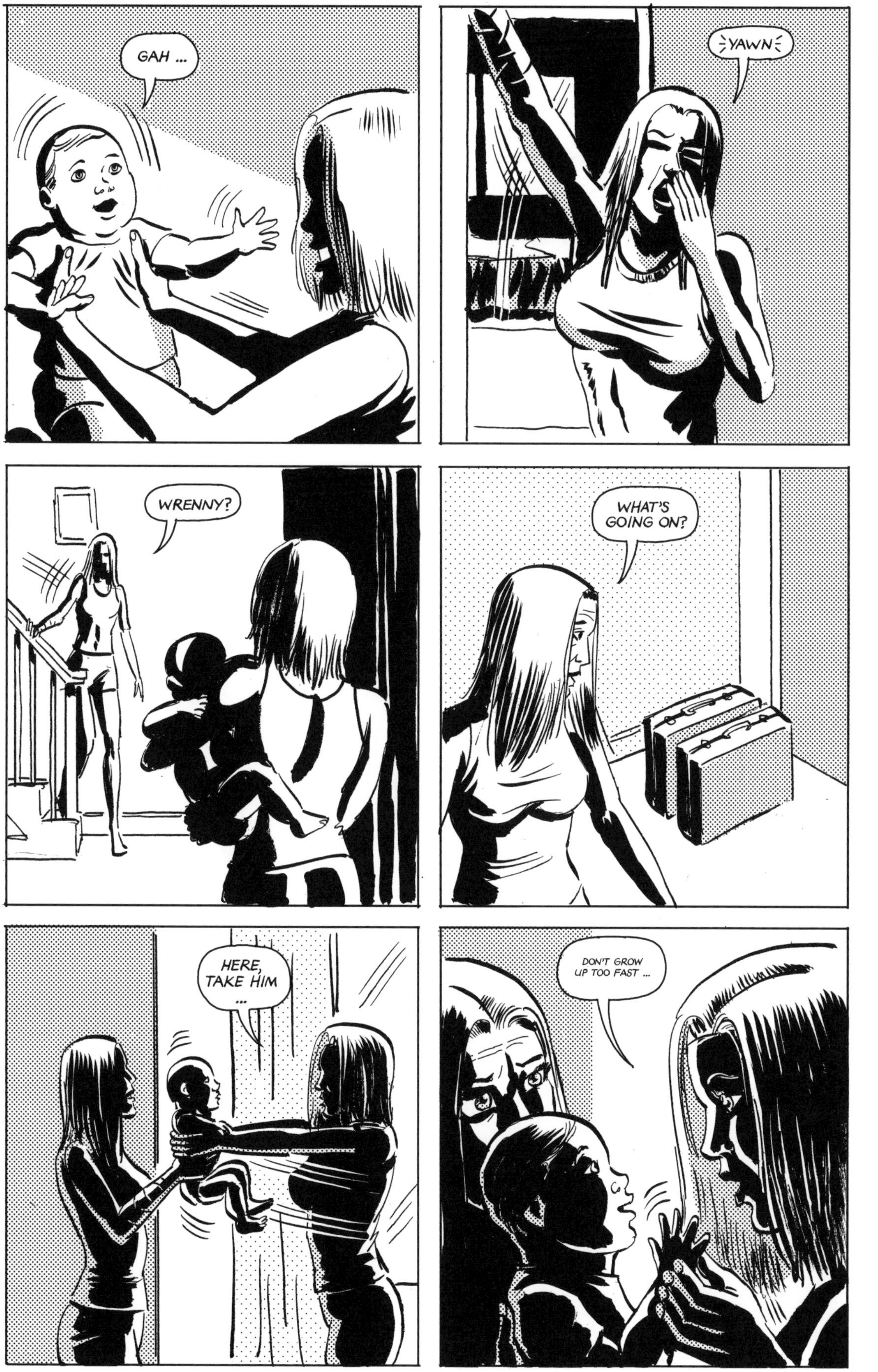
GAH ...
YAWN
WRENNY?
WHAT'S GOING ON?
HERE, TAKE HIM ...
DON'T GROW UP TOO FAST ...

GOODBYE, MOM ...

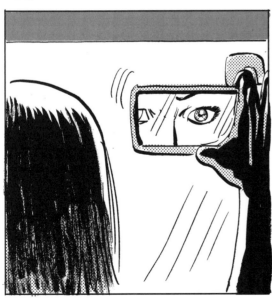

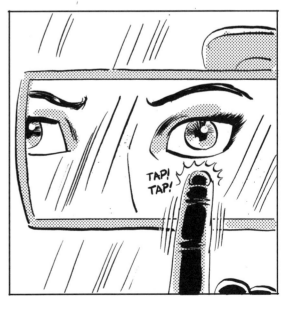

TAP! TAP!

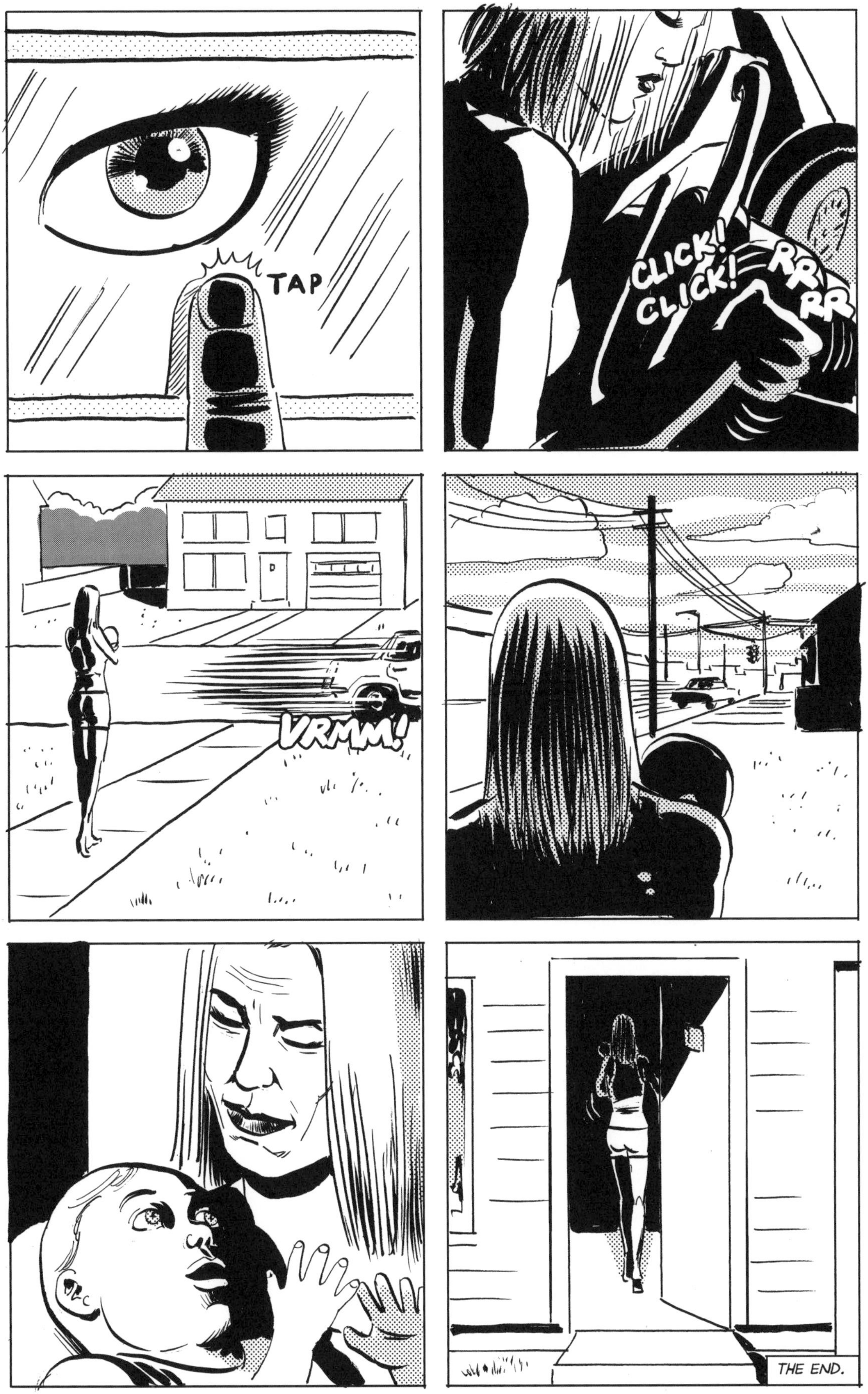
TAP
CLICK!
CLICK!
RRRR
VRMM!
THE END.

ABOUT THE
AUTHORS

DAVID BIRKE is a screenwriter known for the films
Elle (2016), *Slender Man* (2018), and *13 Sins* (2014).
He lives in Tarzana with his wife and two daughters.

NICHOLAS MCCARTHY is a Los Angeles-based
filmmaker and writer known for the feature films
The Pact (2012) and *The Prodigy* (2019), and writer
on Nickelodeon's 2020 reboot of the classic horror
television series *Are You Afraid of the Dark?*

BENJAMIN MARRA is the author of several
acclaimed graphic novels from Fantagraphics,
including *Terror Assaulter (O.M.W.O.T.)*, *Night
Business*, and *American Blood*. He lives in Montreal.

TRADITIONAL COMICS

NeoText

FANTAGRAPHICS BOOKS INC.
7563 Lake City Way NE
Seattle, Washington, 98115
www.fantagraphics.com

EDITOR: Eric Reynolds
DESIGNER: Jacob Covey
PRODUCTION: Paul Baresh
PROMOTION: Jacquelene Cohen
VP / ASSOCIATE PUBLISHER: Eric Reynolds
PRESIDENT / PUBLISHER: Gary Groth

ISBN: 978-1-68396-525-1
LIBRARY OF CONGRESS CONTROL NUMBER:
2021945346
FIRST PRINTING: March 2022
PRINTED IN: Korea